Microsoft Power BI Quick Start Guide

Third Edition

The ultimate beginner's guide to data modeling, visualization, digital storytelling, and more

Devin Knight

Erin Ostrowsky

Mitchell Pearson

Bradley Schacht

BIRMINGHAM—MUMBAI

Microsoft Power BI Quick Start Guide
Third Edition

Senior Publishing Product Manager: Devika Battike
Acquisition Editor – Peer Reviews: Gaurav Gavas
Project Editor: Parvathy Nair
Content Development Editor: Edward Doxey
Copy Editor: Safis Editing
Technical Editor: Aniket Shetty
Proofreader: Safis Editing
Indexer: Manju Arasan
Presentation Designer: Rajesh Shirsath

First published: July 2018
Second edition: October 2020
Third edition: November 2022

Production reference: 1161122

Published by Packt Publishing Ltd.
Livery Place
35 Livery Street
Birmingham
B3 2PB, UK.

ISBN 978-1-80461-349-8

www.packt.com

Contributors

About the authors

Devin Knight is the President of Training at Pragmatic Works. At Pragmatic Works, Devin determines which courses are created, delivered, and updated for customers, including 22+ Power BI courses. This is the eleventh SQL Server and BI book that he has authored. Devin often speaks at conferences such as PASS Summit, PASS Business Analytics Conference, SQL Saturdays, and Code Camps. Making his home in Jacksonville, FL, Devin is a contributor at the local Power BI User Group.

I must give thanks to God; without God in my life, I would not be as blessed as I am daily. Thanks for the amazing team of authors: Mitchell, Brad, and Erin have put in time after hours away from their families to bring this great book together. To my wife, Erin, and three children, Collin, Justin, and Lana, who were all patient during nights that daddy had to spend writing. Finally, I would like to thank Jim Halpert, the best Flonkerton coach a rising star like myself could ask for. This year will surely be our year to win gold.

Erin Angela Ostrowsky recently left her role as the appointed lead for reporting and business intelligence at Nevada Gold Mines, a Barrick Gold Corporation (NYSE: GOLD) and Newmont Corporation (NYSE: NEM) joint venture. She is launching a corporate training company, which focuses on upskilling business and IT teams as they pursue value-driven enterprise data architecture solutions.

Erin's career started with the American City Business Journals as a research director covering 16 industry verticals and over 6,000 businesses across Northeast Florida. Her proven talent for producing and converting primary and secondary research into visually appealing information packages for executive stakeholders eventually led her to training and consulting on the Microsoft Power Platform.

Erin loves to travel and has invested time working on humanitarian projects in the Dominican Republic, Haiti, and France. She is a passionate listener and storyteller who enjoys bridging diverse teams so they can deliver results on time and in budget.

I would like to thank my sisters and cousins, dear friends, mentors, and teachers for their encouragement and honesty along the way — you are truly the greatest gifts God ever gave me.

Mitchell Pearson has worked as a Data Platform Consultant and Trainer for the last 10 years. Mitchell has authored books on SQL Server, Power BI and the Power Platform. His data platform experience includes designing and implementing enterprise level BI solutions with the Microsoft SQL Server stack (T-SQL, SSIS, SSAS, SSRS), the Power Platform, and Microsoft Azure.

Mitchell is very active in the community, presenting at user groups locally and virtually, and creating YouTube videos for Pragmatic Works.

First, I would like to thank God for his grace, provision, and blessings. I would like to thank my wife and children for their patience and support as I worked on this book. I would also like to thank Brian Knight for the opportunity to learn and grow in the field of business intelligence. Finally, I would like to thank Anthony Martin, Dustin Ryan, Bradley Schacht, Devin Knight and the many others not named here, each of these individuals have provided guidance and mentoring through the years and have had a profound impact on my career.

Bradley Schacht is a Principal Program Manager on the Microsoft Azure Synapse Analytics product team based in Jacksonville, FL. Bradley is a former consultant and trainer, and has authored 4 other SQL Server and Power BI books. As a member of the Azure Synapse product team, Bradley works directly with customers to solve some of their most complex data warehousing problems and helps shape the future of the Azure Synapse cloud service. Bradley gives back to the community through speaking at events such as the PASS Summit, SQL Saturdays, Code Camps, and user groups across the country including locally at the Jacksonville SQL Server User Group (JSSUG). He is a contributor on SQLServerCentral.com and blogs on his personal site, BradleySchacht.com.

I give thanks to God, who I would be lost without and who has blessed me in so many ways. Thanks to my beautiful, amazing wife, Nichole, and our two boys, Oliver and Levi, for all the support and encouragement. I can't imagine a life without you. To my co-authors, who all worked hard and sacrificed to make this book possible. Finally, to the Atlanta Braves, for winning the Series last season and proving dreams do come true.

About the reviewers

Back in 2010, **Riccardo Perico** started working in Information Technology. After a brief experience as an ERP consultant, he moved into the data realm. He spent these years exploring the world of datafrom different points of view, both as a DBA and a Business Intelligence Engineer. He is a Microsoft Certified Professional at different levels in databases, BI, and Azure, as well as a Microsoft MVP in the Data Platform category. He is one of the leaders of the Power BI User Group in Italy, and he has been a speaker during the Power Platform World Tour and Power Platform Bootcamp stops in Italy. You can find him speaking at Azure Saturday, SQL Saturday, and Data Saturday events in Europe.

Being part of the reviewer team of this book is another milestone in my career that wouldn't have been possible without my company Lucient Italia (trademark by One4), and my colleagues Danilo, Davide, Elena, Lorenzo, Luca, Massimiliano, Mattia, Saverio, Selena, Sergio, Sergio, and Veronica. Last but not least, special thanks to my girlfriend Jessica for her support during this and all the other journeys of our life.

Greg Deckler is a Microsoft MVP for Data Platform and an active member of the Columbus Ohio IT Community, having founded the Columbus Azure ML and Power BI User Group (CAMLPUG) and presented at many conferences and events throughout the country. An active blogger, You-Tuber and community member interested in helping new users of Power BI, Greg actively participates in the Power BI Community, having authored over 180 Power BI Quick Measures Gallery submissions and over 5,000 authored solutions to community questions. Greg is Vice President of Cloud Services at Fusion Alliance, a regional consulting firm and assists customers in gaining competitive advantage from the cloud and cloud-first technologies like Power BI. Greg has also authored five books on Power BI, including *Learn Power BI*, *DAX Cookbook*, *Power BI Cookbook 2nd Edition* and *Mastering Power BI 2nd Edition*. Finally, Greg has also authored numerous external tool for the Power BI Desktop, including MSHGQM, Power Sort, Conductor, and Metadata Mechanic.

I would like to thank my son, my family, and the entire Power BI community for all of their love and support.

Jonathon Silva is a training specialist and tech consultant at Pragmatic Works, a training company located in Jacksonville, FL, focused on driving technology adoption through education. Prior to working with Pragmatic Works, Jonathon spent 9 years teaching high school history and economics before transitioning into the world of data and analytics. As a lifelong learner, he enjoys taking on new fields of study and challenging himself to master the necessary skills and knowledge to meet all the needs of his clients. Jonathon specializes in Microsoft's Power Platform, specifically with Power BI and Power Automate, and loves to provide a full immersive and tailored experience for all students in his courses.

I would not be here without the love and support of my beautiful wife, Erica. She is the love of my life, mother of our three amazing boys Christian, Justin, and Julian, and the glue that holds our crazy world together. I want to thank her, along with my parents, for all the grace and support through each and every moment of my life.

Join our community on Discord

Join our community's Discord space for discussions with the authors and other readers:

https://packt.link/ips2H

Table of Contents

Preface

As an experienced BI professional, you may have, at one time, considered your skills irreplaceable. However, while you were tirelessly building the most elegant data warehouse solutions, Microsoft was busy building a new suite of self-service business intelligence and analytics tools called Power BI. Quickly, Power BI has become one of the most popular tools in the market, and users are looking to you for advice on how they should implement best practices and scale their own usage of the tool. While your corporate BI solutions will always be the gold standard for your company's enterprise data strategy, you can no longer ignore your company's hunger for self-service data wrangling.

In this book, you will learn how to bridge the gap of your existing corporate BI skillset into what's possible with Power BI. You will understand how to connect to data sources using both import and direct query options. You will then learn how to effectively use the Power BI Query Editor to perform transformations and data-cleansing processes to your data. This will include using R script and advanced M query transforms. Next, you will learn how to properly design your data model to navigate table relationships and use DAX formulas to enhance its usability. Visualizing your data is another key element of this book, as you will learn proper data visualization styles and enhanced digital storytelling techniques. Finally, by the end of this book, you will understand how to administer your company's Power BI environment so that deployment can be made seamless, data refreshes can run properly, and security can be fully implemented.

Who this book is for

This book is intended for business intelligence professionals who have experience with traditional enterprise BI tools in the past and now need a guide to jumpstart their knowledge of Power BI. Individuals new to business intelligence will also gain a lot from reading this book, but knowledge of some industry terminology will be assumed. Concepts covered in this book can also be helpful for BI managers beginning their companies' self-service BI implementation. Prior knowledge of Power BI is helpful but certainly not required for this book.

What this book covers

Chapter 1, Gaining Data Literacy with Power BI, discusses one of the biggest problems organizations are facing, which is the lack of data literacy. The reader will learn why data literacy is so important and then how to address it.

Chapter 2, Connecting to Data, begins by getting the audience oriented with the Power BI Desktop. Next, they will learn how to connect to various common data sources in Power BI. Once a data source is chosen, the options within will be explored, including the choice between data import, direct query, and live connection.

Chapter 3, Data Transformation Strategies, explores the capabilities of the Power Query Editor inside the Power BI Desktop. Using this Power BI Query Editor, the reader will first learn how to do basic transformations, and they will quickly learn more advanced data cleansing practices. By the end of this chapter, the audience will know how to combine queries, use parameters, and read and write basic M queries.

Chapter 4, Building the Data Model, discusses one of the most critical parts of building a successful Power BI solution—designing an effective data model. In this chapter, readers will learn that while designing a data model, they are really setting themselves up for success when it comes to building reports. Specifically, this chapter will teach the audience how to establish relationships between tables, how to deal with complex relationship designs, and how to implement usability enhancements for the report consumers

Chapter 5, Leveraging DAX, teaches that the Data Analysis Expression (DAX) language within Power BI is critical to building data models that are valuable to data consumers. While DAX may be intimidating at first, readers will quickly learn that its roots come from the Excel formula engine. This can be helpful at first, but as you find the need to develop more and more complex calculations, readers will learn that having a background in Excel formulas will only take them so far. This chapter will start with an understanding of basic DAX concepts but quickly accelerate into more complex ideas, such as like Time Intelligence and Filter Context.

Chapter 6, Visualizing Data, describes how to take a finely tuned data model and build reports that properly deliver a message that clearly and concisely tells a story about the data.

Chapter 7, Digital Storytelling with Power BI, covers the capability Power BI has to be much more than just a simple drag-and-drop reporting tool. Using the storytelling features of drillthrough, bookmarks, and the selection pane, you have the ability to design reports that not only display data but also tell engaging stories that make your users crave for more.

Chapter 8, Using a Cloud Deployment with the Power BI Service, examines deploying your solution to the Power BI Service to share what you have developed with your organization. Once deployed, you can build dashboards, share them with others, and schedule data refreshes. This chapter will cover the essential skills a BI professional would need to know to top off a Power BI solution they have developed.

Chapter 9, Data Cleansing in the Cloud with Dataflows, focuses on building reusable data transform logic. Using Power BI dataflows supports large data volumes to perform scalable ETL logic and create robust data source solutions.

Chapter 10, On-Premises Solutions with Power BI Report Server, explores how many organizations have decided that they are not yet ready to move to the cloud. Using the Power BI Report Server cloud, wary organizations get the benefit of Power BI reports without compromising their feelings about the cloud. This chapter will cover deploying to the Power BI Report Server cloud, sharing reports with others, and updating data.

To get the most out of this book

After downloading and installing the Power BI Desktop, you will be able to follow the majority of the examples in this book. By subscribing to the Power BI Pro license, you can follow all examples in this book. There are also supplementary files you can download to follow the book examples.

Download the example code files

The code bundle for the book is hosted on GitHub at `https://github.com/PacktPublishing/Microsoft-Power-BI-Quick-Start-Guide-Third-Edition`. We also have other code bundles from our rich catalog of books and videos available at `https://github.com/PacktPublishing/`. Check them out!

Conventions used

There are a number of text conventions used throughout this book.

`CodeInText`: Indicates code words in the text, database table names, folder names, filenames, file extensions, pathnames, dummy URLs, user input, and Twitter handles. For example: "The `SWITCH` function is preferable to the `IF` function when performing multiple logical tests in a single DAX formula."

A block of code is set as follows:

```
Month Year = RIGHT("0" & 'Date (Order)'[Month Number of Year], 2) & "-"
```

Bold: Indicates a new term, an important word, or words that you see on the screen. For instance, words in menus or dialog boxes appear in the text like this. For example: "With the **Customer** table selected, click on **New Column** from the **Modeling** ribbon."

 Warnings or important notes appear like this.

 Tips and tricks appear like this.

Get in touch

Feedback from our readers is always welcome.

General feedback: Email feedback@packtpub.com and mention the book's title in the subject of your message. If you have questions about any aspect of this book, please email us at questions@packtpub.com.

Errata: Although we have taken every care to ensure the accuracy of our content, mistakes do happen. If you have found a mistake in this book, we would be grateful if you reported this to us. Please visit http://www.packtpub.com/submit-errata, click **Submit Errata**, and fill in the form.

Piracy: If you come across any illegal copies of our works in any form on the internet, we would be grateful if you would provide us with the location address or website name. Please contact us at copyright@packtpub.com with a link to the material.

If you are interested in becoming an author: If there is a topic that you have expertise in and you are interested in either writing or contributing to a book, please visit http://authors.packtpub.com.

Share your thoughts

Once you've read *Microsoft Power BI Quick Start Guide, Third Edition,* we'd love to hear your thoughts! Scan the QR code below to go straight to the Amazon review page for this book and share your feedback.

https://packt.link/r/1804613495

Your review is important to us and the tech community and will help us make sure we're delivering excellent quality content.

Download a free PDF copy of this book

Thanks for purchasing this book!

Do you like to read on the go but are unable to carry your print books everywhere? Is your eBook purchase not compatible with the device of your choice?

Don't worry, now with every Packt book you get a DRM-free PDF version of that book at no cost.

Read anywhere, any place, on any device. Search, copy, and paste code from your favorite technical books directly into your application.

The perks don't stop there, you can get exclusive access to discounts, newsletters, and great free content in your inbox daily

Follow these simple steps to get the benefits:

1. Scan the QR code or visit the link below

https://packt.link/free-ebook/9781804613498

2. Submit your proof of purchase
3. That's it! We'll send your free PDF and other benefits to your email directly

1

Gaining Data Literacy with Power BI

The amount of data produced and collected in the world daily is growing dramatically. As of a 2017 study (`https://www.forbes.com/sites/bernardmarr/2018/05/21/how-much-data-do-we-create-every-day-the-mind-blowing-stats-everyone-should-read/`), the best estimates are that 2.5 quintillion bytes of data are generated each day, but that number is only expected to have grown since that study is a number of years old now and, more importantly, with the popularity of **Internet of Things (IoT)** devices. With such staggering numbers, it produces major problems for organizations trying to ensure their workforce has a high level of data literacy.

Not unlike learning a foreign language, data literacy is the concept of reading, understanding, and communicating with data. In its simplest form, someone with high data literacy skills would know how to take raw data provided to them and convert it into something they can use to drive business decisions. This is a skill that takes time to learn but once an individual masters it, they can become incredibly valuable to an organization. Without high levels of data literacy, organizations can seemingly make decisions on gut feelings without supporting data influencing business plans.

The challenge facing organizations with low data literacy

With the amount of data collected, one would assume that every organization treats the data they collect as an incredibly prized resource. However, that's far from true. Many organizations are struggling to understand the meaning behind key business metrics and how those metrics should serve as indicators for driving timely business decisions.

Many organizations lack the skills required to properly show the value behind their data. Other companies take the approach of having only a select few that specialize in understanding and utilizing their data. While this strategy is better than complete data ignorance, it's still as if every organization has amassed a collection of the world's most important books for gaining knowledge but only a small percentage of employees actually know how to read.

More forward-thinking companies realize that data in the hands of just a few experts creates a bottleneck, and the optimal strategy is to democratize data to the masses. As organizations grow, it's easy to become overwhelmed with these problems, but if companies don't put an emphasis on treating data as an asset, they will quickly fall behind competitors who put a priority on data literacy.

Overcoming low data literacy with a data strategy

So how should organizations facing the challenge of staff with low data literacy respond? The first thing leadership must focus on is developing a data strategy. Data itself has no intrinsic value without a strategy for using it properly. The goal of a data strategy is to provide an organization-wide plan on how data should be collected, stored, protected, and analyzed. Without such a plan, an organization is susceptible to issues like data loss, violating international personal data collection laws, and even data breaches, which you hear about often in the news.

It is important to realize that every organization is different, and each has its own unique set of challenges to working with data. So, you shouldn't stress out about trying to find the definitive data strategy guide because it doesn't exist! There is no one-size-fits-all data strategy approach for all organizations. For example, a data strategy for a university would look very different from a data strategy for a Fortune 500 company. The former is focused on the success of their students while the latter is likely focused on overall profitability. During the planning of a data strategy, an evaluation of each segment of data must be completed to determine how the data will be processed, stored, and shared. This process will often uncover that not all organizational data should be treated the same. For example, timecard entry data from two years ago is far less important than financial statements from the same timeframe. The idea is that a data strategy should be more granular and not make large declarations about all data. Some data is more valuable than others and the time and resources spent should not be the same for all data. An organization's data strategy should be centered around its unique needs, but the point of this chapter is not to give you a step-by-step guide on developing a data strategy. More than anything, this is to stress the importance of simply having one!

The second thing organization leadership should focus on to drive higher data literacy is building a data culture. An organization with a healthy data culture is inclusive, meaning it puts data in the hands of everyone, leaving no one left out. This can be challenging when there is such a skill gap between the typical business user and a professional data analyst or data scientist. So, what do you do to overcome that skill gap?

Anyone can improve their data literacy skills, but the question is: *what is your organization doing to foster an environment that encourages engaging with and thinking about data?* Many organizations are embracing a positive data culture by promoting data enablement programs, which include ways for individuals to improve their skills with both training and mentoring. An enablement program is far more than sending a group of eager data enthusiasts to a class and hoping they learn enough to be productive. A thoughtful data enablement program is an ongoing exercise over the course of weeks and sometimes months to groom your team into becoming citizen developers.

Gartner defines a citizen developer as:

> *"An employee who creates applications capabilities for consumption by themselves or others, using tools that are not actively forbidden by IT or business units. A citizen developer is a persona, not a title or targeted role. They report to a business unit or function other than IT."*

Growing a data culture full of citizen developers doesn't happen all at once. Many organizations often start by building a group of data champions. This group would consist of individuals from multiple departments that are eager to learn and ready to make a commitment to improving their data literacy skills. The primary goal is to grow experts in each department so that way, as new citizen developers emerge, they have a known resource within their department who can help them learn. As you might expect, it's always easier to bounce ideas off someone who knows the kind of data you work with rather than someone who is unfamiliar with your data

Education in data literacy can vary from broad topics that apply to any data analytics tool or more specific tutorials geared toward a particular technology you want your citizen developers leveraging. An example of tool-agnostic learning would be how to spot trends in your data, how to determine outliers in data, or even how to choose the best visualization for the data you are working with. Any of these topics can apply to every data analytics tool on the market. While there are many great data analytics tools on the market, this book spotlights Power BI.

You might have gravitated toward this book for a number of reasons. Maybe you are completely new to Power BI, and you needed a way to kickstart your learning. Perhaps you have been learning about Power BI for some time now but you're completely self-taught, so you are hoping to fill in the gaps of things you just haven't seen yet. This would be the phase of learning where many would say, "I don't know what I don't know." Whatever the case may be for you, the authors of this book hope to give you the essentials necessary for achieving high data literacy within Power BI.

Why choose Power BI

By grabbing this book, there's a bit of an assumption that you have already made the decision that Power BI is the tool you or your organization has chosen. If for some reason you are still on the fence, or perhaps Power BI is one of many business intelligence tools your organization uses, then it's helpful to have an understanding of why so many have already made Power BI their data analytics tool of choice.

Let's start with collaboration. One of Power BI's central goals is to get data in the hands of decision-makers. So even though Power BI does come with a central cloud-based portal that users can visit, it may not make sense to give users a new web page to bookmark in their browser. Collaboration really means bringing Power BI to where your users are rather than forcing them to go somewhere new. The way Power BI does this is with integration into many of the tools you know and love from Microsoft like SharePoint, Excel, PowerPoint, Dynamics, Teams, and even your mobile phone. Within each of these tools, Power BI allows collaboration and discussion to occur around the data visualized on reports. This idea of bringing data to where your users already are is one of the significant ways Power BI helps grow a data culture.

Another reason many are drawn to Power BI is because of its ease of use. As you work your way through this book, you will find that Power BI has a very intuitive interface. It allows you to quickly connect to data, build data cleansing transformations, create relationships between data sources, and visualize your data in minutes. More complex problems can take longer of course, but Power BI tends to follow this 80/20 rule: 80 percent of the problems you encounter in Power BI can be solved with a 20 percent level of Power BI knowledge. The deeper knowledge is important of course, but the times you will actually need it are far rarer.

One of the major considerations when picking a business intelligence tool is price. Fortunately, when comparing many of the other top tools on the market, Power BI wins on cost hands down. The competitor with the closest feature parity is seven times more expensive than Power BI for basic report development.

It is important to note that licensing costs can vary depending on your specific needs so this chapter won't go into more detail on it here. However, we would recommend reviewing licensing details here: `https://powerbi.microsoft.com/en-us/pricing/`.

If these reasons aren't enough, look at the unbiased annual survey performed by Gartner for analytics and BI platforms. Gartner Inc. is a well-recognized technology research firm that conducts research on technologies, which it shares with the public. Power BI continually rates as the highest tool on the market in the categories of "Completeness of Vision" and "Ability to Execute."

Migrating your Excel skills to Power BI

Microsoft Excel is the number one most popular computer program in the world. While Excel is an amazing tool, the millions of users using it to analyze their data are thirsty for more. Fortunately, Power BI was designed with the Excel fanatic in mind. Many of the skills collected over time while designing Excel solutions still apply in Power BI. Concepts like modeling data, writing Excel formulas, and building PivotTables, all have comparable features in Power BI.

Excel was the first self-service business intelligence tool provided by Microsoft. Starting in Excel 2010, features known as Power Pivot and later Power Query were added to enable more advanced data analytics problem solving that traditional Excel could not handle. These two features would later become the core building blocks for what Power BI is today. So much so that even today, any Excel solution developed using Power Pivot and Power Query can be migrated into Power BI via a simple migration wizard.

Having an understanding of these additional Excel features can give someone an incredible head start when learning Power BI. If you are reading this book and feel confident in your Excel skills, pay close attention throughout this book to each tutorial and consider how you would have solved the various use cases in Excel. You will likely find that Power BI is an incredible time saver over how you would have previously solved these problems in Excel.

Summary

While low levels of data literacy continue to be a massive challenge for organizations, there remains hope for improvement! Technologies like Power BI are one, but not the only, ingredient for a successful data literacy recipe. A well-thought-out data strategy cannot be overlooked. Without a proper plan for your organization's data, you are treating one of your biggest assets too nonchalantly. Commitment to a data strategy doesn't happen without buy-in on a culture change within your organization. A strong data culture leads to enablement that scales throughout your organization.

In the next chapter, you will get your first look at the capabilities of Power BI as you learn about the data connectivity options that are available.

Join our community on Discord

Join our community's Discord space for discussions with the authors and other readers:

https://packt.link/ips2H

2

Connecting to Data

Power BI may very well be one of the most aptly named tools ever developed by Microsoft, giving analysts and developers a powerful business intelligence and analytics playground while still packaging it in a surprisingly lightweight application. Using Microsoft Power BI, the processes of data discovery, modeling, visualization, and sharing are made elegantly simple using a single product. These processes are so commonplace when developing Power BI solutions that this book has adopted sections that follow this pattern. However, from your perspective, the really exciting thing may be that development problems that would have previously taken you weeks to solve in a corporate BI solution can now be accomplished in only hours.

Using the Power BI Desktop application enables you to define your data discovery and data preparation steps, organize your data model, and design engaging data visualizations based on your reports. In this chapter, the development environment will be introduced, and the data discovery process will be explored in depth. The topics detailed in this chapter include the following:

- Getting started
- Importing data
- DirectQuery
- Composite models
- Live connection
- Choosing a data connection method

Let's first start by learning about Power BI at a high level, and understanding what you need on your machine to get started.

Getting started

Power BI is a **Software as a Service (SaaS)** offering in the Azure cloud and, as such, the Microsoft product team follows a strategy of *cloud first* as they develop and add new features to the product. Power BI is also one of five members of Microsoft's Power Platform:

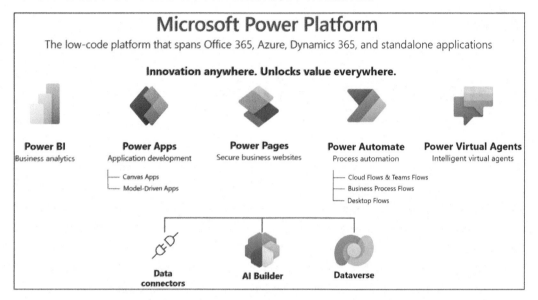

Figure 2.1: Microsoft's Power Platform suite of tools

Each of the tools within the Power Platform solves distinctly different problems, but what they have in common is who their core user audience is intended to be. The Power Platform and all the tools included within it are designed and built so business users can solve and design solutions on their own rather than relying solely on their IT department. All five tools within the Power Platform leverage Microsoft's cloud architecture and allow for seamless integration between the different tools. Leveraging the features of each Power Platform tool (Power BI, Power Apps, Power Pages, Power Automate, and Power Virtual Agents) can give your business incredible advantages over the competition.

However, since this book's focus is on Power BI, if you're interested in learning more about the other members of the Power Platform, we would recommend reviewing other titles by Packt to explore each.

While Power BI is primarily a cloud application, this does not mean that Power BI is only available in the cloud. Microsoft presents two options for sharing your results with others. The first, most often utilized method is the cloud-hosted Power BI service, which is available to users for a low monthly subscription fee. The second option is the on-premises Power BI Report Server, which can be obtained through either your SQL Server Enterprise licensing with Software Assurance or a subscription level known as Power BI Premium. Both solutions require a development tool called Power BI Desktop, which is available for free, and is generally where you will start to design your solutions.

Power BI Desktop can be found via a direct download link at Power BI (`https://powerbi.microsoft.com/en-us/desktop/`), or by installing it as an app from the Microsoft Store. There are several benefits of using the Microsoft Store Power BI Desktop app, including automatic updates, no requirement for admin privileges, and making it easier for a planned IT rollout of Power BI.

 If you are using the on-premises Power BI Report Server for your deployment strategy, then you must download a different Power BI Desktop, which is available by clicking the advanced download options link at `https://powerbi.microsoft.com/en-us/report-server/`. A separate installation is required because updates are released less frequently to the non-cloud version of Power BI (Power BI Report Server). This book will be written primarily under the assumption that you are using the cloud-hosted Power BI service as your deployment strategy.

Once you've downloaded, installed, and launched Power BI Desktop, you will likely be welcomed by the start-up screen, which is designed to help new users find their way.

Close this start-up screen so that we can review some of the most commonly used features of the application:

Figure 2.2: First view of the Power BI Desktop

Following the preceding screenshot, let's learn the names and purposes of some of the most important features in Power BI Desktop:

1. **Get data**: Used for selecting data connectors and configuring data source details.

2. **Transform data**: Launches the Power Query Editor, which is used to apply data transformations to incoming data.

3. **Report view**: Report canvas used for designing data visualizations. This is the default view that's open when Power BI Desktop is launched.

4. **Data view**: Provides a view of the data in your model. This looks similar to a typical Excel spreadsheet, but it is read-only.

5. **Model view**: Primarily used when your data model has multiple tables and relationships that need to be defined between them.

Now that you have a little familiarity with the basic controls within Power BI Desktop, let's learn about the options you have for connecting to your various data sources. Power BI is best known for the impressive data visualizations and dashboard capabilities it has. However, before you can begin building reports, you first need to connect to the necessary data sources.

Within Power BI Desktop, a developer has many unique data connectors to choose from, including traditional file types, database engines, big data solutions, cloud sources, data stored on a web page, and other SaaS providers. This book will not cover all the connectors that are available, but it will highlight some of the most popular and common ways to connect to data.

When establishing a connection to a data source, you may be presented with one of three different options regarding how your data will be treated: **Import**, **DirectQuery**, or **Live Connection**. The sections that follow will focus specifically on these options.

Importing data

Choosing to import data, which is the most common option and default behavior, means that Power BI will physically extract rows of data from the selected source and store it in an in-memory storage engine within Power BI. Power BI Desktop uses a special method for storing data, known as xVelocity, which is an in-memory technology that not only increases the performance of your query results but can also highly compress the amount of space taken up by your Power BI solution. In *some* cases, the compression that takes place can even lower the required disk space by up to one-tenth of the original data source size. This data compression occurs automatically, meaning there is no required configuration step you must do to receive this benefit. The xVelocity engine uses a local unseen instance of **SQL Server Analysis Services (SSAS)** to provide these in-memory capabilities.

There are consequences to using the **Import** option within Power BI that you should also consider. These consequences will be discussed later in this chapter, but as you read on, consider the following:

- How does data that has been imported into Power BI get updated?
- What if I need a dashboard to show near real-time analytics?
- How much data can really be imported into an in-memory storage system?

Now that you are familiar with the underlying mechanics of importing data, let's try it out with a few of the most common data source types, starting with Excel.

Excel as a source

Believe it or not, Excel continues to be the most popular application in the world and, as such, you should expect that at some point, you will be using it as a data source:

1. To get started, open Power BI Desktop and close the start-up screen if it automatically appears.

2. Under the **Home** ribbon, you will find the **Get data** button, which you already learned is used for selecting and configuring data sources. Selecting the down arrow next to the button will show you the most common data connectors, but selecting the center of the button will launch the full list of all available connectors. Regardless of which way you select the button, you will find **Excel workbook** at the top of both lists.

3. Navigate to and open the file called AdventureWorksDW.xlsx from this book's resources. This will launch the **Navigator** dialog, shown in the following screenshot, which is used for selecting the objects in the Excel workbook you wish to take data from:

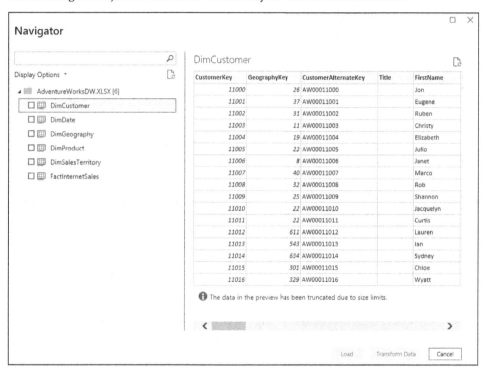

Figure 2.3: The Navigator dialog is used for selecting spreadsheets or tables

4. In this example, you can see six separate spreadsheets you can choose from. Clicking once on the spreadsheet name will give you a preview of the data it stores, while clicking the checkbox next to the name will include it as part of the data import. For this example, select the checkboxes next to all of the available objects, then notice the options available at the bottom right.

5. Selecting **Load** will immediately take the data from the selected spreadsheets and import them as separate tables into your Power BI data model. Choosing **Transform Data** will launch an entirely new window called the Power Query Editor, which allows you to apply data cleansing business rules or transforms to your data prior to importing it. You will learn much more about the Power Query Editor in *Chapter 3, Data Transformation Strategies*. Since you will learn more about this later, simply select **Load** to end this example.

Another topic you will learn more about in *Chapter 8, Using a Cloud Deployment with the Power BI Service*, is the concept of data refreshes. This is important because, when you import data into Power BI, that data remains static until another refresh is initiated. This refresh can either be initiated manually or set on a schedule. This may also require the installation of a data gateway, the application in charge of securely pushing data into the Power BI service. Feel free to skip to *Chapter 8, Using a Cloud Deployment with the Power BI Service*, if configuring a data refresh is a subject you need to know about now.

SQL Server as a source

Another common source designed for relational databases is Microsoft SQL Server:

1. To connect to SQL Server, select the **Get data** button again, but this time choose **SQL Server**.

2. On your first use of SQL Server, you are asked to choose the type of **Data Connectivity mode** you would like. As mentioned previously, **Import** is the default mode, but you can optionally select **DirectQuery**. DirectQuery will be discussed in greater detail later in this chapter. Expanding the **Advanced** options provides a way to insert a SQL statement that may be used as your source.

The following screenshot shows that you must provide the server, but the database is optional and can be selected later. For the following example, the **Server** name property is the only property populated before clicking **OK**:

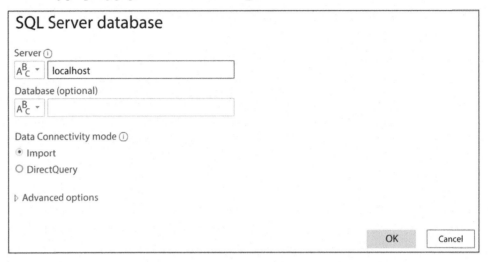

Figure 2.4: Establishing a connection to SQL Server

3. Next, you will be prompted, as shown in the following screenshot, to provide the credentials you are using to connect to the database server you provided on the previous screen:

Figure 2.5: Providing credentials to SQL Server

4. Click **Connect** after providing the proper credentials. You may be prompted with a warning stating that Power BI is only able to access the data source using an unencrypted connection. Click **OK** if you encounter this to launch the same **Navigator** dialog that you may remember from when you connected to Excel. Here, you will select the tables, views, or functions within your SQL Server database that you wish to import into your Power BI solution. Once again, the final step in this dialog allows you to choose to either **Load** or **Transform Data**.

Dataverse as a source

Microsoft Dataverse is becoming an increasingly popular data source to use within Power BI. You can think of Dataverse as the database of Dynamics 365 as well as the Power Platform. Often, Power Apps developers will leverage Dataverse for storing the data they collect from users during their usage of the apps they design. Let's review the process of connecting to Dataverse within Power BI:

1. To connect to Dataverse, select the **Get data** button and choose **Dataverse**.

2. Next, you will be prompted to sign in with your organization's Azure Active Directory account. After providing your account details you will click **Connect**.

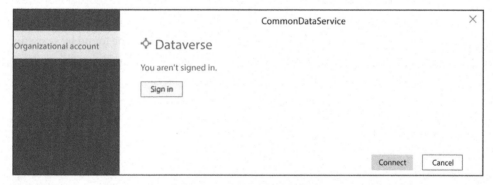

Figure 2.6: Authenticating to Dataverse

3. This will yet again bring you to the **Navigator** dialog where you can choose from your Dynamics 365 or Power Platform Dataverse database that you have permission to access. After choosing a database, you can then choose which tables you wish to bring into Power BI from this same screen.

Now that you have a better understanding of how to connect to some of the most common data sources, let's look at one that is rather unique.

Web as a source

One pleasant surprise to many Power BI developers is the availability of a web connector. Using this connection type allows you to source data from files that are stored on a website, or even data that has been embedded into an HTML table on a web page. Using this type of connector can often be helpful when you would like to supplement your internal corporate data sources with information that can be publicly found on the internet.

For this example, imagine you are working for a major automobile manufacturer in the United States. You have already designed a Power BI solution using data internally available within your organization that shows historical patterns in sales trends. However, you would like to determine whether there are any correlations between periods of historically higher fuel prices and lower automobile sales. Fortunately, you found that the United States Department of Labor publicly posts the historical average consumer prices of many commonly purchased items, including fuel prices:

1. Now that you understand the scenario within Power BI Desktop, select the **Get data** button and choose **Web** as your source. You will then be prompted to provide the **URL** where the data can be found. In this example, the data can be found by searching on the website `https://www.data.gov/`. Alternatively, to save you some time, use the direct link: `https://download.bls.gov/pub/time.series/ap/ap.data.2.Gasoline`. Once you provide the **URL**, click **OK**, as shown in the following screenshot:

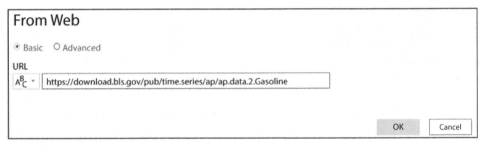

Figure 2.7: Providing the URL where your data can be found

2. Next, you will likely be prompted with an **Access Web content** dialog box. This is important when you are using a data source that requires someone to log in to access it. Since this data source does not require a login to find the data, you can simply select **Anonymous access**, which is the default, and then click **Connect**.

3. Notice on the next screen that Power BI Desktop recognizes the URL you provided as a tab-delimited file. This can now easily be added to any existing data model you have designed by selecting **Load**:

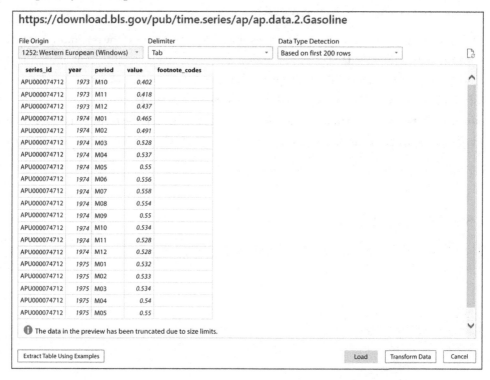

Figure 2.8: A preview of the data is shown before you import it into Power BI

Now that you've learned how to connect to various data sources, it is important to discuss in more depth the different data storage modes.

DirectQuery

Many of you have likely been trying to envision how you may implement these data imports in your environment. You may have asked yourself questions such as the following:

*   If data imported into Power BI uses an in-memory technology, has my company provided me with a machine that has enough memory to handle this?
*   Am I really going to import my source table with tens of billions of rows into memory?
*   How do I handle the requirement of displaying results in real time from the source?

These are all excellent questions that would have many negative answers if the only way to connect to your data was by importing your source into Power BI. Fortunately, there is another way. Using DirectQuery, Power BI allows you to connect directly to a data source so that no data is imported or copied into Power BI Desktop.

Why is this a good thing? Consider the questions that were asked at the beginning of this section. Since no data is imported to Power BI Desktop, this means it is less important how powerful your personal laptop is. This is because all query results are now processed on the source server instead of your laptop. As you can imagine, a database server likely has far more resources than your personal workstation. It also means that there is no need to refresh the results in Power BI since any reports you design are always pointing to a live version of the data source. That's a huge benefit!

The following screenshot shows a connection to a SQL Server database with the **DirectQuery** option selected:

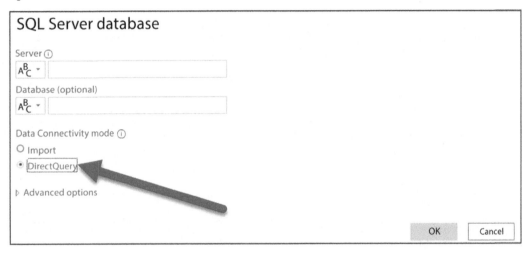

Figure 2.9: SQL Server Data Connectivity mode allows you to switch to DirectQuery mode

Earlier in this chapter, the on-premises data gateway application was mentioned as a requirement for scheduling data refreshes for sources that used the **Import** option. This same application is also needed with **DirectQuery** if your data is an on-premises source. Even though there is no scheduled data refresh, the on-premises data gateway application is still required to access on-premises data in the cloud. Again, this will be discussed in more depth in *Chapter 8, Using a Cloud Deployment with the Power BI Service.*

Limitations

So, if DirectQuery is so great, why not choose it every time? Well, with every great feature, you will also find limitations. The first glaring limitation is that not all data sources support DirectQuery. At the time this book was written, the following data sources support DirectQuery in Power BI:

Actian	IBM Netezza
Amazon Athena	Impala
Amazon Redshift	Indexima
AtScale cubes	Intersystems IRIS
Azure Analysis Services	Jethro ODBC
Azure Data Explorer (Kusto)	Kyligence Enterprise
Azure Databricks	MariaDB
Azure HDInsight Spark	MarkLogic ODBC
Azure SQL Database	Oracle
Azure Synapse	PostgreSQL
BI Connector	Power BI datasets
Data Virtuality LDW	QubolePresto
Microsoft Dataverse	SAP Business Warehouse Message Server
Denodo	SAP Business Warehouse Server
Dremio	SAP HANA
Essbase	Snowflake
Exasol	Spark
Google BigQuery	SQL Server
Hive LLAP	Starburst Enterprise
HDInsight Interactive Query	Teradata Database
IBM DB2	Vertica

Note that this list will be updated from time to time. The most up-to-date list of the data sources supported by DirectQuery can be found here: https://docs.microsoft.com/en-us/power-bi/connect-data/power-bi-data-sources

Depending on the data source you choose, there is a chance of slower query performance when using DirectQuery compared to the default data import option. Keep in mind that when the **Import** option is selected, it leverages a highly sophisticated in-memory storage engine. When selecting DirectQuery, performance will depend on the source type you have chosen from the preceding list.

Another limitation worth noting is that not all Power BI features are supported when you choose DirectQuery. For example, depending on the selected source, some of the Power Query Editor features are disabled and could result in the following message: **This step results in a query that is not supported in DirectQuery mode.** The following screenshot shows this response:

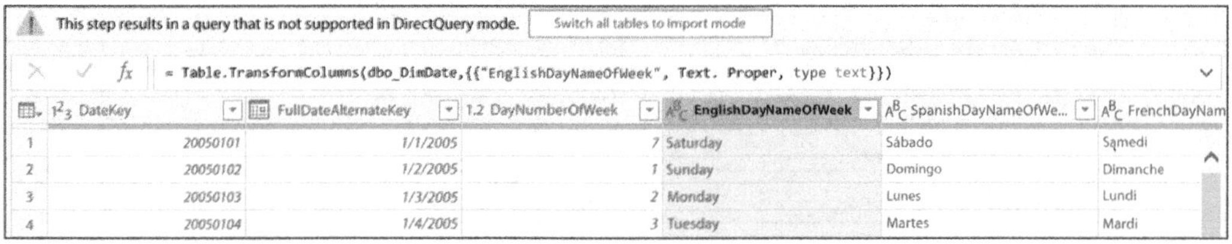

Figure 2.10: Certain transforms may force a user out of DirectQuery mode

The reason for this limitation is that DirectQuery automatically attempts to convert any Power Query steps into a query in the data source's native language. So, if the source of this solution was SQL Server, then Power BI would attempt to convert this data transformation into a comparable T-SQL statement. Once Power BI realizes the Power Query Editor used a function that is not compatible with the source, the error is generated. There are other less notable limitations found when working with DirectQuery that you can find by reviewing Microsoft's documentation on DirectQuery.

Composite models

Occasionally, you may find it helpful for your data model to take a hybrid approach regarding how it stores data. For example, you want sales transactions to be displayed in near real time on your dashboard, so you set your `SalesTransaction` table to use DirectQuery. However, your `Product` table rarely has values that are added or changed. Having values that do not change often makes it a great candidate for the imported data storage method to take advantage of the performance benefits.

This describes a perfect scenario for utilizing a feature called composite models. Composite models allow a single Power BI solution to include both DirectQuery and import table connections within one data model. From the Power BI developer's perspective, you can take advantage of the best parts of each data storage mode within your design.

Another effective use case for composite models is found when using the feature called aggregations. Leveraging aggregations is one of the best ways to manage extremely large datasets in Power BI. You will learn more about designing aggregations in *Chapter 4, Building the Data Model*.

Within the Power BI Desktop, it is clear a solution is leveraging composite models if we view the storage mode in the bottom-right corner of the tool. Clicking the text **Storage Mode: Mixed**, shown in the following screenshot, will allow you to switch all tables to **Import** mode instead. Optionally, if you need to change the storage mode of individual tables, this can be accomplished in the **Model** view by selecting individual tables:

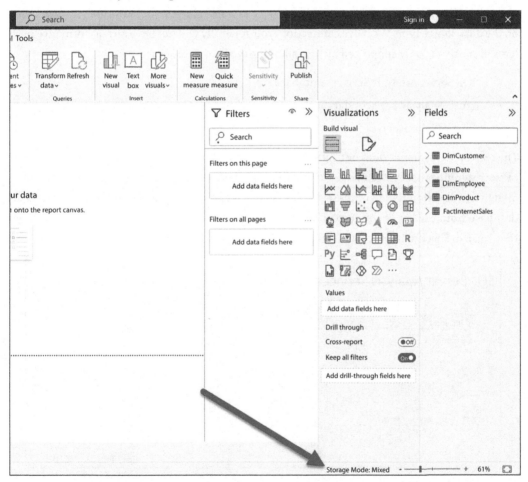

Figure 2.11: The bottom-right corner allows you to switch storage modes for the entire model

While composite models give you the best of DirectQuery and import models, there's a third storage mode that is often used for data sources that are highly groomed by IT.

Live connection

The basic concept of **live connection** is very similar to that of DirectQuery. Just like DirectQuery, when you use a live connection, no data is actually imported into Power BI. Instead, your solution points directly to the underlying data source and leverages the Power BI Desktop simply as a data visualization tool. So, if these two things are so similar, why give them different names? The answer is that even though the basic concept is the same, DirectQuery and live connection vary greatly.

One difference that should quickly be noticeable is the query performance experience. It was mentioned in a previous section that DirectQuery can often have poor performance, depending on the data source type. With live connection, you generally will not have any performance problems because it is only supported by the following types of data sources:

- SQL Server Analysis Services database
- Azure Analysis Services database
- Power BI datasets

The reason performance does not suffer with these data sources is that they either use the same xVelocity engine that Power BI does or another high-performance storage engine. To set up your own live connection to one of these sources, you can choose the **SQL Server Analysis Services database** from the list of connectors after selecting **Get data**. The following screenshot shows that you can specify that the connection should be set to **Connect live**:

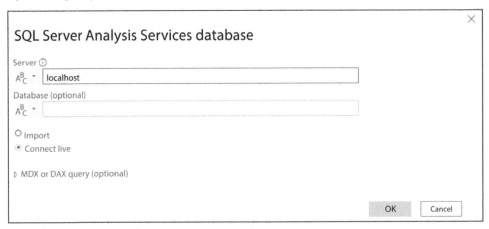

Figure 2.12: SQL Server Analysis Services Data Connectivity mode allows you to switch to Connect live mode

Of course, these benefits don't come without a cost. Let's discuss some of the limitations of live connection.

Limitations

So far, this sounds great! You have now learned that you can connect directly to your data sources without importing data into your model and that you won't face significant performance consequences. Of course, these benefits don't come without giving something up, so what are the limitations of a live connection?

What you will encounter with live connections are limitations that are generally a result of the fact that Analysis Services is an Enterprise BI tool. Thus, if you are going to connect to it, then it has probably already gone through significant data cleansing and modeling by your IT team.

Modeling capabilities such as defining relationships are not available because these would be designed in an Analysis Services model. Also, Power Query Editor is not available at all against a live connection source. While, at times, this may be frustrating, it does make sense that it works this way. This is because any of the changes you may desire to make to relationships or in the Power Query Editor should be done in Analysis Services, not Power BI.

Choosing a data connection method

Now that you have learned about the three different ways to connect to your data, you are left wondering which option is best for you. It's fair to say that the choice you make will really depend on the requirements of each individual project you have.

To summarize, some of the considerations that were mentioned in this chapter are listed in the following table:

Consideration	Import Data	DirectQuery	Live connection
Best performance	Yes	No	Yes
Best design experience	Yes	No	No
Best for keeping data up to date	No	Yes	Yes
Data source availability	Yes	No	No
Most scalable	No	Yes	Yes

Some of the items you'll consider may be more important than others. So, to make this more personal, try using the Data Connectivity - Decision Matrix file that is included with this book.

In this file, you can rank (from 1 to 10) the importance of each of these considerations to help you choose which option is best for you.

Since the **Import Data** option presents the most available features, going forward, this book primarily uses this option. In *Chapter 3, Data Transformation Strategies*, you will learn how to implement data transformation strategies to ensure all the necessary business rules are applied to your data.

Summary

Often, Power BI developers have questions concerning various data sources and what unique challenges come with each connection. The great news is once you have established a connection to your data source, regardless of which one it is, everything after that point typically follows that same pattern of steps. The point is don't let any one data source overly intimidate you. Once you connect to it, the rest of your Power BI solution design will follow the same processes mentioned earlier in this chapter: data discovery, data modeling, data visualization, and sharing.

Power BI provides users with a variety of methods for connecting to data sources with natively built-in data connectors. The connector you choose for your solution will depend on where your data is located. Once you've connected to a data source, you can decide on what type of query mode best suits your needs. Some connectors allow for little to no latency in your results with options like DirectQuery or live connection. In this chapter, you learned about the benefits and disadvantages of each query mode, and you were given a method for weighting these options using a decision matrix. In the next chapter, you will learn more about how data transformations may be applied to your data import process so that incoming data will be properly cleansed.

Join our community on Discord

Join our community's Discord space for discussions with the authors and other readers:

https://packt.link/ips2H

3

Data Transformation Strategies

Within any **business intelligence** (BI) project, it is essential that the data you are working with has been properly scrubbed to ensure accurate results on your reports and dashboards. Applying data cleansing business rules, also known as transformations, is the primary method for correcting inaccurate or malformed data, but the process can often be the most time-consuming part of any corporate BI solution. However, the data transformation capabilities built into Power BI are both very powerful and user-friendly. Using the Power Query Editor, tasks that would typically be difficult or time-consuming in an enterprise BI tool are as simple as right-clicking on a column and selecting the appropriate transform for the field. While interacting with the user interface, the Power Query Editor automatically writes queries using a language called M behind the scenes.

Through the course of this chapter, you will explore some of the most common features of the Power Query Editor that make it so highly regarded by its users. Since one sample dataset cannot provide all the problems you will run into, you will be provided with several small, disparate examples to show you what is possible. This chapter will detail the following topics:

- The Power Query Editor
- Transformation basics
- Advanced data transformation options
- The R programming language
- AI Insights
- The M formula language

To get started, let's get familiar with the interface known as the Power Query Editor.

The Power Query Editor

The **Power Query Editor** is the primary tool that you will utilize for applying transformations and cleansing processes to your data. This editor can be launched as part of establishing a connection to your data, or by simply clicking **Transform Data** on the **Home** ribbon of Power BI Desktop. When the Power Query Editor is opened, you will notice that it has its own separate environment for you to work in. The environment encapsulates a user-friendly method for working with all of the queries that you will define. Before you dive deep into the capabilities of the Power Query Editor, let's first start by reviewing the key areas of the Power Query Editor interface:

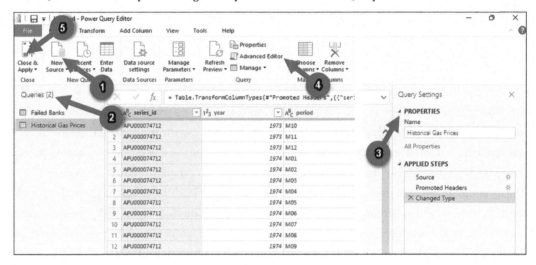

Figure 3.1: First view of the Power Query Editor

Following the numbered labels, let's review some of the most important features of the Power Query Editor:

1. **New Source**: This launches the interface to establish your connection details, which is the same interface as the **Get data** button that you learned about in *Chapter 2*, *Connecting to Data*.

2. The **Queries** pane: A list of all the queries that you have connected to. From here, you can rename a query, disable the load and modify report refresh capabilities, and organize your queries into groups.

3. **Query Settings**: Within this pane, you can rename the query, but more importantly, you can see and change the list of steps, or transforms, that have been applied to your query. If you ever accidentally close this pane, you can relaunch it from the **View** menu.

4. **Advanced Editor:** By launching the **Advanced Editor**, you can see the query that is automatically written for you by the Power Query Editor.

5. **Close & Apply:** Choosing this option will close the Power Query Editor and load the results into the data model.

With this basic navigation understood, let's start to discuss some of the basics of working with various transforms.

Transformation basics

Applying data transformations within the Power Query Editor can be a surprisingly simple thing to do. However, there are a few things to consider as we begin this process. The first is that there are multiple ways to solve a problem. As you work your way through this book, we have tried to show you the fastest and easiest methods of solving the problems that are presented, but these solutions will certainly not be the only ways to reach your goals.

The next thing you should understand is that every click you do inside the Power Query Editor is automatically converted into a formula language called M. Virtually all the basic transforms you will need can be accomplished by simply interacting with the Power Query Editor user interface, but for more complex business problems there is a good chance you may have to modify the M queries that are written for you by the editor. You will learn more about M later in this chapter.

Finally, the last important consideration to understand is that all transforms that are created within the editor are stored in the **Query Settings** pane located on the right side under a section called **Applied Steps**. Why is this important to know? The **Applied Steps** section has many features, but here are some of the most critical to know for now:

- **Deleting transforms:** If you make a mistake and need to undo a step, you can click the **Delete** button next to a step.
- **Modifying transforms:** This can be done with any step that has a gear icon next to it.
- **Changing the order of transforms:** If you realize that it is better for one step to execute before another one, you can change the order of how the steps are executed.
- **Selecting previous steps:** Clicking on any step prior to the current one will allow you to see how your query results would change one step earlier in the process.

With this understanding, you will now get hands-on with applying several basic transforms inside the Power Query Editor. The goal of these first sets of examples is to get you comfortable with the Power Query Editor user interface before the more complex use cases are covered.

Data Transformation Strategies

Use First Row as Headers

Organizing column names or headers is often an important first task when managing your dataset. Providing relevant column names makes many of the downstream processes, such as building reports, much easier. Often, column headers are automatically imported from your data source, but sometimes you may be working with a more unique data source that makes it difficult for Power BI to capture the column header information. This walk-through will show how to deal with such a scenario:

1. Launch Power BI Desktop, and click **Get data** on the **Home** ribbon.

2. Choose **Excel workbook**, then navigate to and select **Open** on the Failed Bank List.xlsx file that is available in the book source files, available here: https://github.com/PacktPublishing/Microsoft-Power-BI-Quick-Start-Guide-Third-Edition.

3. In the **Navigator** window, select the table called **Data**, then choose **Transform Data**. When the Power Query Editor launches, you should notice that the column headers are not automatically imported. In fact, the column headers are in the first row of the data.

4. To push the column names that are in the first row of data to the header section, select the transform called **Use First Row as Headers** from the **Home** ribbon as shown in *Figure 3.2*:

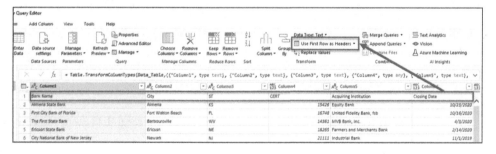

Figure 3.2: Leveraging the Use First Row as Headers transform

Once complete, you will see the first row of the dataset has been promoted to the column header area. This is a very common transform that you can expect to use often with flat files. Next, let's look at another commonly used transform, **Remove Columns**.

Remove Columns

Often, the data sources you will connect to will include many columns that are not necessary for the solution you are designing. It is important to remove these unnecessary columns from your dataset because these unused columns needlessly take up space inside your data model.

There are several different methods for removing columns in the Power Query Editor. This example will show one of these methods using the same dataset from the previous demonstration:

1. Multi-select (*Ctrl* + click) the column headers of the columns you wish to keep as part of your solution. In this scenario, select the columns **Bank Name**, **City**, **ST**, and **Closing Date**.

2. With these four columns selected, right-click on any of the selected columns headers and choose **Remove Other Columns**, as shown in *Figure 3.3*:

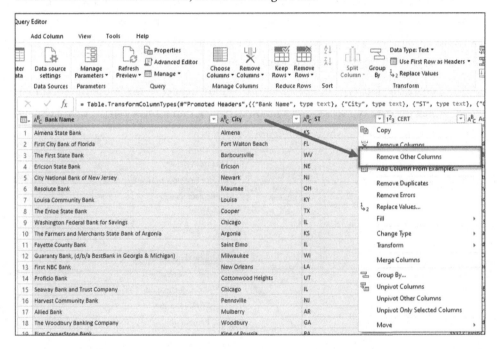

Figure 3.3: Selecting the Remove Other Columns transform

Once this transform is completed, you should be left with only the columns you need.

Another popular method for removing columns is clicking the **Choose Columns** button on the **Home** ribbon of the Power Query Editor. This option provides a list of all the columns, and you can choose the columns you wish to keep or exclude.

You can also select the columns you wish to remove; right-click on one of the selected columns and click **Remove**. This seems like the more obvious method. However, this option is not as user-friendly in the long run because it does not provide an option to edit the transform in the **Applied Steps** section as the first two methods do.

With any data cleansing tool, data type manipulation is critical and can help save you from many headaches later in the development of your solution. In the next section, you will learn about how to change data types.

Change Type

Defining column data types properly early on in your data scrubbing process can help to ensure proper business rules can be applied and data is presented properly in reports. The Power Query Editor has various numeric, text, and date-time data types for you to choose from. In our current example, all of the data types were automatically interpreted correctly by the Power Query Editor, but let's look at where you could change this if necessary:

1. Locate the data type indicator on the column header to the left of the column name.

2. Click the data type icon, and a menu will open that allows you to choose whichever data type you desire, as shown in *Figure 3.4*:

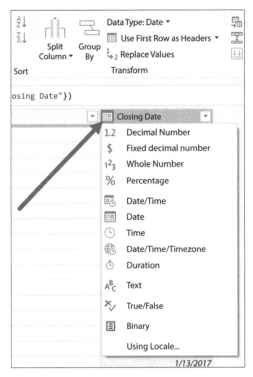

Figure 3.4: Choosing a different data type

You will not need to make a change to the data type for this example but now you know where to go when you are required to.

Another method you can use for changing column data types is to right-click on the column you wish to change, then select **Change Type**, and choose the new data type. You should always be careful when changing data types to ensure your data supports the change.

For instance, if you change a column data type to **Whole Number** while it has letters stored in it, Power BI will produce an error.

 If you want to change multiple column data types at once, you can multi-select the necessary columns, then select the new data type from the **Data Type** property on the **Home** ribbon.

Many of the transforms you will encounter in the future are contextually based on the column data types you are working with. For example, if you have a column that is a date, then you will be provided with special transforms that can only be executed against a date data type, such as extracting the month name from a date column.

Understanding how to properly set data types in Power BI is often the first step to using more exciting transforms. In the next section, you will learn how Power BI can read from an example you provide to automatically create transform rules.

Add Column From Examples

One option that can make complex data transformations seem simple is the feature called **Add Column From Examples**. Using **Add Column From Examples**, you can provide the Power Query Editor with a sample of what you would like your data to look like, and it can then automatically determine which transforms are required to accomplish your goal. Continuing with the same failed banks example, let's walk through a simple example of how to use this feature:

1.   Find and select the **Add Column** tab in the Power Query Editor ribbon.

2. Select the **Column From Examples** button and, if prompted, choose **From All Columns**. This will launch a new **Add Column From Examples** interface:

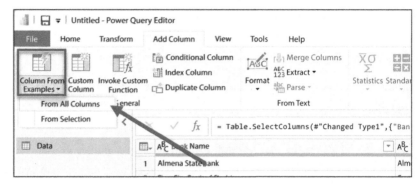

Figure 3.5: Choosing the Column From Examples transform

3. Our goal is to leverage this feature to combine the City and ST columns. In the first empty cell, type Almena, KS and then hit *Enter*. In *Figure 3.6* you will notice that the text you typed has automatically been translated into an M query and applied to every row in the dataset.

4. Once you click **OK**, the transform is finalized and automatically added to the overall M query that has been built through the user interface. The newly merged column will be added with the rest of your columns and you can optionally rename the column to something more appropriate by double-clicking on the column header:

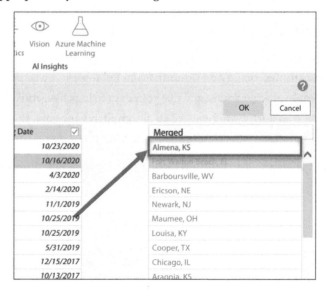

Figure 3.6: Add Column From Examples

As you can see, the **Add Column From Examples** feature is great because you don't have to be an expert in which transforms are appropriate because Power BI will automatically choose them for you!

 Sometimes, you may encounter scenarios where the **Add Column From Examples** feature needs more than one example to properly translate your example into an M query function that accomplishes your goal. If this happens, simply provide additional examples of how you would like the data to appear in different rows, and the Power Query Editor should adjust to account for outliers.

Now that you have learned some basic transformations, let's explore some more complex design patterns that are still used quite frequently.

Advanced data transformation options

Now that you should be more comfortable working within the Power Query Editor, let's take the next step and discuss more advanced options. Often, you will find the need to go beyond these basic transforms when dealing with data that requires more care. In this section, you will learn about some common advanced transforms that you may have a need for, which include **Conditional Columns**, **Fill Down**, **Unpivot**, **Merge Queries**, and **Append Queries**.

Add Conditional Columns

Using the Power Query Editor **Conditional Columns** functionality is a great way to add new columns to your query that follow logical if/then/else statements. This concept of if/then/ else is common across many programming languages, including Excel formulas. Let's review a real-world scenario where you would be required to do some data cleansing on a file before it could be used. In this example, you will be provided with a file of all the counties in the United States, and you must create a new column that extracts the state name from the county column and places it in its own column:

1. Start by connecting to the FIPS_CountyName.txt file that is found in the book files using the **Text/CSV** connector.

2. Launch the Power Query Editor by selecting **Transform Data**, then start by changing the data type of Column1 to **Text**. When you do this, you will be prompted to replace an existing type conversion. You can accept this by clicking **Replace current**. Notice that many of the values had leading zeros that were not visual before changing the data type.

3. Now, on Column2, filter out the value **UNITED STATES** from the column by clicking the arrow next to the column header and unchecking **UNITED STATES**. Then, click **OK**.

4. Remove the state abbreviation from Column2 by right-clicking on the column header and selecting **Split Column | By Delimiter**. Choose **-- Custom --** for the delimiter type, and type a comma followed by a space before clicking **OK**, as shown in *Figure 3.7*:

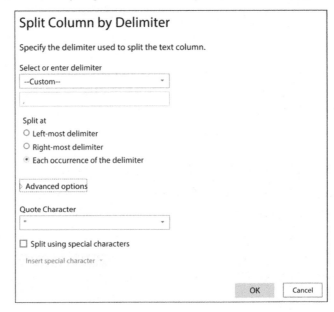

Figure 3.7: Splitting a column based on a delimiter

5. Next, rename the column names Column1, Column 2.1, and Column 2.2 to County Code, County Name, and State Abbreviation, respectively.

6. To isolate the full state name into its own column, you will need to implement **Conditional Column**. Go to the **Add Column** ribbon and select **Conditional Column**.

7. Change the **New column name** property to State Name and implement the logic If State Abbreviation equals null Then return County Name Else return null, as shown in *Figure 3.8*. To return the value from another column, you must select the icon in the **Output** property, then choose **Select a column**. Once this is complete, click **OK**:

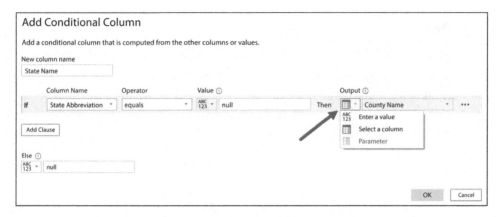

Figure 3.8: Adding a conditional column

This results in a new column called **State Name**, which has the fully spelled-out state name only appearing on rows where the State Abbreviation is null:

	ABC County Code	ABC County Name	ABC State Abbreviation	123 State Name
	fx = Table.AddColumn(#"Renamed Columns", "State Name", each if [State Abbreviation] = null ∨			
1	01000	ALABAMA	null	ALABAMA
2	01001	Autauga County	AL	null
3	01003	Baldwin County	AL	null
4	01005	Barbour County	AL	null
5	01007	Bibb County	AL	null
6	01009	Blount County	AL	null
7	01011	Bullock County	AL	null
8	01013	Butler County	AL	null
9	01015	Calhoun County	AL	null
10	01017	Chambers County	AL	null
11	01019	Cherokee County	AL	null
12	01021	Chilton County	AL	null
13	01023	Choctaw County	AL	null
14	01025	Clarke County	AL	null
15	01027	Clay County	AL	null
16	01029	Cleburne County	AL	null
17	01031	Coffee County	AL	null

Figure 3.9: End result of following these steps

This is only setting the stage to fully scrub this dataset. To complete the data cleansing process for this file, read on to the next section about **Fill Down**. However, for the purposes of this example, you have now learned how to leverage the capabilities of the **Conditional Column** transform in the Power Query Editor.

Fill Down

Fill Down is a rather unique transform in how it operates. By selecting **Fill Down** on a particular column, a value will replace all `null` values below it until another non-`null` appears. When another non-`null` value is present, that value will then fill down to all subsequent `null` values. To examine this transform, you will pick up from where you left off in the **Conditional Column** example in the previous section:

1. Right-click on the **State Name** column header and select **Transform | Capitalize Each Word**. This transform should be self-explanatory.

2. Next, select the **State Name** column and, in the **Transform** ribbon, select **Fill | Down**. This will take the value in the **State Name** column and replace all non-null values until there is another **State Name** value that it can switch to. After performing this transform, scroll through the results to ensure that the value of `Alabama` switches to `Alaska` when appropriate.

3. To finish this example, filter out any `null` values that appear in the **State Abbreviation** column. The final result should look like *Figure 3.10*, as follows:

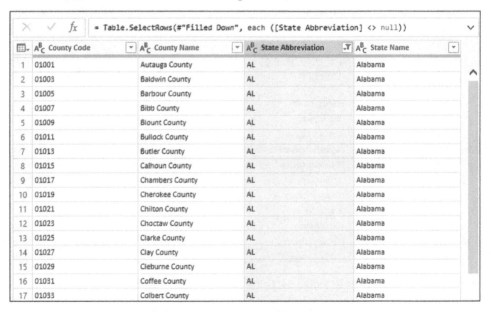

Figure 3.10: End result of following these steps

In this example, you learned how you can use **Fill Down** to replace all of the null values below a non-null value. You can also use **Fill Up** to do the opposite, which would replace all the null values above a non-null value. One important thing to note is that the data must be sorted properly for **Fill Down** or **Fill Up** to be successful. In the next section, you will learn about another advanced transform, known as **Unpivot**.

Unpivot

The **Unpivot** transform is an incredibly powerful transform that allows you to reorganize your dataset into a more structured format best suited for BI. Let's discuss this by visualizing a practical example to help understand the purpose of **Unpivot**. Imagine you are provided with a file that contains the populations of US states and territories by decades, as shown in *Figure 3.11*:

Year	Alabama	Alaska	American Samoa	Arizona
1960	3,266,740	226,167	20,051	1,302,161
1970	3,444,165	300,382	27,159	1,770,900
1980	3,893,888	401,851	32,297	2,718,215
1990	4,040,587	550,043	46,773	3,665,228
2000	4,447,100	626,932	57,291	5,130,632
2010	4,779,736	710,231	55,519	6,392,017
2020	5,024,279	733,391	49,710	7,151,502

Figure 3.11: Example data that will cause problems in Power BI

The problem with data stored like this is you cannot very easily answer simple questions. For example, how would you answer questions like, *What was the total population for all states and territories in the US in 2020?* or *What was the average state and territory population in 2010?* With the data stored in this format, simple reports are made rather difficult to design. This is where the **Unpivot** transform can be a lifesaver.

Using **Unpivot**, you can change this dataset into something more acceptable for an analytics project, as shown in *Figure 3.12*:

A^B_C Name	1²₃ Year	1²₃ Population
Minnesota	1960	3413864
Colorado	1960	1753947
Rhode Island	1960	859488
Mississippi	1960	2178141
Oklahoma	1960	2328284
North Carolina	1960	4556155
South Carolina	1960	2382594
Iowa	1960	2757537
Massachusetts	1960	5148578
Kansas	1960	2178611
South Dakota	1960	680514
New Jersey	1960	6066782
American Samoa	1960	20051
Louisiana	1960	3257022
Vermont	1960	389881
Montana	1960	674767
Pennsylvania	1960	11319366
Kentucky	1960	3038156

Figure 3.12: Results of unpivoted data

Data stored in this format can now easily answer the questions posed earlier by simply dragging a few columns into your visuals. Accomplishing this in other programming languages would often require fairly complex logic, while the Power Query Editor does it in just a few clicks.

There are three different methods for selecting the **Unpivot** transform that you should be aware of, and they include the following options:

- **Unpivot Columns**: Turns any selected column's headers into row values and the data in those columns into a corresponding row. With this selection, any new columns that may get added to the data source *will* automatically be included in the **Unpivot** transform.

- **Unpivot Other Columns**: Turns all column headers that *are not* selected into row values and the data in those columns into a corresponding row. With this selection, any new columns that may get added to the data source *will* automatically be included in the **Unpivot** transform.

- **Unpivot Only Selected Columns**: Turns any selected columns' headers into row values and the data in those columns into a corresponding row. With this selection, any new columns that may get added to the data source *will not* be included in the **Unpivot** transform.

Let's walk through two examples of using the **Unpivot** transform to show you the first two of these methods, and provide an understanding of how this complex problem can be solved with little effort in Power BI. The third method mentioned for doing **Unpivot** will not be shown since it's so similar to the first option:

1. Launch a new instance of Power BI Desktop, and use the Excel Workbook connector to import the workbook called Income Per Person.xlsx found in the book source files. Once you select this workbook, choose the spreadsheet called **Data** in the **Navigator** window, and then select **Transform Data** to launch the Power Query Editor. *Figure 3.13* shows what our data looks like before the **Unpivot** operation:

	A^B_C Column1	1.2 Column2	1.2 Column3	1.2 Column4
1	GDP per capita PPP, with projections	1764	1765	1766
2	Abkhazia	null	null	null
3	Afghanistan	null	null	null
4	Akrotiri and Dhekelia	null	null	null
5	Albania	null	null	null
6	Algeria	null	null	null
7	American Samoa	null	null	null
8	Andorra	null	null	null
9	Angola	null	null	null
10	Anguilla	null	null	null
11	Antigua and Barbuda	null	null	null
12	Argentina	null	null	null
13	Armenia	null	null	null
14	Aruba	null	null	null
15	Australia	null	null	null
16	Austria	1403.59853	1404.448052	1405.298088

Figure 3.13: Example before Unpivot is performed

2. Now, make the first row of data into column headers by selecting the transform called **Use First Row as Headers** on the **Home** ribbon.
3. Rename the **GDP per capita PPP, with projections** column to **Country/Region**.
4. If you look closely at the column headers, you can tell that most of the column names are actually years and the values inside those columns are the income for those years. This is not the ideal way to store this data because it would be incredibly difficult to answer a question like, *What is the average income per person for Belgium?* To make it easier to answer this type of question, right-click on the **Country/Region** column and select **Unpivot Other Columns**.
5. Rename the columns Attribute and Value to Year and Income, respectively.

6. To finish this first example, you should also rename this query **Income**. The results of these first steps can be seen in *Figure 3.14*:

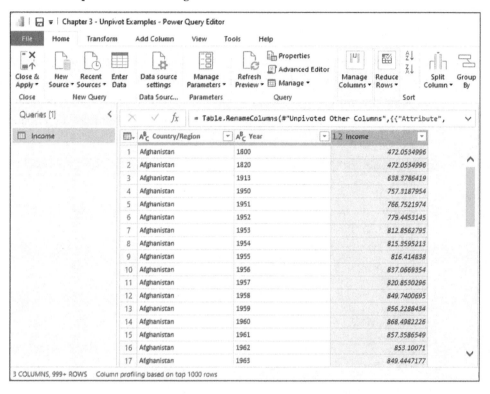

Figure 3.14: Results of unpivoted data

This first method walked you through what can often be the fastest method for performing an **Unpivot** transform, which is by using the **Unpivot Other Columns** option. In this next example, you will learn how to use the **Unpivot Columns** method as well:

1. Remain in the Power Query Editor, and select **New Source** from the **Home** ribbon. Use the Excel Workbook connector to import the Total Population.xlsx workbook from the book source files. Once you select this workbook, choose the spreadsheet called **Data** in the **Navigator** window, and then select **OK**. *Figure 3.15* shows the dataset before **Unpivot** has been added:

	A^B_C Column1	1$^2_3$ Column2	1$^2_3$ Column3	1$^2_3$ Column4
1	Total population	1086	1100	1290
2	Abkhazia	null	null	null
3	Afghanistan	null	null	null
4	Akrotiri and Dhekelia	null	null	null
5	Albania	null	null	null
6	Algeria	null	null	null
7	American Samoa	null	null	null
8	Andorra	null	null	null
9	Angola	null	null	null
10	Anguilla	null	null	null
11	Antigua and Barbuda	null	null	null
12	Argentina	null	null	null
13	Armenia	null	null	null
14	Aruba	null	null	null
15	Australia	null	null	null
16	Austria	null	null	null

Figure 3.15: Example before Unpivot is performed

2. Like the last example, you will again need to make the first row of data into column headers by selecting the transform called **Use First Row as Headers** on the **Home** ribbon.

3. Then, rename the column **Total population** to **Country/Region**.

4. This time, multi-select all the columns except **Country/Region**, then right-click on one of the selected columns and choose **Unpivot Columns**, as shown in *Figure 3.16*.

The easiest way to multi-select these columns is to select the first year column and then hold *Shift* before clicking the last column:

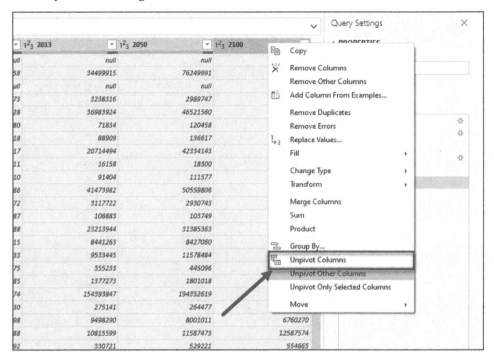

Figure 3.16: Using the Unpivot Columns transform

5. Rename the columns from **Attribute** and **Value** to **Year** and **Population**, respectively, to match the results shown in *Figure 3.17*:

	A^B_C Country/Region	A^B_C Year	1.2 Population
1	Afghanistan	1800	3280000
2	Afghanistan	1820	3280000
3	Afghanistan	1870	4207000
4	Afghanistan	1913	5730000
5	Afghanistan	1950	8151455
6	Afghanistan	1951	8276820
7	Afghanistan	1952	8407148
8	Afghanistan	1953	8542906
9	Afghanistan	1954	8684494
10	Afghanistan	1955	8832253
11	Afghanistan	1956	8986449
12	Afghanistan	1957	9147286

Figure 3.17: Shows the final result of these steps

6.   Finalize this query by renaming it **Population** in the **Query Settings** pane.

In this section, you learned about two different methods for performing an **Unpivot**. To complete the data cleansing process on these two datasets, it's recommended that you continue to the next section on merging queries.

Merge Queries

Another common requirement when building BI solutions is the need to join two tables together to form a new outcome that includes some columns from both tables in the result. Fortunately, Power BI makes this task very simple with the **Merge Queries** feature. Using this feature requires that you select two tables and then determine which column or columns will be the basis of how the two queries are merged.

After determining the appropriate columns for your join, you will select a join type. The join types are listed here with the description that is provided within the product:

- **Left Outer** (all rows from the first table, only matching rows from the second)
- **Right Outer** (all rows from the second table, only matching rows from the first)
- **Full Outer** (all rows from both tables)
- **Inner** (only matching rows from both tables)
- **Left Anti** (rows only in the first table)
- **Right Anti** (rows only in the second table)

Many of you may already be very familiar with these different join terms from the SQL programming you have learned in the past. However, if these terms are new to you, I recommend reviewing *Visualizing Merge Join Types in Power BI*, courtesy of Jason Thomas in the *Power BI Data Story Gallery*: https://community.powerbi.com/t5/Data-Stories-Gallery/Visualizing-Merge-Join-Types-in-Power-BI/m-p/219906. This visual aid is a favorite of many users that are new to these concepts.

To examine the **Merge Queries** option, you will pick up from where you left off with the **Unpivot** examples in the previous section:

1.   With the **Population** query selected, find and select **Merge Queries | Merge Queries as New** on the **Home** ribbon.

2. In the **Merge** dialog box, select the **Income** query from the drop-down selection in the middle of the screen.

3. Then, multi-select the **Country** and **Year** columns on the **Population** query, and do the same under the **Income** query. This defines which columns will be used to join the two queries together. Ensure that the number indicators next to the column headers match, as demonstrated in *Figure 3.18*. If they don't, you could accidentally attempt to join the incorrect columns.

4. Next, select **Inner (only matching rows)** for **Join Kind**. This join type will return rows only when the columns you chose to join on have values that exist in both queries. Before you click **OK**, confirm that your screen matches *Figure 3.18*:

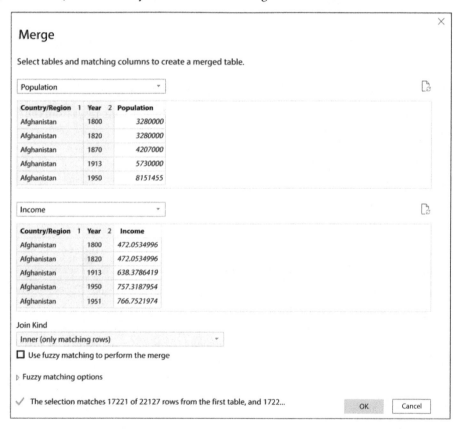

Figure 3.18: Configuring a merge between two queries

5. Once you select **OK**, this will create a new query called Merge1 that combines the results of the two queries. Go ahead and rename this query Country Statistics.

6. You will also notice that there is a column called Income that has a value of Table for each row. This column is actually representative of the entire Income query that you joined to. To choose which columns you want from this query, click the **Expand** button on the column header. After clicking the **Expand** button, uncheck **Country, Year**, and **Use original column name as prefix**, then click **OK**.

7. Rename the column called Income.1 to Income. *Figure 3.19* shows this step completed:

	A⁸꜀ Country/Region	A⁸꜀ Year	1.2 Population	1.2 Income
1	Afghanistan	1800	3280000	472.0534996
2	Afghanistan	1820	3280000	472.0534996
3	Afghanistan	1913	5730000	638.3786419
4	Afghanistan	1950	8151455	757.3187954
5	Afghanistan	1951	8276820	766.7521974
6	Afghanistan	1952	8407148	779.4453145
7	Afghanistan	1953	8542906	812.8562795
8	Afghanistan	1954	8684494	815.3595213
9	Afghanistan	1955	8832253	816.414838
10	Afghanistan	1956	8986449	837.0669354

Figure 3.19: Configuring a merge between two queries

8. Finally, since you chose the option **Merge Queries as New** in *Step 1*, you can disable the load option for the original queries that you started with. To do this, right-click on the **Income** query in the **Queries** pane and click **Enable load** to disable it. Do the same thing for the **Population** query, as shown in *Figure 3.20*. Disabling these queries means that the only query that will be loaded into your Power BI data model is the new one, called **Country Stats:**

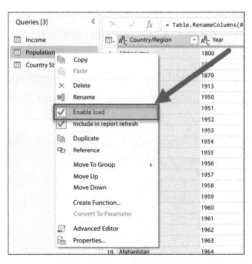

Figure 3.20: Uncheck to disable the loading of this query into the data model

To begin using this dataset in a report, you would click **Close & Apply**. You will learn more about building reports in *Chapter 6, Visualizing Data*.

By default, merging queries together relies on exact matching values between your join column(s). However, you may work with data that does not always provide perfect matching values. For example, a user enters data and misspells their country as Unite States instead of United States. In those cases, you may consider the more advanced feature called **fuzzy matching**. With fuzzy matching, Power BI can perform an approximate match and still join on these two values based on their similarity. In this section, you learned how the **Merge Queries** option is ideal for joining two queries together. In the next section, you will learn how to solve the problem of performing a union of two or more queries.

Append Query

Occasionally, you will work with multiple datasets that need to be appended to each other. Here's a scenario: you work for a customer service department for a company that provides credit or loans to customers. You are regularly provided with .csv and .xlsx files that give summaries of customer complaints regarding credit cards and student loans. You would like to analyze both of these data extracts at the same time but, unfortunately, the credit card and student loan complaints are provided in two separate files. In this example, you will learn how to solve this problem by performing an append operation on these two different files:

1. Launch a new instance of Power BI Desktop, and use the Excel Workbook connector to import the workbook called Student Loan Complaints.xlsx found in the book source files. Once you select this workbook, choose the spreadsheet called **Student Loan Complaints** in the **Navigator** window, and then select **Transform Data** to launch the Power Query Editor.

2. Next, import the credit card data by selecting **New Source | Text/CSV**, then choose the file called Credit Card Complaints.csv found in the book source files. Click **OK** to bring this data into the Power Query Editor.

3. With the Credit Card Complaints query selected, find and select **Append Queries | Append Queries as New** on the **Home** ribbon.

4. Select **Student Loan Complaints** as the table to append to, then select **OK,** as shown in *Figure 3.21*:

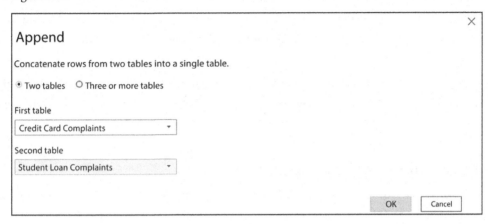

Figure 3.21: Configuring an append between two queries

5. Rename the newly created query **All Complaints** and view the results, as seen in *Figure 3.22*:

Figure 3.22: Configuring an append between two queries

6. Similar to the previous example, you would likely want to disable the load option for the original queries that you started with. To do this, right-click on the **Student Load Complaints** query in the **Queries** pane and click **Enable load** to disable it.

7. Do the same to the **Credit Card Complaints** query, and then select **Close & Apply**.

Now that you have learned about the various methods for combining data, the next section will discuss a more advanced method of working with data using the R programming language.

The R programming language

R is a very powerful scripting language that is primarily used for advanced analytics tools but also has several integration points within Power BI. One such integration is the ability to apply business rules to your data with the R language.

Why is that important? Well, with this capability, you can extend beyond the limits of the Power Query Editor and call functions and libraries from R to do things that would not normally be possible. In the next two sections, you will explore how to set up your machine to leverage R within Power BI and then walk through an example of using an R script transform.

 There are many additional books and references you can read to learn more about the R scripting language, but for the purposes of this book, our goal is to inform you of what is possible when R and Power BI are combined.

Installation and configuration

To use R within Power BI, you must first install an R distribution for you to run and execute scripts against. In this book, we will leverage Microsoft's distribution, **Microsoft R Open**. It is an open source project and free for anyone to use. Once Microsoft R Open has been installed, you can then configure Power BI to recognize the home directory where R libraries may be installed. Let's walk through these setup steps together:

1. Navigate to https://mran.microsoft.com/download/ to download and install Microsoft R Open.

2. For the purposes of our example, you will select **Download** next to **Windows**.

3. Once the download has completed, run the installation and accept all default settings and user agreements.

4. Next, launch a new instance of Power BI Desktop to set up the R integration with Power BI. Click the menu options **File | Options and settings | Options**.

5. Choose the **R scripting** section and ensure that the **Detected R home directories** property is filled with the R instance you just installed, as shown in *Figure 3.23*:

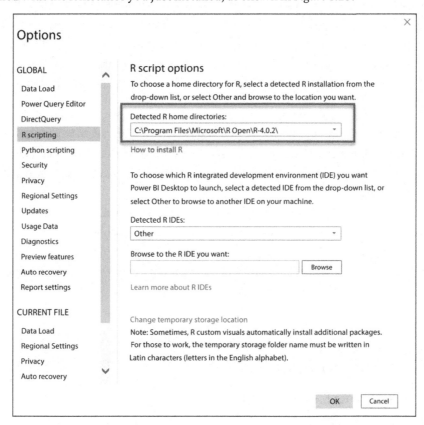

Figure 3.23: Mapping the R home directories in Power BI

6. Once this is completed, click **OK**.

With this setup now complete, let's see how we can take advantage of R within Power BI.

The R script transform

With the R distribution now installed and configured to integrate with Power BI, you are now ready to see what's possible with these new capabilities. In this example, you will be looking at data from the European stock market. The problem with this dataset, which calls for it to be corrected with R, is that the file provided to you has missing values for certain days. So, to get a more accurate reading of the stock market, you will use an R package called MICE to impute the missing values:

1. Before beginning in Power BI, you should ensure that the MICE library is installed and available in the R distribution you set up in the last section. To do this, launch Microsoft R Open from your device. This is the basic RGui that was installed for you to run R scripts with.

    Although we will be using Microsoft R Open, for many developers, the preferred method for writing R scripts is a free open source tool called RStudio. RStudio includes a code editor and debugging and visualization tools that many find easier to work with. You can download RStudio from https://www.rstudio.com/.

2. Type the following script in the **R Console** window, and then hit *Enter*:

    ```
    install.packages("mice")
    ```

    This input is illustrated in the following screenshot:

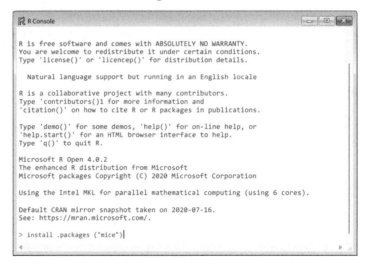

Figure 3.24: Running the library install in RGui

3. If you are prompted to install in a personal library, select **yes**.

4. You can close the **R Console** window and return to Power BI Desktop after it returns an output like the following:

```
package 'mice' successfully unpacked and MD5 sums checked
```

5. In Power BI Desktop, start by connecting to the required data source called EuStockMarkets_ NA.csv from the book source files using the Text/CSV connector. Once you connect to the file, click **Transform Data** to launch the Power Query Editor.

6. You will notice that there are a few days that are missing values in the **SMI (Stock Market Index)** column. We would like to replace values that show **NA** with approximate values using an R script. Go to the **Transform** ribbon, and select the **Run R Script** button on the far right.

7. Use the following R script to call the MICE library that you recently installed to detect what the missing values in this dataset should be:

```
# 'dataset' holds the input data for this script
library(mice)
tempData <- mice(dataset,m=1,maxit=50,meth='pmm',seed=100)
completedData <- complete(tempData,1)
output <- dataset
output$completedValues <- completedData$"SMI missing values"
```

8. Click **OK**. If you are prompted with a warning indicating **Information is required about data privacy**, click **Continue**. You may also be prompted with a **Privacy levels** dialog box. If so, select **Ignore Privacy Levels checks for this file** and then click **Save**.

9. Next, click on the hyperlink on the table value next to the completedData row to see the result of the newly implemented transform for detecting missing values.

This new output has replaced the missing values with new values that were detected based on the algorithm used within the R script. To now build a set of report visuals on this example, you can click **Close & Apply** on the **Home** ribbon.

This is just one simple way that R can be used with Power BI. You should note that in addition to using R as a transform, it can also be used as a data source and as a visual within Power BI.

While this book highlights the programming language R to extend the capabilities of Power BI, some might prefer Python. Python is another programming language that allows for extensibility into Power BI to create new data connectors, transforms, and visuals. So, should you choose R or Python? That depends on which you are more comfortable with. If you have already spent time learning Python, then stick with that! In the next section of this chapter, you will learn about Power BI's AI integration features, which give you the ability to call on components of Azure Cognitive Services with the Power Query Editor.

AI Insights

As you learned in the previous section, Power BI integrates and takes advantage of outside tools to enhance the capabilities within itself. That continues to be the case with the **AI Insights** features. Leveraging the AI Insights capabilities gives you the ability to tap into core features and algorithms within **Azure Cognitive Services** and expose them within Power BI. So how can this be useful to you?

Imagine you work for a company that runs a vacation rentals website. Customers can book trips and post reviews of them on your website. With thousands of customers and hundreds of rental homes, it can be difficult to manage all the reviews that come in to make sure your locations are all meeting the standards your customers expect. With AI Insights you can run algorithms that can perform **sentiment analysis, key phrase extraction, language detection**, and even **image tagging**.

So, if you have international customers that post reviews, you can use language detection to understand what language the post was written in. Then you can use sentiment analysis to capture whether the review was positive or negative. Finally, using phrase extraction, you can pull out key terms in the reviews to see if the same locations continue to receive feedback regarding similar problems. Furthermore, if your feedback system allows photos to be posted in the reviews, the image tagging capabilities can return a list of characteristics found in the images posted. This would allow for the automated categorization of images using AI.

As you can see, these are very powerful features that take your analytics processing to the next level. There are limitations, however, that you should be aware of before exploring these features. As of the time that this book was published, Cognitive Services integration is only supported for Power BI Premium capacity nodes EM2, A2, or P1 and above. You may also use the Power BI Premium Per User license to work with these features. This means if your company is not currently leveraging Power BI Premium, then these features are not available to you.

Before using the AI Insights features in Power BI, you will need to change the capacity settings in the Power BI admin portal to enable the AI workload. After turning on the AI workload setting, you can also set the maximum amount of memory you would like to give the workload. The general recommendation is a memory limit of 20%.

In the next section, you will learn how to leverage an AI Insights Text Analytics feature called Sentiment Analysis.

Sentiment Analysis with Text Analytics

The **Text Analytics** features within the AI Insights features can be incredible time-savers. Imagine having to read paragraphs of information and conclude what was important or whether it was written in a positive or negative light. These are exactly the type of things that this feature can do for you. In this next example, you are going to test out one of these features by running a sentiment analysis algorithm on hotel reviews to see how customers feel about staying at your hotel locations:

1. Launch a new instance of Power BI Desktop, and use the Excel Workbook connector to import the workbook called Hotel Ratings.xlsx found in the book source files. Once you select this workbook, choose the spreadsheet called **Reviews** in the **Navigator** window, and then select **Transform Data** to launch the Power Query Editor.

2. Select **Text Analytics** on the **Home** ribbon of the Power Query Editor. If this is your first time using this feature, you may be prompted to sign into a Power BI account that has Power BI Premium capacity assigned to it.

3. Next, you will be prompted to choose which Text Analytics algorithm you would like to use. Select **Score sentiment**, as shown in *Figure 3.25*, and ensure the **ReviewText** field is the **Text** that will be analyzed. Then click **OK**:

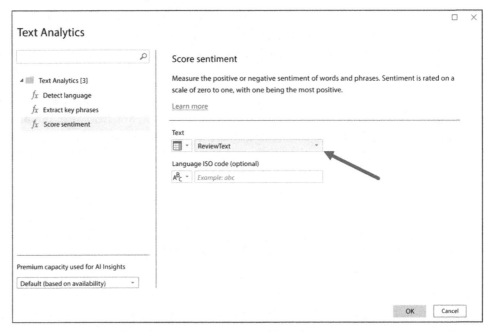

Figure 3.25: Using the Text Analytics feature

4. If prompted with a data privacy warning, click **Continue** and then select **Ignore Privacy Levels check** for this file before clicking **Save**. This type of warning can occur when you combine two disparate sources or services together and is to ensure it is OK for these data sources to be combined.

This transform will produce a new numeric column with a value between 0 and 1 for every row in the dataset.

A sentiment score of .50 is considered neutral, while any score lower is negative and any score higher is generally positive:

ReviewText	Title	Score sentiment
Everything that has been written by other reviewers was spot on. It is...	Very accommodating	0.124835461
This place needs a complete overhaul from top to bottom. It is run do...	OLD, RUN-DOWN SMELLS MUSTY - AV_	0.00153321
I can't say enought good things about the Fort Conde Inn!! The place it...	A True Gem	0.803139627
We've stayed in several of the hotels in Griffin, I feel this is one of the ...	One of the best in Griffin	0.787136734
I travel a lot and see a lot hotels. However this was the worst bathroo...	Not good at all	0.226432294
My family and I recently moved to Jacksonville and experienced some...	Great Experience!	0.974209011
Beds were had as rocks, light came in through the wind since there we...	Felt more like a boarding house	0.90875572
I knew when I booked this hotel, a few several months in advance, I kn...	Buyer Beware	0.083024442
This was a terrific place to stay. Just minutes from Spearfish Canyon an...	great place to stay	0.99323523
If you just need a room in an modestly accessible area, this property d...	Amenities Lacking	0.5
Love how I can count on La Quinta for a great nights sleep. Best beds!	Great Room	0.98553443
We enjoyed a one night stay while passing through. Very convenient o...	Very nice property	0.950750291
Comfortable accommodations and friendly, excellent staff. Stayed for ...	Enjoyable	0.992243648
Hampton Inn and suites were a vet pleasant surprise for us. The king s...	Best place in town	0.988350809
The staff was very friendly.	Comfortable Suite Hotel	0.923171163
A very pleasant stay, convenient to everything in Albany.	My six night stay at Days Inn	0.948374689
My husband spent 6 days at Hyatt Place Northpoint. The staff was extr...	Great place to stay	0.940660596
I was visiting family at a nearby Army base and wanted to stay at a hot...	A great find!	0.14485395
Undenvhelmed. This hotel smells bad, has some loud, partying guests.	Don't Bother Staying Here....	0.025672793
This is our 3rd year returning to Gatlinburg and I must say this is the b...	Love!!!!!!	0.169369876

Figure 3.26: Results of Score sentiment

Looking at *Figure 3.26*, it looks like the AI integration, with a few exceptions, did a good job determining how to rate each review.

Next, in the final section of this chapter, you will be introduced to the M formula language.

The M formula language

The Power Query Editor is the user interface that is used to design and build data imports. However, you should also know that every transform you apply within this editor is actually, quietly and behind the scenes, writing an **M** query for you. The letter M here is a reference to the language's data mash-up capabilities.

For simple solutions, it is unlikely that you will ever need to even look at the M query that is being written, but there are some more complex cases where it's helpful to understand how to read and write your own M. For the purposes of this book, covering just the Power BI essentials, you will learn how to find the M query editor within your solution and then understand how to read what it is doing for you.

For the purposes of this example, you can open up any previously built example; however, the screenshot used here is from the very first example in this chapter on basic transforms:

1. Using any Power BI solution you have designed, launch the Power Query Editor.

2. On the **Home** ribbon, select **Advanced Editor** to see the M query that has been written by the user interface. *Figure 3.27* shows an example of what your **Advanced Editor** might show:

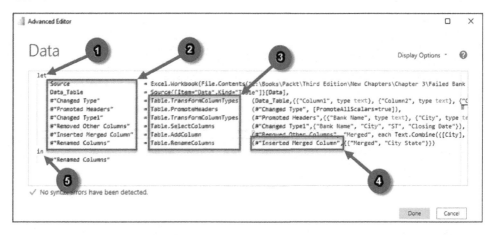

Figure 3.27: Understanding the elements of M

This query has been formatted to make it easier to read. Let's review the key elements that are present here:

1. The **let** expression: Encapsulates a set of values or named expressions to be computed.

2. **Named expressions or variables**: The name given to a set of operations in a step. These names can be anything, but you should note that if you wish to have a space in the name of a step then it must be surrounded by #"". For example, if I wanted something to be called *Step 1*, then I would have to name an expression #"Step 1". If a space is not required in the name of your step, then double quotes are not required.

3. **M functions**: The operations that are used to manipulate the data source.

4. **Prior step reference**: The M query language generally executes its functions as serial operations, meaning each operation is executed one after the other sequentially. You can see this when you look at a query because each call to an M function always references the prior-named expression, to pick up where it left off.

5. The **in** expression: Oddly, the in expression is actually a reference to what the query will output. Whichever named expression is referenced in the in expression will be what is returned in the Power Query Editor preview.

 It is important to realize that M is case-sensitive. That means if you ever make a change to a query or write one from scratch, you should be careful because there is a difference between "a" and "A."

Exploring the M Query library with #shared

As mentioned previously, this book will not dive deep into writing your own M queries since that would be far beyond the essentials of Power BI. However, there is a great method for exploring the M functions that are available, and how to use them. Within the Power Query Editor, you can use the #shared function to return documentation on every available function in the M library. Let's walk through how you can leverage this tool:

1. In a new instance of Power BI Desktop, select **Get data** and then choose **Blank Query**. This will launch the Power Query Editor with an empty formula bar waiting for you to provide your own M.

2. In this formula bar, type = #shared, then hit *Enter*. Remember that M is case-sensitive so you must use a lowercase s when typing shared.

3.   This will return a list of all the available M functions. By selecting the cell that has the hyperlink text of a certain function, you can see documentation on how to use each function. *Figure 3.28* shows an example of this:

Figure 3.28: Example of function documentation

This is a great method for learning what M functions are available, and how each may be used. If you are stumped on how to solve a problem using M, then make this your first stop to explore what options you have.

Summary

In this chapter, you learned that the Power Query Editor is an extremely powerful tool for applying business rules to incoming data. Implementing data cleansing techniques can be as simple as right-clicking on a column, or more complex, such as when building a conditional column. While the Power Query Editor does have a vast library of transforms available, you also learned that you can tap into the capabilities of R to extend what's possible when designing queries. Finally, this chapter discussed the AI capabilities within the Power Query Editor that allow you to leverage several algorithms available within Azure Cognitive Services. In the next chapter on building the data model, you will learn about proper techniques for developing a well-designed Power BI data model to ensure your solutions can solve all your reporting needs.

Join our community on Discord

Join our community's Discord space for discussions with the authors and other readers:

https://packt.link/ips2H

4

Building the Data Model

In this chapter, you are now going to create a coherent and intelligent data model. Creating a data model is primarily the process of creating necessary relationships between the different data sources that are leveraged in your model.

Self-service BI would not be possible without a functional data model. Historically, BI projects focused on building data models could take months and even years to develop when working within the rigid structure and constraints of a corporate business intelligence environment. Unfortunately, studies show that about 50 percent of all enterprise BI projects fail. These projects fail because the costs are often too high; these projects can cost anywhere from hundreds of thousands of dollars to millions of dollars due to the costs associated with the infrastructure, licensing, and labor. Another reason for the low success rate is that the business and end users often won't see any results for many months and can grow frustrated with the lack of visibility in key business areas. These longer project timelines are a result of the time it takes to work through the gathering of requirements, architecting a complex data model, and cleaning up the original data sources. For the enterprise BI projects that do make it all the way to completion, they will often not deliver on promised deliverables and lack the components needed to perform the analytical tasks requested by the business.

Fortunately, Power BI Desktop removes all of the barriers that have resulted in the high failure rate of traditional enterprise BI projects. Power BI Desktop provides you with a much more agile approach to building your data model. Therefore, project completion is measured in days not months or years, the cost is exponentially cheaper, and any missing components can easily be added as needed. The topics detailed in this chapter are as follows:

* Organizing data with a star schema

- Building relationships
- Working with complex relationships
- Usability enhancements
- Improving data model performance

Power BI Desktop and the self-service agile approach greatly improve the success of BI projects and this is due to the flexibility of Power BI. Power BI allows you to easily and quickly create meaningful relationships with the different tables that have been imported into your data model. In this section, you will learn how to build relationships in Power BI Desktop.

Organizing data with a star schema

We have worked with consultants who have spent their entire career building data models specifically designed for reporting and analytical purposes. These same consultants would tell you that you are always learning new ways to model data based on business requirements, technology enhancements, and the data. Building a data model is much more an art than it is a science.

However, you don't need 20 years of data modeling experience to be successful in Power BI. You just need to understand the fundamentals of the **star schema**.

The star schema is a way of modeling data that is designed specifically for making it easier to build reports and retrieve analytical value from your data. The star schema way of designing your data model makes the entire model easier to understand and work with. The star schema method of modeling is part of a much broader topic called **dimensional modeling**. Dimensional modeling has two main types of tables; those tables are facts and dimensions.

Simply put, facts are events you want to measure. This can be the sale of goods, a student attending a class, an interaction with a member, or any other type of event that you need to measure. The type of event you want to measure can vary wildly across business units and industries.

On the other hand, dimensions are what describe your facts (events). If a company made five million in sales, you might ask for what year, what country, which products, or which salesperson. Each of these critically important questions about the data tells us exactly what type of dimension (descriptive) tables we need to build into our model. Here, we identified four separate dimension tables:

- Date (year)
- Geography (country)

- Employee (salesperson)
- Products (product)

The model that is used throughout this book represents a dimensional model with a fact and multiple dimension tables. When you look at the model view, the tables can appear to be in the shape of a star, hence where the term "star schema" comes from.

In this section, we briefly discussed dimensional modeling and the star schema. A deeper dive is outside the scope of this book but keep these ideas in mind as you progress through the remainder of this book and start building your own data models!

Building relationships

A relationship in Power BI simply defines how different tables are related to one another. For example, your customer table may be related to your sales table on the customer key column. You could argue that the building of relationships is the most important aspect of Power BI Desktop. It is this process, the building of relationships, that makes everything else work like magic in Power BI. The automatic filtering of visuals and reports, the ease with which you can author measures with **Data Analysis Expressions (DAX)**, and the ability to quickly connect disparate data sources are all made possible through properly built relationships in the data model.

Sometimes, Power BI Desktop will create the relationships for you automatically. It is important to verify these *auto-detected relationships* to ensure accuracy.

There are a few characteristics of relationships that you should be aware of, which will be discussed in this section:

- Auto-detected relationships
- There may be only one active relationship between two tables
- There may be an unlimited number of inactive relationships between two tables
- Relationships may only be built on a single column, not multiple columns
- Relationships automatically filter from the *one side* of the relationship to the *many side*

Now, to examine some of the key elements of relationships in Power BI, open up the pbix file Chapter 4 - Building the Data Model.pbix found in your class files:

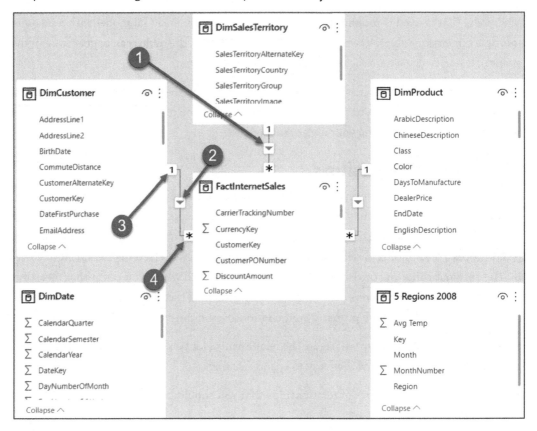

Figure 4.1: Reviewing relationships

Following the numbering, let's take a closer look at each of the four items highlighted in the preceding *Figure 4.1*:

1. **Relationship**: The line between two tables represents that a relationship exists.

2. **Direction**: The arrow indicates in which direction filtering will occur.

3. **One side**: The 1 indicates the **DimCustomer** table as the *one side* of the relationship. This means the key from the *one side* of the relationship is always unique in that table.

4. **Many side**: The * indicates that the **FactInternetSales** table is the *many side* of the relationship. The key will appear in the sales table for each transaction; therefore, the key appears many times.

The first thing you should do after importing data is to verify that all auto-detected relationships have been created correctly. From the **Home** ribbon, select **Manage relationships**, as seen in *Figure 4.2*. When in the **Report** view, **Manage relationships** will appear on the **Modeling** ribbon. When in the **Data** view, **Manage relationships** appears on the **Table tools** ribbon, and when in the **Model** view, **Manage relationships** appears on the **Home** ribbon:

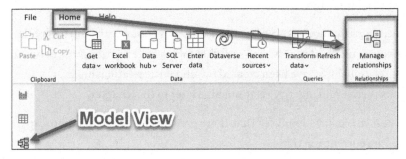

Figure 4.2: Launch the Manage relationships editor

This will open up the **Manage relationships** editor. The relationship editor is one of two places where you will go to create new relationships and edit or delete existing relationships. In this demo, the relationship editor will be used to verify the relationships that were automatically created by Power BI Desktop.

Figure 4.3 provides a view of the **Manage relationships** editor:

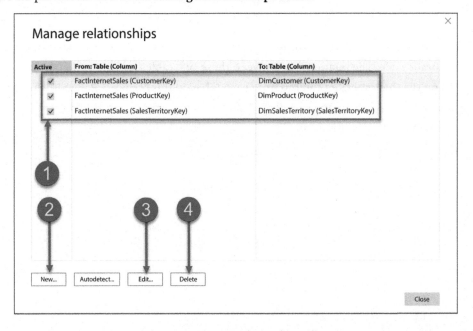

Figure 4.3: Manage relationships editor

Let's break down the editor using the numbered figure:

1. Current relationships in the data model

2. Create a new relationship

3. Edit an existing relationship

4. Delete a relationship

First, you need to verify auto-detected relationships. In *Figure 4.3*, the top half of the relationship editor gives you a quick and easy way to see what tables have relationships between them, what columns the relationships have been created on, and if the relationship is an active relationship. We will discuss active and inactive relationships later in this chapter.

Take a look at *Figure 4.4*; you will see that there are currently three relationships, and all three relationships are currently active:

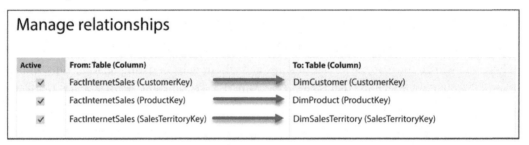

Manage relationships

Active	From: Table (Column)		To: Table (Column)
✓	FactInternetSales (CustomerKey)	→	DimCustomer (CustomerKey)
✓	FactInternetSales (ProductKey)	→	DimProduct (ProductKey)
✓	FactInternetSales (SalesTerritoryKey)	→	DimSalesTerritory (SalesTerritoryKey)

Figure 4.4: Verifying relationships

The first row in *Figure 4.4* displays the relationship between the **FactInternetSales** table and the **DimCustomer** table. The relationship between these two tables was created automatically by Power BI on the **CustomerKey** column from each table. In this scenario, Power BI has correctly chosen the correct column names. However, if the relationship was created in error, then you would need to edit that relationship.

Now, let's take a look at how to edit an existing relationship.

Editing relationships

In this example, you will edit the relationship between **FactInternetSales** and **DimCustomer**. To edit an existing relationship, select that relationship and then click on **Edit...**:

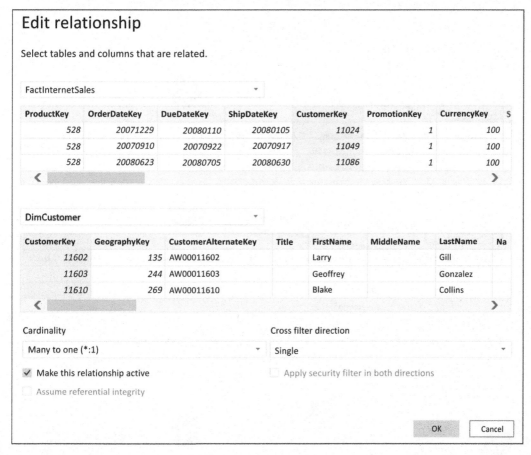

Figure 4.5: Editing a relationship

Once you select **Edit...** you will receive a new dialog box; this is the **Edit relationship** editor. In this view, you will see how to change an existing relationship, how to change a relationship to active or inactive, and the cardinality of the current relationship; this is also where you can change the **Cross filter direction**:

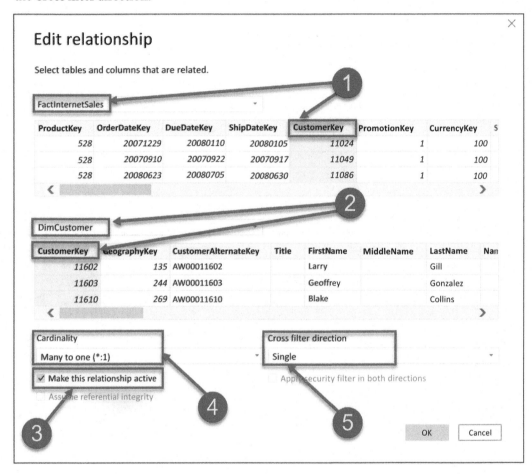

Figure 4.6: Editing a relationship

There are five numbered items we will review from *Figure 4.6*:

1. This identifies the **FactInternetSales** table and the column that the relationship was built on, **CustomerKey**.

2. This identifies the **DimCustomer** table and the column that the relationship was built on, also **CustomerKey**.

3. This checkbox identifies whether the relationship is active or inactive.

4. This is the current cardinality between the two tables. Here, we see that there is a *many-to-one* relationship between **FactInternetSales** and **DimCustomer**. Power BI does an excellent job of identifying the correct cardinality, but it is important to always verify that the cardinality is correct.

5. The cross-filter direction can be **Single** or **Both**. The *one side* of a relationship always filters the *many side* of the relationship, and this is the default behavior in Power BI. The cross-filter option allows you to change this behavior. Cross-filtering will be discussed later in this chapter.

If you need to change an existing relationship, then you would do that in the relationship editor seen in *Figure 4.6*. To change the column that a relationship has been created on, simply select a different column. It is important to point out that a relationship between two tables may only be created on a single column. Therefore, if you have a relationship that needs to be defined on multiple columns, also known as a composite key, then you would need to first combine those keys into a single column before creating your relationship. You saw how to combine columns in *Chapter 3, Data Transformation Strategies*.

Creating a new relationship

In the previous section, you saw how to verify existing relationships, and even how to edit them. In this section, you are going to learn how to create a new relationship. There are six tables in the data model thus far, and Power BI automatically created a relationship for all the tables, except for two. Let's begin by creating a relationship between the FactInternetSales and DimDate tables.

The FactInternetSales table stores three different dates: OrderDate, ShipDate, and DueDate. There can be only one active relationship between tables in Power BI, and all filtering occurs through the active relationship. In other words, which date do you want to see your total sales, profit, and profit margin calculations on? If it's OrderDate, then your relationship will be on the OrderDate column from the FactInternetSales table to the FullDateAlternateKey column in the DimDate table. To create a new relationship, open **Manage relationships** from the **Home** ribbon.

Now, let's create a relationship from the **OrderDate** column in **FactInternetSales** to the **Full-DateAlternateKey** column in **DimDate**. With the **Manage relationships** editor open, click on **New...** to open the **Create relationship** editor:

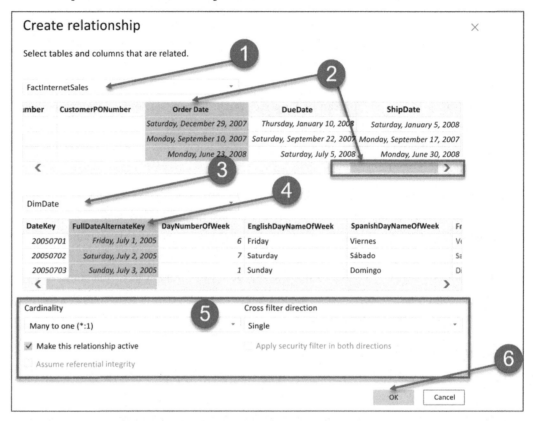

Figure 4.7: Creating a new relationship

Complete the following steps to create a new relationship:

1. Select **FactInternetSales** from the list of tables in the dropdown.

2. Select **OrderDate** from the list of columns; use the scroll bar to scroll all the way to the right.

3. Select **DimDate** from the next drop-down list.

4. Select **FullDateAlternateKey** from the list of columns.

5. **Cardinality**, **Cross filter direction**, and whether the relationship is active or inactive are updated automatically by Power BI; remember to always verify these items.

6. Click **OK** to close the editor.

Now, let's take a look at creating the relationship on the date key rather than the Date column.

Creating a relationship on the date key

The astute reader may have noticed that the previous demo used the actual date columns from each table instead of the date keys. This is because most Power BI models will not contain a date key. However, if you are retrieving your data from a relational database or data warehouse, then a date key will most likely exist on both tables, and the relationship can be created on the date key.

 In data modeling, we generally store dates as integer values. More specifically, you can store the date as a **smart key**, for example, 20200706. This type of integer value is called a smart key because the date is stored as an integer, but you can still derive the date from the integer value. For example, the first four characters are the year, the next two represent the month, and the final two represent the day number of the month. Storing your dates as integer values is a best practice and will help save space in the model.

In *Figure 4.8*, you see an example of creating a relationship on the date keys in each table:

FactInternetSales

ProductKey	OrderDateKey	DueDateKey	ShipDateKey	CustomerKey	PromotionKey	CurrencyKey	S
528	20071229	20080110	20080105	11024	1	100	
528	20070910	20070922	20070917	11049	1	100	
528	20080623	20080705	20080630	11086	1	100	

DimDate

DateKey	Date	DayNumberOfWeek	EnglishDayNameOfWeek	SpanishDayNameOfWeek
20050701	Friday, July 1, 2005	6	Friday	Viernes
20050702	Saturday, July 2, 2005	7	Saturday	Sábado
20050703	Sunday, July 3, 2005	1	Sunday	Domingo

Figure 4.8: Creating a new relationship using the date keys

The date table in the Power BI data model is important for developing time intelligence calculations. When you define your relationship on the date key, rather than the date column, it is important to also mark your date table as a date table! If this step is not performed, some built-in time intelligence functions may not work as expected.

Time intelligence is discussed in further detail in *Chapter 5, Leveraging DAX*.

At the time of writing, marking a table as a date table can only be accomplished in the **Report** view or **Data** view. There are two ways to mark a table as a date table. First, you can right-click on the date table and choose **Mark as date table | Mark as date table**:

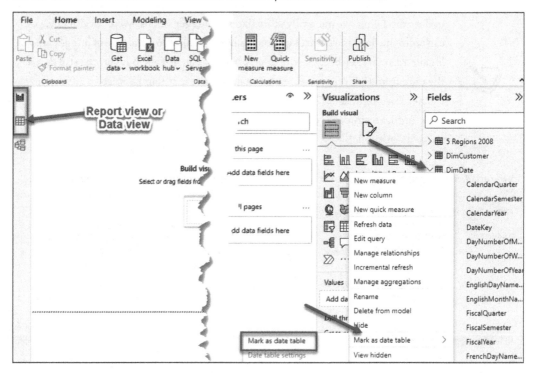

Figure 4.9: Mark as date table

Secondly, you can select the date table; go to the **Table tools** ribbon and select **Mark as date table**:

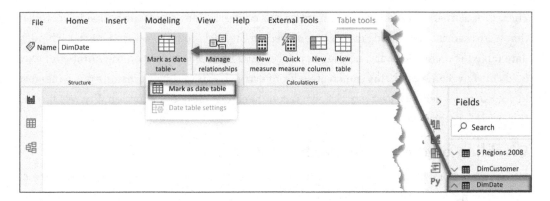

Figure 4.10: Mark as date table, alternate method

Once **Mark as date table** is selected, you will then be prompted to select the **Date column** from your date table:

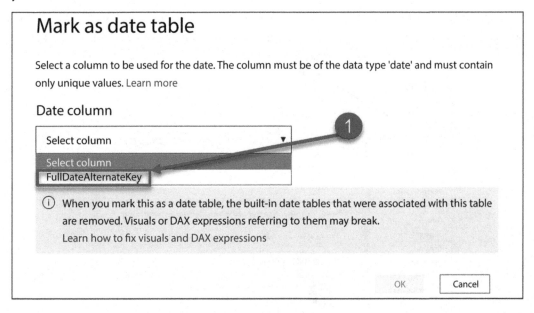

Figure 4.11: Select valid date column from date table

Power BI will automatically limit the list of available options to columns that are set to a date type and have only unique values.

There is one other important thing to note on this configuration screen: the built-in date tables that were associated with this table are removed. In the background, Power BI creates a hidden date table for each field that has a date or date/time field. Depending on the number of date fields in your data model, this can create a lot of extra objects and will consume more memory in your data model! As a best practice, we recommend disabling this functionality. We'll cover this process in the next section.

Disabling automatically created date tables

As mentioned previously, Power BI automatically creates hidden date tables for each date or date/time field in your data model. The date tables created by Power BI can be disabled from the **Options** menu. This functionality is automatically enabled on your current Power BI file and will be enabled on future files. Therefore, you will need to disable the auto date/time capability in two separate locations from the **Options** menu.

To open the **Options** menu, in Power BI Desktop, go to **File | Options and Settings | Options**. Once the **Options** window has been opened, complete the following steps, as seen in *Figure 4.12*:

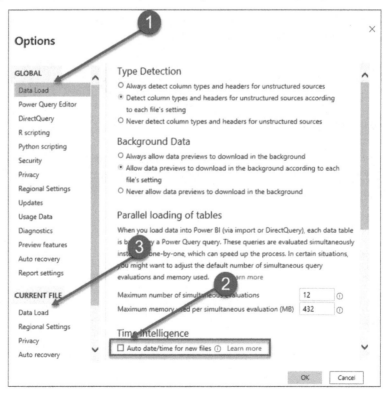

Figure 4.12: Disable automatically created hidden date tables

1. Under **GLOBAL**, choose **Data Load**.
2. Uncheck **Auto date/time for new files**.
3. Under **CURRENT FILE**, choose **Data Load** and uncheck **Auto date/time**.

In this section, you learned how to verify automatically created relationships and how to create new relationships in Power BI Desktop. In the next section, you will learn about working with complex relationships.

Working with complex relationships

There are many complex scenarios that need to be addressed when building a data model, and Power BI is no different in this regard. In this section, you will learn how to handle many-to-many relationships and role-playing tables in Power BI.

Many-to-many relationships

Before we discuss how to build a relationship between two tables that have a many-to-many relationship, let's discuss specifically what a many-to-many relationship is. A many-to-many relationship is when multiple rows in one table are associated with multiple rows in another table. An example of a many-to-many relationship can be observed in the relationship between products and customers. A product can be sold to many customers; likewise, a customer can purchase many products. This relationship between products and customers is a many-to-many relationship. In a one-to-many relationship, a relationship can be created directly between the two tables. However, in a many-to-many relationship, an indirect relationship is often created through a bridge table. This section will focus on how to set up a many-to-many relationship and how to gain analytical value from such relationships!

A more common example of a many-to-many relationship is when you have two separate fact tables that share a similar key. For example, if you have a **FactSales** table and a **FactReturns** table, both tables may contain a product key. From an analytical perspective, how do you now build a report that shows your sales and returns by year, by customer, or by store? The simple answer is, you drill across both tables using your dimension tables. A deep dive into the star schema is outside the scope of this book; however, it is very common for a Power BI data model to have multiple fact tables that have many-to-many relationships between them.

 To learn more about many-to-many relationships, take a look at the following Microsoft link: https://learn.microsoft.com/en-us/power-bi/guidance/relationships-many-to-many.

In the previous section, you learned how to create a relationship between two tables that had a one-to-many relationship. Immediately, once a one-to-many relationship has been defined in your data model, filtering occurs automatically. This adds a tremendous amount of value to Power BI. However, the analytical value achieved through many-to-many relationships does not happen automatically and requires an extra step. Let's take a look at filtering in general and then how to effectively develop many-to-many relationships in Power BI.

Filtering behavior

Before you can learn how to handle many-to-many relationships in Power BI, you must first understand the basic behavior of filtering. Filtering will be discussed in more detail in the next chapter, but now let's take a minor detour to explain how filtering works in this context. In *Figure 4.13*, the total **SalesAmount** of all transactions is **$29,358,677.22**. The visual you see in *Figure 4.13* is simply the sum of the column SalesAmount from the FactInternetSales table:

SalesAmount
29,358,677.22

Figure 4.13: Total unfiltered SalesAmount

To view the total SalesAmount for all transactions broken down by country, all you would need to do is simply add the SalesTerritoryCountry column from the DimSalesTerritory table. This behavior in Power BI is awesome, and this is automatic filtering at work. Take a look at *Figure 4.14*:

SalesTerritoryCountry	SalesAmount
Australia	9,061,000.58
Canada	1,977,844.86
France	2,644,017.71
Germany	2,894,312.34
United Kingdom	3,391,712.21
United States	9,389,789.51
Total	**29,358,677.22**

Figure 4.14: SalesAmount filtered by Country

Please note that this only works because a valid relationship exists between the FactInternetSales and DimSalesTerritory tables. If a relationship had not been created, or if the relationship created was invalid, then you would get entirely different results and they would be confusing. Let's take a look at what would happen if no relationship had previously existed.

In *Figure 4.15*, the **SalesTerritoryCountry** has been removed and replaced with the **Temperature Range** column from the 5 Regions 2008 table:

Temperature Range	SalesAmount
Cold	29,358,677.22
Cool	29,358,677.22
Hot	29,358,677.22
Warm	29,358,677.22
Total	**29,358,677.22**

Figure 4.15: Replacing Country with Temperature Range

Notice how the total sales amount is repeated for each temperature range. This behavior indicates that the 5 Regions 2008 table is unable to filter the FactInternetSales table. This inability to filter can happen for a number of different reasons:

- Because a relationship does not exist between the tables
- Because an existing relationship is invalid
- Because an existing relationship does not allow the filtering to pass through an intermediate table

If you see the repeated value behavior demonstrated in *Figure 4.15*, then go back to the relationship view and verify that all relationships have been created and are valid.

Cross-filtering direction

Now that you understand the basics of automatic filtering in Power BI, let's take a look at an example of a many-to-many relationship. In this data model, DimProduct and DimCustomer have a many-to-many relationship. A product can be sold to many customers. For example, bread can be sold to Jessica, Kim, and Tyrone. A customer can purchase many products. Kim could purchase bread, milk, and cheese.

A bridge table can be used to store the relationship between two tables that have a many-to-many relationship, just like tools you have worked with in the past.

The relationship between `DimProduct` and `DimCustomer` is stored in the `FactInternetSales` table. The `FactInternetSales` table is a large, many-to-many bridge table:

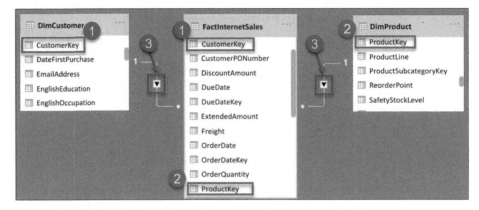

Figure 4.16: Relationship between DimCustomer and FactInternetSales

Figure 4.16 shows the relationship between these two tables; see the following explanation for the numbered points:

1. The relationship between **DimCustomer** and **FactInternetSales**
2. The relationship between **DimProduct** and **FactInternetSales**
3. The cross-filter direction is set to single

The following report in *Figure 4.17*, displays the total sales, total transactions, and customer count for each product:

EnglishProductName	Total Sales	Total Transactions	Customer Count
Adjustable Race			18484
All-Purpose Bike Stand	$39,591.00	249	18484
AWC Logo Cap	$19,688.10	2190	18484
BB Ball Bearing			18484
Bearing Ball			18484
Bike Wash - Dissolver	$7,218.60	908	18484
Blade			18484

Figure 4.17: Customer count for each product

Let's take a closer look at *Figure 4.17*, and note the numbered points:

1. **EnglishProductName** from the `DimProduct` table
2. **Total Sales** is the SUM of the `SalesAmount` column from the `FactInternetSales` table

3. **Total Transactions** is the COUNT of associated rows from the FactInternetSales table

4. **Customer Count** is the COUNT of the CustomerKey column from the DimCustomer table

Total Sales and Total Transactions are returning the correct results for each product. Customer Count is returning the same value for all products (18,484). This is due to the way that filtering works. The calculations for Total Sales and Total Transactions are derived from columns or rows that come from the FactInternetSales table. The Product table has a one-to-many relationship with Internet Sales, and therefore filtering occurs automatically. This explains why those two calculations are being filtered properly, but it does not explain why the count of customers is returning the same repeated value for all products, not entirely anyway.

Let's take another look at the relationship between DimProduct and DimCustomer. Notice in *Figure 4.18* that the relationship between these two tables flows through the FactInternetSales table. This is because they have a many-to-many relationship. In this scenario, the table FactInternetSales is acting as a large, many-to-many bridge table. DimProduct filters FactInternetSales. DimCustomer also filters FactInternetSales, and FactInternetSales is currently unable to filter the customer table:

Figure 4.18: Filtering behavior in Power BI

The repeated value for customer count occurs because FactInternetSales is unable to filter the DimCustomer table. DimProduct filters FactInternetSales, and a list of transactions are returned for each product. Unfortunately, the filtering does not pass from FactInternetSales to DimCustomer. This is because FactInternetSales is on the many side of the relationship with DimCustomer. Therefore, when our calculation performs a count on the customer key, the table is not filtered and the calculation sees every customer key in the DimCustomer table (18,484).

Do you remember the cross-filter direction property that was briefly covered earlier in this chapter? That little property is there to provide many-to-many support. By simply enabling cross-filtering in both directions, the FactInternetSales table will be able to filter the customer table and the customer count will work.

Enabling filtering from the many side of a relationship

To enable cross-filtering, open the relationship editor. Remember, the **Manage relationships** option can be found from the **Report** view, **Data** view, or **Model** view from different ribbons as discussed at the beginning of this chapter. When in **Report** view, **Manage relationships** will appear on the **Modeling** ribbon, when in **Data** view, **Manage relationships** appears on the **Table tools** ribbon, and when in **Model** view, **Manage relationships** appears on the **Home** ribbon.

See *Figure 4.19* for a refresher on where to find it:

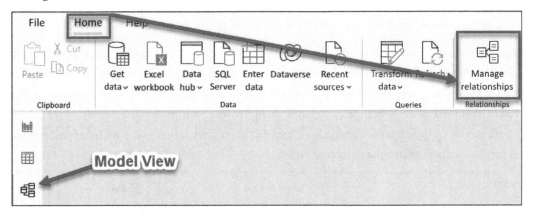

Figure 4.19: Open the relationship editor

Select the relationship between FactInternetSales and DimCustomer, and then click **Edit**. Once the relationship editor has launched, change the **Cross filter direction** from **Single** to **Both**:

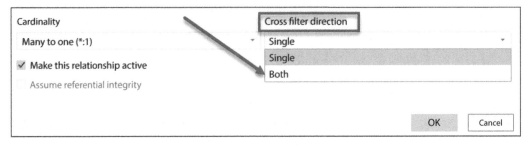

Figure 4.20: Enabling cross-filtering

Back in the **Report** view, you will now see the correct Customer Count for each product, as shown in *Figure 4.21*:

EnglishProductName	Total Sales	Total Transactions	Customer Count
All-Purpose Bike Stand	$39,591.00	249	243
AWC Logo Cap	$19,688.10	2190	2132
Bike Wash - Dissolver	$7,218.60	908	875
Classic Vest, L	$12,382.50	195	195
Classic Vest, M	$12,636.50	199	199
Classic Vest, S	$10,668.00	168	168
Fender Set - Mountain	$46,619.58	2121	2110

Figure 4.21: Customer Count for each product

As a best practice, it is not recommended to enable cross-filtering in your data model. Cross-filtering can cause ambiguity in your results and can cause some time intelligence functions to not function properly; the date table must have a contiguous range of dates and therefore cannot be filtered by other tables. Use the Data Analysis Expression language when possible to return the results seen in *Figure 4.21*. DAX is discussed in *Chapter 5, Leveraging DAX*.

Now that you have learned how to handle many-to-many relationships in Power BI Desktop, let's take a look at how to handle another type of complex relationship. In this section, you will learn what role-playing tables are and how to handle them in Power BI Desktop.

Role-playing tables

A role-playing table is a table that can play multiple roles, which helps to reduce data redundancy. Most often, a date table is a role-playing table. For example, the FactInternetSales table has three dates to track the processing of an order. There is the Order Date, Ship Date, and Due Date and, without role-playing tables, you would need to have three separate date tables instead of just one. The additional tables take up valuable resources, such as memory, as well as adding an extra layer of administrative upkeep.

Each of these dates is very important to different people and different departments within an organization. For example, the finance department may wish to see total sales and profit by the date that a product was purchased, the order date. However, your shipping department may wish to see product quantity based on the ship date. How do you accommodate requests from different departments in a single data model?

One of the things I loved about working with SQL Server Analysis Services multidimensional mode was the ease with which it handled role-playing tables; perhaps you also come from a background where you have worked with tools that had built-in support for role-playing tables. Unfortunately, role-playing tables are not natively supported in Power BI; this is because all filtering in Power BI occurs through the active relationship and you can only have one active relationship between two tables.

There are generally two ways you can handle role-playing tables in Power BI:

- Import the table multiple times and create an active relationship for each table
- Use DAX and inactive relationships to create calculations that show calculations by different dates

The first way, and the method we will show here, is importing the table multiple times. Yes, this means that it will take up more resources. The data model will have three date tables, one table to support each date in the FactInternetSales table. Each date table will have a single active relationship to the FactInternetSales table.

Some of the benefits of importing the table multiple times are as follows:

- It is easier to train and acclimate end users with the data model. For example, if you want to see sales and profit by the ship date, then you would simply use the date attributes from the ship date table in your reports.
- Most of your DAX measures will work across all date tables, so there is no need to create new measures. The exception here is your time intelligence calculations; they will need to be rebuilt for each date table.
- The analytical value of putting different dates in a matrix. For example, sales ordered and sales shipped by date. For clarification, see *Figure 4.22*:

Year	2005 (ShipDate)	2006 (ShipDate)	2007 (ShipDate)	2008 (ShipDate)	Total
2005 (OrderDate)	$3,105,587	$160,786			$3,266,374
2006 (OrderDate)		$6,416,193	$114,151		$6,530,344
2007 (OrderDate)			$9,403,398	$387,663	$9,791,060
2008 (OrderDate)				$9,770,900	$9,770,900
Total	$3,105,587	$6,576,979	$9,517,549	$10,158,562	$29,358,677

Figure 4.22: Sales by ShipDate and OrderDate

In *Figure 4.22* you can observe the analytical benefit of having a shipping date table and an order date table in the same data model. In this example, the total sales are being displayed in a matrix visual with the year from the order date table on the rows and the year from the shipping date table on the columns:

1. The value of $3,266,374 is the number of total sales that were made in the year 2005.

2. The value of $3,105,587 is the number of total sales that were shipped in the year 2005.

3. If you take a look at the column 2006 (ShipDate), you will notice that $6,576,979 of sales shipped in 2006. Upon closer inspection, $160,786 of what shipped in 2006 was actually ordered in 2005 and the remaining $6,416,193 was ordered in 2006.

Some of the cons of importing the table multiples times are:

- **Resources**: Additional memory and space will be used.

- **Administrative changes**: Any modifications made to one table will need to be repeated for all tables, as these tables are not linked. For example, if you create a hierarchy in one table, then you would need to create a hierarchy in all date tables.

- **Time Intelligence**: Time intelligence calculations will need to be rewritten for each date table.

The report in *Figure 4.23* shows total sales and total transactions by year, but which year? Is this the year that a product was purchased or the year a product was shipped? The active relationship is on the order date, so the report is displaying the results based on when the product was purchased:

CalendarYear	Total Sales	Total Transactions
2005	$3,266,373.66	1013
2006	$6,530,343.53	2677
2007	$9,791,060.30	24443
2008	$9,770,899.74	32265
Total	**$29,358,677.22**	**60398**

Figure 4.23: Total sales and total transactions by year

The previous visualization is correct but it is ambiguous. To remove any uncertainty from our reports, the data model can be further improved by renaming columns. In the next section, you will learn how to make small changes in your data model so that the visuals are more specific.

Importing the date table

In this section, we are going to import a date table to support the analysis of data based on when an order shipped. From the **Get data** option, select **Excel** and open the AdventureWorksDW Excel file; the file can be found in the directory location Microsoft-Power-BI-Start-Guide-Second-Edition-main\Data Sources.

Next, select **DimDate** from the list of tables, and then click **Load** as seen in *Figure 4.24*:

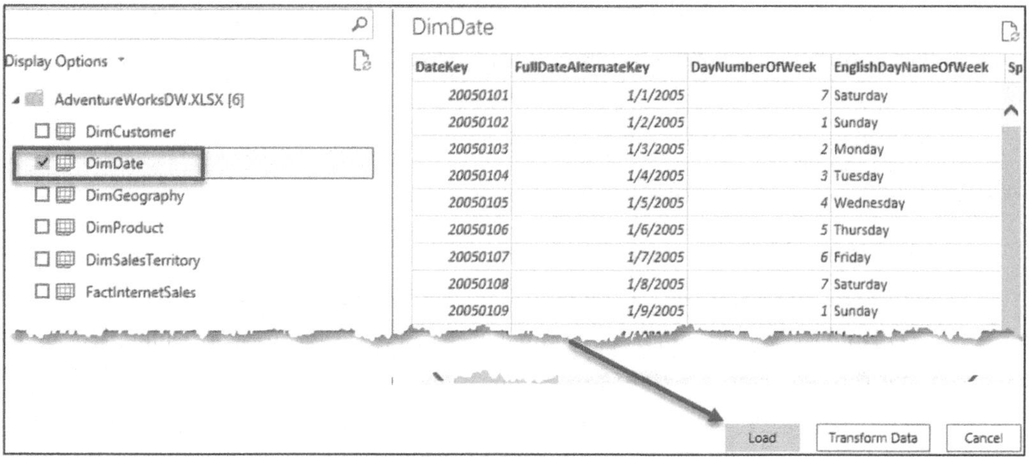

Figure 4.24: Importing DimDate into Power BI

Now that the data has been imported, the next step is creating a valid relationship. Open **Manage relationships** from either the **Home** or **Modeling** ribbon, depending on which view you are currently in. From the relationship editor, click **New** to create a new relationship. For a reminder on how to create a new relationship, refer to *Figure 4.7*. Complete the following steps:

1. Select **FactInternetSales** from the drop-down list
2. Select the **ShipDate** column; use the scroll bar to scroll all the way to the right
3. Select **DimDate (2)** from the drop-down list
4. Select the **FullDateAlternateKey** column
5. Click **OK** to close the **Create relationship** window

I took the liberty of changing the table and column names here, for clarity. You will learn how to rename tables and columns in the following *Usability enhancements* section. DimDate has been renamed Date (Order). DimDate (2) has been renamed Date (Ship).

The data model now has two date tables, each with an active relationship to the FactInternetSales table. If you wish to see sales by Order Year, then you would bring in the year column from the Order Date table, and if you wish to see sales by the Ship Year, then you would bring in the year column from the Ship Date table; see *Figure 4.25*:

Filtered by Order Date			Filtered by Ship Date		
Order Year	Total Sales	Total Transactions	Ship Year	Total Sales	Total Transactions
2005	$3,266,373.66	1013	2005	$3,105,587.33	962
2006	$6,530,343.53	2677	2006	$6,576,978.98	2665
2007	$9,791,060.30	24443	2007	$9,517,548.53	23313
2008	$9,770,899.74	32265	2008	$10,158,562.38	33458
Total	**$29,358,677.22**	**60398**	**Total**	**$29,358,677.22**	**60398**

Figure 4.25: Displaying the ship year column

Importing the same table multiple times is the easiest solution to implement for new users to Power BI because this method doesn't require writing any DAX. This method is easy to explain to end users and allows you to reuse most of your existing DAX calculations.

The alternative method is to create inactive relationships and then create new calculations (measures) using the DAX language. This method of leveraging inactive relationships can become overwhelming from an administrative point of view. Imagine having to create copies of the existing measures in the data model for each relationship between two tables. In the current data model, FactInternetSales stores three dates, and this would possibly mean having to create and maintain three copies of each measure, one to support each date.

In this section, you learned about role-playing tables; this is an important request in most models. Now let's take a look at other usability enhancements that can improve your data model.

Usability enhancements

Usability enhancements are those enhancements that can significantly improve the overall user experience when interacting with the data model. In order to ensure a successful handoff and adoption of the work you have done, it is important to not overlook these rather basic improvements.

In this section, we are going to cover the following usability enhancements:

- Hiding tables and columns
- Renaming tables and columns
- Changing the default summarization property
- Displaying one column but sorting by another
- Setting the data category of fields
- Creating hierarchies

Let's begin by considering how to hide tables and columns.

Hiding tables and columns

Some tables are available in the data model simply in a support capacity and would never be used in a report. For example, you may have a table to support many-to-many relationships, weighted allocation, or even dynamic security. Likewise, some columns are necessary for creating relationships in the data model but would not add any analytical value to the reports. Tables or columns that will not be used for reporting purposes should be hidden from the **Report** view to reduce complexity and improve the user experience.

To hide a column or table, simply right-click on the object you wish to hide, and then select **Hide in report view**. If you are in the **Report** view already, the available option will simply say **Hide**.

Navigate to the **Model** view, find the **FactInternetSales** table, and right-click on **CurrencyKey**, then select **Hide in report view** as seen in *Figure 4.26*:

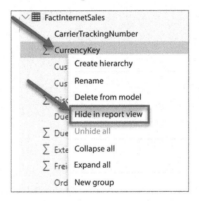

Figure 4.26: Select Hide in report view

Columns that are hidden are still visible in the data and model views. Hidden columns will have a visibility icon that appears to the right of the column name, as seen in *Figure 4.27*:

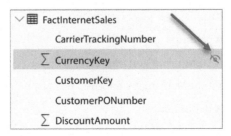

Figure 4.27: Hidden columns

Next, go to each table and hide all remaining key columns, except for `FullDateAlternateKey`.

 When working in the **Model** view, you can multi-select columns by holding down the *Ctrl* key while selecting columns. Therefore, you can select all columns that need to be hidden first, then hide them all in a single action.

Renaming tables and columns

The renaming of tables and columns is an important step in making your data model easy to use. Different departments often have different terms for the same entity, therefore it is important to consider multiple departments when renaming objects. For example, you may have a column with a list of customer names and you decide to name this column `Customer`. However, the sales team may have named that column `Prospect` or `Client`, or any number of other terms. Remember to keep your end users and consumers of your reports in mind when renaming tables and columns.

You may rename tables or columns in the **Report, Data,** or **Model** view. Navigate to the **Model** view and right-click on **FactInternetSales**, then select **Rename**, as seen in *Figure 4.28*. Rename the table `Internet Sales`:

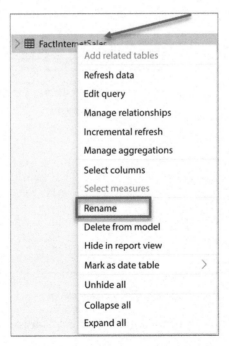

Figure 4.28: Renaming FactInternetSales

Next, rename the remaining tables, removing the `Dim` prefix and adding spaces where applicable. The table below is provided for reference:

Original names	New name
FactInternetSales	Internet Sales
DimDate	Date (Order)
DimDate (2)	Date (Ship)
DimProduct	Product
DimCustomer	Customer
DimSalesTerritory	Sales Territory
5 Regions 2008	Temperature

The next step is necessary, but could be a somewhat tedious process. If you come from a programming or development background, then you will be used to eliminating spaces in table and column names. End users and consumers of reports will expect to see spaces and, for that reason, it is recommended to add spaces where applicable. Spaces need to be added to any column that is visible, not hidden, in the **Report** view. To rename a column, right-click on it and then select **Rename**. In *Figure 4.29*, spaces have been added to **CarrierTrackingNumber** and **CustomerPONumber**:

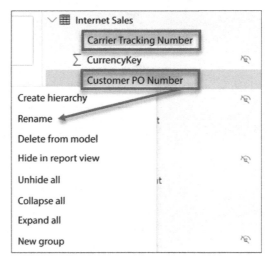

Figure 4.29: Renaming columns

Complete the following steps to rename the rest of your columns:

1. Repeat this process of adding spaces for the remaining columns in each table
2. Rename `FullDateAlternateKey` to simply `Date`

Renaming columns is a simple yet effective step for improving user experience! Now, let's take a look at another important usability enhancement for your data model, changing the default summarization on numeric columns.

 Using the Power Query Editor, you may be able to automate the process of renaming your columns in Power BI. Here is a quick YouTube video outlining this process: https://youtu.be/GF5S2ktPTB0.

Default summarization

By default, Power BI assigns a default summarization to numeric columns that do not have a relationship or appear on the one side of a relationship. This default summarization is usually a sum operation. Columns that have been assigned a default summarization are denoted by Power BI with a Sigma symbol (Σ), as seen in the **Report** view. This default summarization behavior can be observed in the **Temperature** table. In *Figure 4.30*, the columns **Avg Temp** and **Month Number** have been assigned a default summarization by Power BI:

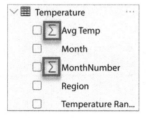

Figure 4.30: Default aggregations assigned to columns

This automatic assignment of default summarizations has pros and cons. The benefit is that fields like Sales Amount or Total Cost will be automatically aggregated when they are added to a visual in a report, thus making the report building process a little easier. The downside is that very commonly, a data model will contain numeric columns that are descriptive in nature and it could cause confusion for report developers in Power BI when these columns are automatically aggregated when added to a report. The columns identified in *Figure 4.30* are descriptive attributes that help to explain the data; these columns should not be aggregated. Take a look at the following screenshot:

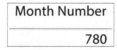

Figure 4.31: Sum of months from the Temperature table

In *Figure 4.31*, the Month Number column from the Temperature table has been added to a table visual, and the expected behavior is to see a distinct list of the month numbers (1, 2, 3, 4, 5, 6, 7, 8, 9, 10, 11, 12). Instead of returning a distinct list, the report returns a sum of all records from the Month Number column in the Temperature table resulting in a final value of 780. Fortunately, the default aggregation can be changed. See *Figure 4.32* and the accompanying steps:

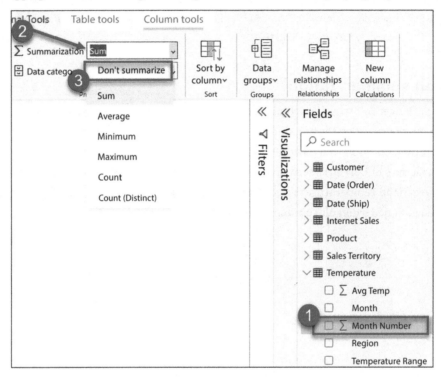

Figure 4.32: Adjust the default summarization

Let's take a look at the numbered items in *Figure 4.32* to learn how to change the default summarization:

1.   Expand the **Temperature** table and select the **Month Number** column. Make sure to click on the column name here, not the checkbox. Once the column has been selected, the **Column tools** ribbon will appear across the top of Power BI Desktop.

2.   Select the **Column tools** ribbon.

3. Click the dropdown for **Summarization** and select **Don't summarize**.

Repeat the above process for each column in your data model that has been assigned a default aggregation but should not be summarized.

 Columns that are in tables on the one side of a relationship will automatically have a default summarization of Don't summarize! Take a look at the date table and you will notice that each of the numeric columns, like Calendar Year and Month Number, have a default summarization of Don't summarize. This is yet another benefit of properly defining relationships in Power BI.

Now that you have learned how to update the default summarization, let's take a look at yet another important usability enhancement. In this section, you will learn how to configure columns in your data model so that the data is properly sorted in visualizations.

How to display one column but sort by another

Oftentimes, you want to display the name of one column but sort by another. For example, the month name is sorted alphabetically when added to a report visual; see *Figure 4.33*:

English Month Name
April
August
December
February
January
July
June
March
May
November
October
September

Figure 4.33: Month names sorted alphabetically when added to a report visual

The desired behavior is for the month to be sorted chronologically instead. Therefore, the report should display the month name but sort by the month number of the year. Take a look at the numbered items in *Figure 4.34* and the accompanying steps:

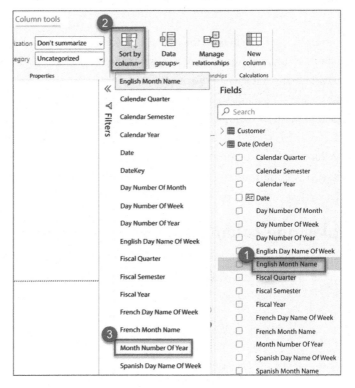

Figure 4.34: Changing the sort order of a column

In order to change the sort order of a column, complete the following steps:

1. Expand the **Date** table and select **English Month Name**, as seen in *Figure 4.34*
2. Select the **Column tools** ribbon
3. Click the dropdown for **Sort by column** and select **Month Number Of Year**

In this section, you learned how to reorder the values of a column, this will be very helpful and is a very common request. Now, let's take a look at how to categorize columns to further improve the report consumer experience.

Data categorization

Power BI makes some assumptions about your columns based on data types, column names, and relationships in the data model. These assumptions are used in the **Report** view when building visualizations to improve your default experience with the tool. Once you start building visualizations, you will notice that Power BI selects different types of visuals for different columns; this is by design. Power BI also decides column placement within the fields section of a visual—you will learn more about the creation of visuals in *Chapter 6, Visualizing Data*. As you saw previously in this chapter, when Power BI detects a column that has numeric values on the *many* side of a relationship, a default aggregation is assigned. Power BI assumes you will want to aggregate that data, and will automatically place these numeric columns into the Values area of a report visual.

The classification of data allows you to improve the user experience, as well as improving accuracy. There are thirteen different options available for data categorization at the time of writing.

Figure 4.35 provides a full list of the data categories available in Power BI:

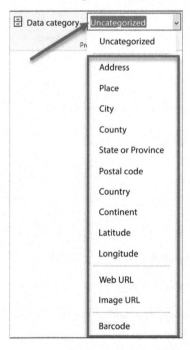

Figure 4.35: Options for data categorization

The most common use for data categorization is the classification of geographical data. When geographical data is added to a map, Bing maps may have to make some assumptions about how to map that data. This can sometimes cause inaccurate results. However, through data classification, you can reduce and possibly eliminate inaccurate results.

One extremely useful method is combining multiple address columns (`City`, `State`) into a single column, and assigning the new column a data categorization of **Place**. See the following blog post for more tips on mapping geographical data: `https://tinyurl.com/pbiqs-categoryplace`.

To update a column's data category, see *Figure 4.36*:

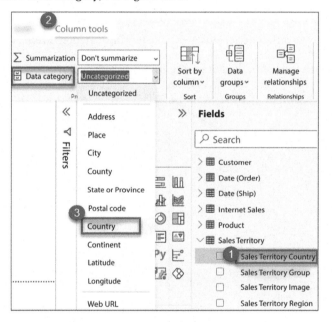

Figure 4.36: Modifying the data category

Take the following steps to complete this process:

1. Expand the **Sales Territory** table and select **Sales Territory Country**
2. Select the **Column tools** ribbon
3. Click the dropdown for **Data category** and select **Country**

Explicitly classifying each of the geographical columns in your data model will help Bing Maps to properly map your data correctly. When geographical classifications are not used, it is much more likely that data could be incorrectly mapped. The blog previously mentioned in this chapter shows data that was incorrectly mapped by Bing Maps and how proper classification of data solved the mapping issue.

Creating hierarchies

Predefining hierarchies can provide several key benefits. Some of those benefits are listed here:

1. Hierarchies organize attributes and show relationships in the data
2. Hierarchies allow easy drag-and-drop interactivity
3. Hierarchies add significant analytical value to the visualization layer through drilling down and rolling up data, as necessary

Hierarchies store information about relationships in the data that users may not have otherwise known. Imagine working for a client in the telecommunication industry with **Base Transceiver Stations (BTSes)** and **sectors**. Without clear direction from the client, how would you know which came first, the BTS or the sector? Did a BTS contain multiple sectors, or did a sector contain multiple BTSes? Once a hierarchy is added to the data model, you will no longer have to worry about remembering the relationship because the relationship was stored in the hierarchy. Here is a list of common hierarchies:

- Category | Subcategory | Product
- Country | State | City
- Year | Quarter | Month | Day

In order to create a new hierarchy, consider *Figure 4.37*:

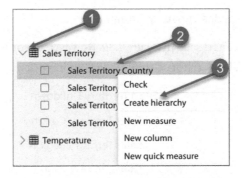

Figure 4.37: Create a new hierarchy

To create a hierarchy, complete the numbered steps:

1. Expand the **Sales Territory** table.
2. Right-click on the **Sales Territory Country** column.
3. Select **Create hierarchy**.

A new hierarchy has been created with a single column and given a default name of Sales Territory Country Hierarchy. Right-click on the hierarchy created and rename it Sales Territory Drilldown. The next step is to add additional columns/attributes to the hierarchy:

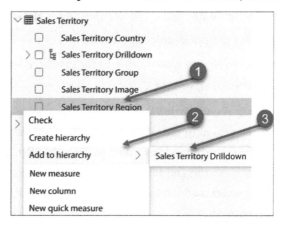

Figure 4.38: Adding columns/attributes to the hierarchy

Complete the following steps as seen in *Figure 4.38*:

1. Within the **Sales Territory** table, right-click on **Sales Territory Region**.
2. Click on **Add to hierarchy**.
3. Select **Sales Territory Drilldown**.
4. Repeat *steps 1-3* for **Sales Territory Group**.

The completed hierarchy can be seen in *Figure 4.39*. However, the order of the attributes is incorrect; the order should be **Sales Territory Group** | **Sales Territory Country** | **Sales Territory Region**:

Figure 4.39: Completed hierarchy

To correct the order of the attributes, go to the model view:

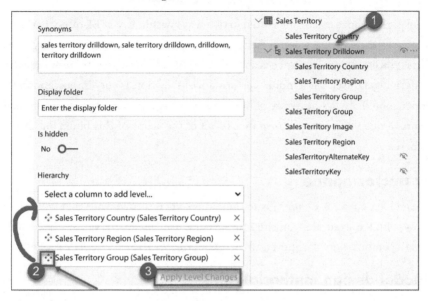

Figure 4.40: Reordering a hierarchy

Take the following steps:

1. From the model view, select the **Sales Territory Drilldown** from the **Sales Territory** table.
2. From the **Properties** pane, drag and drop the **Sales Territory Group** to the top of the hierarchy.
3. Click **Apply Level Changes**.

In *Figure 4.41* you can see the correctly arranged hierarchy:

Figure 4.41: Completed Sales Territory hierarchy

In this section, you learned how many small but effective modifications can be leveraged to improve the readability and effectiveness of the data model. These necessary usability enhancements help to improve the user experience by making the model intelligent and easier to understand.

Now let's transition to discussing some considerations for data model performance.

Improving data model performance

Data model performance can be measured in two ways within Power BI, query performance and processing performance. Query performance is how quickly results are returned by visualizations and reports. Processing performance is a measure of how long it takes to perform a data refresh on the underlying dataset. Data model performance as a whole is very important and the Power BI developer should always be aware of how design decisions may affect performance today or in the future. A deep dive into performance is out of the scope of this book, but an overview is provided here.

Query performance

As you learned in *Chapter 2, Connecting to Data*, there are multiple ways that you can connect to data in Power BI. For example, you can import data, use DirectQuery, use a live connection, or you can use a combination of import and direct queries with the composite model.

Data model design methodologies

Data models in Power BI are specifically designed for the purpose of extracting analytical value out of data to make informed business decisions. Therefore, the data should be modeled in such a way as to effectively and efficiently report data. In Power BI, there are three types of data models that commonly appear and those are flat models, star schemas, and snowflake schemas.

A flat or completely denormalized model is where the entire data model is a single table with no supporting tables. Therefore, all your measurable items and all the descriptive attributes are in the same table. This model is very common and is a result of a lot of Excel users importing data directly into Power BI from their Excel worksheets. This method is highly inefficient and has several drawbacks:

- A flat model does not scale well; as the number of records in the table increases, the data model will consume significantly more resources due to the repetitiveness of data and the number of columns.
- A flat model is not flexible and does not hold up well to future changes.
- A flat model is not intelligent, simply meaning it's not easily understandable.
- Time series analysis calculations like Year to Date and Year over Year are much more difficult to author.

The next type of model is a star schema. This method was discussed earlier in this chapter and we will review it in this section for completeness. The star schema is the preferred way to model data in Power BI. The term star schema is derived from dimensional modeling. Dimensional modeling is the way enterprises and organizations have been designing their analytical data warehouses for over 30 years. A star schema has two types of tables, fact tables and dimension tables. The reason these data models are called star schemas is that the dimension tables surround the fact table and appear to represent a star. See *Figure 4.42*:

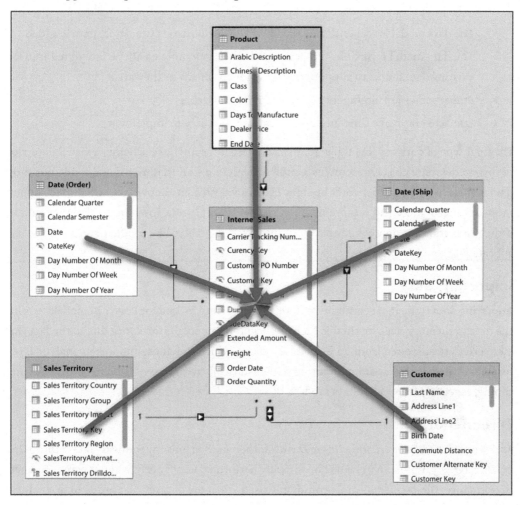

Figure 4.42: Star schema

Fact tables store metrics, the measurable items in your data model like sales, tax amount, duration of a phone call, and so on... A dimension table stores descriptive attributes that help you to explain your metrics. In a dimension table, related attributes are stored in their own separate and distinct table. For example, product name, color, size, weight, and other product-related columns would be stored in a product table.

Taking the time to build a star schema in Power BI Desktop has several advantages; please note that the following list is not a comprehensive list of all the advantages of a star schema:

- The data model is scalable, meaning it will be flexible to grow as more data is added
- The data model is flexible and additional tables can more easily be integrated into the existing data model to support analytical requirements as they arise
- Star schemas are intelligent and easily understandable
- Star schemas make time intelligence calculations easy to implement

The final type of data model I'd like to mention here is a snowflake schema, a visual depiction of this model more closely resembles a snowflake than a star. In dimensional modeling, most data models begin as star schemas but may evolve over time into snowflake schemas to support more advanced analytical requirements. A simple example of a snowflake schema would be if the product dimension were broken out into multiple tables like product category, product subcategory, and product.

Importing data

Importing data is the most common method of connecting to data for Power BI models, storing the data in memory. This method is highly efficient for query performance due to the fact that all queries are answered from an in-memory cache, which provides unmatched analytical performance! Models that contain imported data historically require very little to no performance tuning, especially for smaller data models.

DirectQuery

As discussed in *Chapter 2, Connecting to Data*, another method for connecting to data is DirectQuery. DirectQuery, unfortunately, has historically performed very poorly when it comes to query performance. DirectQuery is most commonly used when the dataset that needs to be analyzed is too large to import into Power BI.

Aggregations

Creating aggregations in Power BI provides a powerful mechanism for improving query performance. Aggregations can be used with imported or DirectQuery models, for massive performance gains!

Effectively implementing aggregations requires an understanding of the data and understanding how end users will generally query the data. With this knowledge, an aggregated table can be designed and used to answer a large number of user requests, rather than the original table storing many more rows of data.

Let's look at a hypothetical example: imagine a transaction table that has 100 million rows of data for the last year. If most visualizations will be performing counts and sums by date, then an aggregation can be built that returns total sales and total transactions grouped by date. In this scenario, the aggregate table would return 365 rows of data, 1 row for each day in the last year instead of the original 100-million-row transaction table. In most data models, it is unlikely that the date alone would suffice to answer most queries from end user requests. Therefore, additional attributes may need to be added to the aggregate table, for example, maybe adding the geography key is the missing ingredient. The aggregate table would now be total sales and total transactions grouped by date and geography. This would of course increase the size of the table significantly, depending on how many unique records exist in your geography table, but it would still be significantly smaller than your original transactional table and likely small enough to import the aggregated data into Power BI.

 The steps for effective implementation of aggregations would not fit within the scope of this book; however, to learn more about aggregations, take a look at the following blog by Shabnam Watson: https://shabnamwatson.wordpress.com/2019/11/21/aggregations-in-power-bi/.

Now let's take a look at data modeling considerations for improving processing performance.

Processing performance

Imported datasets must go through a data refresh operation to load the most recent data into the data model. In today's "data-driven culture," organizations want more data and they want it faster than ever before. If a dataset takes hours to refresh, then you would be limited in how often you can refresh the dataset. On the other hand, if a dataset only takes minutes to refresh, you can refresh it more often throughout the day, providing richer insights and more time-sensitive access to the underlying data.

Query folding

As you learned previously in this book, query folding is the process of pushing work back to the underlying data source. Query folding is very important when the underlying data source supports query folding. A relational database like Microsoft SQL Server is one example of a data source that supports query folding. Pushing the work back to SQL Server can significantly improve the processing performance of a data model.

Incremental refresh

Historically, refreshing a data model in Power BI requires that all data be refreshed. Therefore, if a data model contains five years of data, then all five years of data and the associated rows would be refreshed each time a refresh occurs. As you can imagine, this can require a lot of overhead. What if a data refresh operation could take less than a minute, instead of hours?

I have seen the process of incremental refresh reduce data refresh operations from hours to only minutes. This is because incremental refresh does not reprocess all the data in the model. Instead, only the most recent data is loaded, while not touching the historical data. This would include new records or records that have been updated.

 Further reading: Implementation of incremental refresh is outside the scope of this book; however, you can learn more about incremental refresh by taking a look at the following blog: https://docs.microsoft.com/en-us/power-bi/admin/service-premium-incremental-refresh.

Best practices

There are a few recommended best practices that can help speed up data refresh operations. This is by no means a comprehensive list, but this list provides you with a starting point for building data models:

- Only import necessary columns for reporting; remove all other columns from your model.
- Likewise, only import necessary rows of data; filter out data that is not needed.
- Try to avoid highly unique columns; they have low compression and take up valuable resources.
- Disable **Auto date/time for new files**; see *Figure 4.12*.
- Create new columns in the Power Query Editor, rather than in DAX, when possible.

Summary

In this chapter, you learned that data models in Power BI Desktop should be understandable and designed for scalability and flexibility. You learned how to create new relationships and edit existing relationships. You also learned about how to handle and model complex relationships like many-to-many and role-playing tables. This chapter discussed the importance of usability enhancements like sorting columns, adjusting default summarization, data categorization, and hiding and renaming columns and tables. Finally, the chapter ended with a short discussion on performance considerations for querying and processing your data model. You are now prepared and ready to start building data models in Power BI Desktop!

These data relationships, combined with simple yet critical usability enhancements, allow you to build a data model that is both coherent and intelligent. Historically, business intelligence projects have cost significant resources in terms of time and money. With Power BI Desktop and through a self-service approach to BI, you now have the tools necessary to build your own BI project within hours and immediately extract value from that model to make informed business decisions.

In the next chapter, you will learn about how to leverage data analysis expressions to further extend the analytical capabilities of your data model.

Join our community on Discord

Join our community's Discord space for discussions with the authors and other readers:

https://packt.link/ips2H

5

Leveraging DAX

Data Analysis Expressions (DAX) is a formula language that made its debut back in 2010 with the release of Power Pivot within Excel. Much of DAX is similar to Excel's functions, and therefore, learning DAX is an easy transition for Excel users and Power users alike. In fact, DAX is so similar to Excel that we have seen new students become comfortable with the language and begin writing DAX within minutes.

The goal of this chapter is to introduce you to DAX and give you the confidence to start exploring this language on your own. Because of the limited scope of this chapter, there will not be any discussions on in-depth DAX concepts and theory. There are, of course, many other books that are dedicated to just that.

Now, let's take a look at what is covered in this chapter:

- Building calculated columns
- Creating calculated measures
- Understanding filter context
- Working with time intelligence functions
- Role-playing tables with DAX

Now, let's take a look at writing DAX by building calculated columns.

Building calculated columns

In this section, you will learn how to create calculated columns in Power BI using DAX. The building of calculated columns is a great way of extending the analytical capability of Power BI and by the end of this chapter, you will feel very comfortable with creating new columns through DAX. The writing of calculated columns logically occurs after the data model has been developed, therefore, in order to follow along with this section, you will need to open the pbix file `Chapter 5 - Leveraging DAX.pbix` from the `Microsoft-Power-BI-Quick-Start-Guide-Third-Edition\ Starting Examples` directory.

Calculated columns are stored in the table in which they are assigned, and the values are static until the data is refreshed. You will learn more about refreshing data in a later chapter.

There are many use cases for calculated columns, but the two most common are as follows:

- Adding descriptive columns
- Creating concatenated key columns

Now you are going to create your first calculated column. Before you get started though, you need to first know that Power BI Desktop provides the **IntelliSense** feature. IntelliSense will help you out a lot when writing code, as you will discover very soon. This built-in functionality will autocomplete your code as you go and will also help you explore and discover new functions in the DAX language. In order to take advantage of IntelliSense, you simply need to start typing in the formula bar. Now you are ready to start writing DAX!

Click on **Data view**—this is located on the left navigation pane of the Power BI Desktop screen. Next, click on the `Customer` table from the **Fields** list. Once the `Customer` table has been selected, click on **New column**—this is found on the **Table tools** ribbon, as shown in *Figure 5.1*:

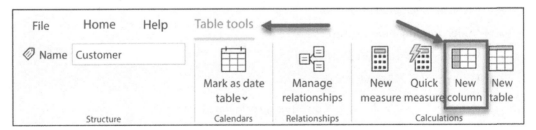

Figure 5.1: New calculated column

You will now see the text `Column` = in the formula bar. First, name the new column by replacing the default text of `Column` with `Full Name`. Then, move your cursor to after the equals sign and type a single quote character. Immediately after typing the single quote character, a list of auto-complete options will appear underneath the formula bar. This is IntelliSense at work. The first option in this list is the name of the table you currently have selected—`Customer`. Press the *Tab* key and the name of the table will automatically be added to the formula bar, as shown in *Figure 5.2*:

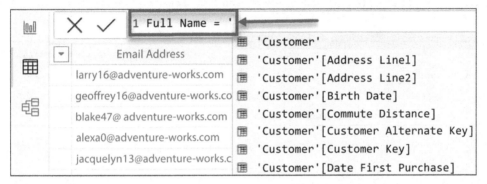

Figure 5.2: Using IntelliSense

> At some point, you will inevitably discover that you can reference just the column name. As a best practice, we recommend always referencing both the table and column name anytime you use a column in your DAX code.

Next, type an opening square bracket into the formula bar followed by the capital letter F, making [F. Once again, you will immediately be presented with autocomplete options. The list of options has been limited to only columns that contain the letter *f*, and the first option available from the dropdown is `First Name`. Press the *Tab* key to autocomplete. The formula bar should now contain the following formula:

```
Full Name = 'Customer'[First Name]
```

The next step is to add a space, followed by the last name. There are two options in DAX for combining string values. The first option is the concatenate function. Unfortunately, concatenate only accepts two parameters; therefore, if you have more than two parameters, your code will require multiple concatenate function calls. On the other hand, you also have the option of using the ampersand sign (&) to combine strings.

The ampersand will first take both input parameters and convert them into strings. After this data conversion step, the two strings are then combined into one. Let's continue with the rest of the expression. Remember to use the built-in autocomplete functionality to help you write code.

Next, add a space and the last name column. To add a space—or any string literal value for that matter—into a DAX formula, you will use quotes on both sides of the string. For example, " " inserts a space between the first and last name columns. The completed DAX formula will look like *Figure 5.3*:

Figure 5.3: Completed DAX example for Full Name

In *Figure 5.4*, you see the results of the completed expression in the Customer table:

Address Line1	Address Line2	Phone	Date First Purchase	Commute Distance	Full Name
29, avenue de la Gare		1 (11) 500 555-0180	Sunday, November 18, 2007	2-5 Miles	Latasha Suarez
Am Gallberg 645		1 (11) 500 555-0125	Friday, January 11, 2008	2-5 Miles	Larry Gill
1538 Golden Meadow		1 (11) 500 555-0131	Friday, July 21, 2006	0-1 Miles	Geoffrey Gonzalez
6543 Jacobsen Street		1 (11) 500 555-0117	Thursday, July 6, 2006	2-5 Miles	Edgar Sanchez
4519 Lydia Lane		1 (11) 500 555-0140	Thursday, July 13, 2006	0-1 Miles	Blake Collins
111, rue des Pyrenees		1 (11) 500 555-0195	Friday, January 25, 2008	2-5 Miles	Shelby Bailey
Residenz StraBe 98		1 (11) 500 555-0191	Monday, April 21, 2008	2-5 Miles	Alexa Watson

Figure 5.4: Results of the Full Name calculated column in the Customer table

Now, let's take a look at an example of using string functions in DAX to create calculated columns.

Creating calculated columns with string functions

Now that you have completed your first calculated column, let's build a calculated column that stores the month-year value. The goal is to return a month-year column with the two-digit month and four-digit year separated by a dash, making MM-YYYY. Let's build this calculation incrementally.

Select the **Date (Order)** table and then click on **New column** from the **Table tools** ribbon. Write the following code in the formula bar and then hit *Enter*:

```
Month Year = 'Date (Order)'[Month Number of Year]
```

As you begin validating the code, you will notice that this only returns the single-digit month with no leading zero. Your next attempt may look something like the following:

```
Month Year = "0" & 'Date (Order)'[Month Number of Year]
```

This will work for single-digit months; however, double-digit months will now return three digits. Take a look at *Figure 5.5*:

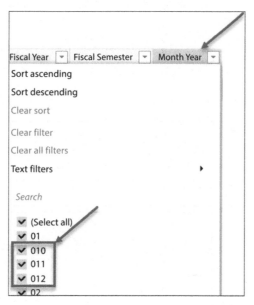

Figure 5.5: Displaying Month Year

To improve upon this and only return the two-digit month, you can use the RIGHT function. The RIGHT function returns a specified number of characters from the right side of a string; in the example below, two characters are returned from the expression. Modify your existing DAX formula to look like the following:

```
Month Year = RIGHT("0" & 'Date (Order)'[Month Number of Year], 2)
```

 For a full list of text functions in DAX, please go to the following link: `https://tinyurl.com/pbiqs-text`

The rest of this formula can be completed quite easily. First, to add a dash, the following DAX code can be used:

```
Month Year = RIGHT("0" & 'Date (Order)'[Month Number of Year], 2) & "-"
```

Complete the Month Year formula by combining the current string with the Year column. The completed example is seen in *Figure 5.6*:

```
1  Month Year =
2  RIGHT("0" & 'Date (Order)'[Month Number Of Year], 2) &
3      ("-" &
4          'Date (Order)'[Year]
```

Figure 5.6: Displaying Month Year

In *Figure 5.7*, you see the results of the completed expression in the Date table:

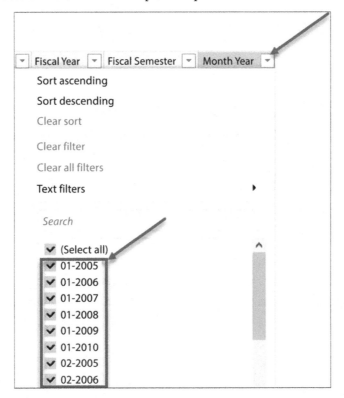

Figure 5.7: Results of the Month Year calculated column in the Date table

You may have noticed that the Year column has a data type of a whole number, and you may have expected that this numeric value would need to be converted to a String prior to the combine operation. However, remember that the ampersand operator will automatically convert both inputs into a String before performing the combine operation!

In this example, you learned how to create a Month Year column using a combination of the Right function with the ampersand operator. Next, you will learn an easier method for achieving the same goal with the FORMAT function.

Using the FORMAT function in DAX

As with any other language, you will find that there are usually multiple ways to do something. Now you are going to learn how to perform the calculation that we saw in the previous section using the FORMAT function. The FORMAT function allows you to take a number or Date column and customize it in a number of ways. A side effect of the FORMAT function is that the resulting data type will be text. Therefore, this may affect numerical-based calculations that you wish to perform on those columns at a later time. Let's perform the preceding calculation again, but this time, using the FORMAT function.

Make sure you have the **Date (Order)** table selected, and then click on **Create a New Calculated Column** by selecting **New column** from the **Table tools** ribbon. In the formula bar, write the following expression:

```
Month Year Format = FORMAT('Date (Order)'[Date], "MM-YYYY")
```

If you would like to take a full look at all the custom formatting options available using the FORMAT function, please take a look at https://tinyurl.com/pbiqs-format

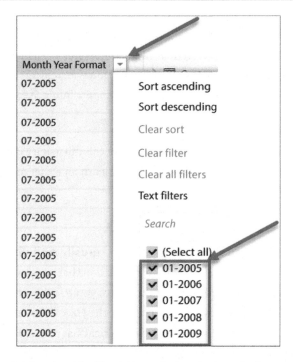

Figure 5.8: Results of the Month Year calculated column in the Date table

Now, let's take a look at the DATEDIFF function and how to implement conditional logic with the IF function in DAX.

Implementing conditional logic with IF()

Next, you are going to determine each customer's age. The Customer table currently contains a column with the birth date of each customer. This column, along with the TODAY function and some DAX, will allow you to determine each customer's age. Your first attempt at this calculation may be to use the DATEDIFF function in a calculation that looks something like the following:

```
Customer Age = DATEDIFF('Customer'[Birth Date], TODAY(), YEAR)
```

The TODAY function returns the current date and time. The DATEDIFF function returns the count of the specified interval between two dates; however, it does not look at the day and month and therefore, does not always return the correct age for each customer.

Let's rewrite the previous DAX formula in a different way. In this example, you are going to learn how to use conditional logic and the FORMAT function to return the proper customer age. Please keep in mind that there are many ways to perform this calculation.

Select the **Customer Age** column from the previous step and rewrite the formula to look like *Figure 5.9*:

```
1  Customer Age =
2  IF(
3      FORMAT('Customer.[Birth Date], "MMDD") <= FORMAT(TODAY(), "MMDD"), //Logical Test
4      DATEDIFF('Customer'[Birth Date], TODAY(), YEAR),                   //Result If True
5      DATEDIFF('Customer'[Birth Date], TODAY(), YEAR),-1)               //Result If False
```

Figure 5.9: Customer Age calculation column

Formatting code is very important for readability and maintaining code. Power BI Desktop has built-in functionality to help out with code formatting. When you press *Shift + Enter* to navigate down to the next line in your formula bar, your code will be indented automatically where applicable.

When completed, the preceding code returns the correct age for each customer. The FORMAT function is used to return the two-digit month and two-digit day for each date (the birth date and TODAY's date). Following the logical test portion of the IF statement are two expressions. The first expression is triggered if the logical test evaluates to true, and the second expression is triggered if the result of the test is false. Therefore, if the customer's month and day combo is less than or equal to today's month and day, then their birthday has already occurred this year, and the logical test will evaluate to true, which will trigger the first expression. If the customer's birthday has not yet occurred this year, then the second expression will execute.

In the preceding DAX formula, comments were added by using two forward slashes in the code. Comments are descriptive and are not executed with the rest of the DAX formula. Commenting code is always encouraged and will make your code more readable and easier to maintain.

In this example, you learned how to implement conditional logic with the IF function. Now let's look at the SWITCH function, which can be used as an alternative method to IF.

Implementing conditional logic with SWITCH()

Now that you have the customer's age, it's time to put each customer into an age bucket. For this example, there will be four separate age buckets:

- 18-34

- 35-44
- 45-54
- 55+

The SWITCH function is preferable to the IF function when performing multiple logical tests in a single DAX formula. This is because the SWITCH function is easier to read and makes debugging code much easier.

With the **Customer** table selected, click on **New Column** from the **Modeling** ribbon. Type in the completed DAX formula as seen in *Figure 5.10*:

```
1  Age Breakdown =
2  SWITCH(TRUE(),
3      'Customer'[Customer Age] >= 55, "55 +",    //If 55 or older then 55+
4      'Customer'[Customer Age] >= 45, "45-54",   //If 45-54 then 45-54
5      'Customer'[Customer Age] >= 35, "35-44",   //If 35-44 then 35-44
6      "18-34")                                   //18-34
```

Figure 5.10: Conditional logic with SWITCH

The preceding formula is very readable and understandable. There are three logical tests, and if a customer's age does not evaluate to true on any of those logical tests, then that customer is automatically put into the 18-34 age bucket.

The astute reader may have noticed that the second and third logical tests do not have an upper range assigned. For example, the second test simply checks whether the customer's age is 45 or greater. Naturally, you may assume that a customer whose age is 75 would be incorrectly assigned to the 45-54 age bucket. However, once a row evaluates to true, it is no longer available for subsequent logical tests. Someone who is 75 would have been evaluated to true on the first logical test (55+) and would no longer be available for any further tests.

    If you would like a better understanding of using the SWITCH statement instead of nesting multiple IF statements, then you can check out a blog post by Rob Collie at https://tinyurl.com/pbiqs-switch.

Let's take a look at another important task in DAX: retrieving data from a column in another table. In Excel, you would just use the VLOOKUP function, and in SQL, you would use a join. In DAX, you use navigation functions to retrieve this data.

Leveraging existing relationships with navigation functions

It's finally time to create a relationship between the Temperature table and the Internet Sales table. The key on the Temperature table is a combination of the region name and the month number of the year.

This column combination makes a single row unique in this table, as shown in *Figure 5.11*:

Region	Month	MonthNumber	Key	Avg Temp	Temperature Range
Northeast	Jan	1	Northeast1	26.3	Cold
Northeast	Feb	2	Northeast2	25.4	Cold
Northeast	Mar	3	Northeast3	31.4	Cold
Northeast	Apr	4	Northeast4	48.1	Cool
Northeast	May	5	Northeast5	52.8	Cool

Figure 5.11: Column combination that makes a single row unique

Unfortunately, neither of those two columns currently exists in the Internet Sales table. However, the Internet Sales table has a relationship with the Sales Territory table, and the Sales Territory table has the region. Therefore, you can determine the region for each sale by doing a simple lookup operation. Well, it should be that simple, but it's not quite that easy. Let's take a look at why.

Calculated columns do not automatically use the existing relationships in the data model. In contrast to calculated columns, calculated measures automatically see and interact with all relationships in the data model. Now let's take a look at why this is important. Calculated measures will be covered in the next section.

In the following screenshot, we have created a new column in the Internet Sales table and we are trying to return the region name from the Sales Territory table. Take a look at *Figure 5.12*:

```
1 Temperature Key = 'Sales Terr
```

Figure 5.12: Sales Territory table

Note that there is no IntelliSense and that the autocomplete functionality is unavailable as we type in Sales Territory. The reason for this is the calculated column creates a row context and by default does not use the existing relationships in the data model. There is a much more complicated explanation behind all this, but for now, it is sufficient to say that navigation functions (RELATED and RELATEDTABLE) allow calculated columns to interact with and use existing relationships.

If we rewrite the following DAX formula with the RELATED function, then you will notice that IntelliSense has returned, along with the autocomplete functionality that was previously discussed. The IntelliSense can be seen in *Figure 5.13*:

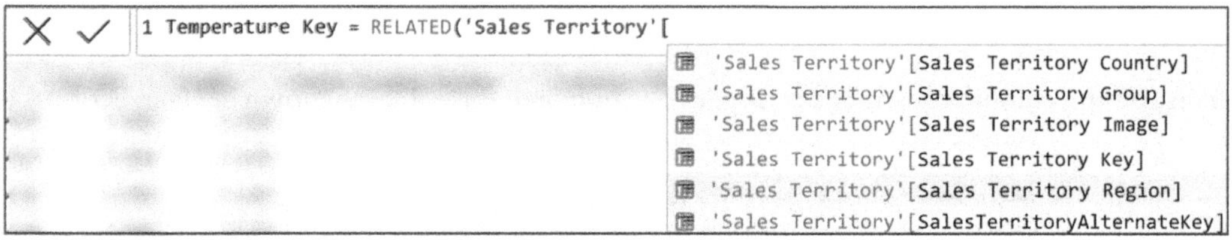

```
✕ ✓   1 Temperature Key = RELATED('Sales Territory'[

                         ▦  'Sales Territory'[Sales Territory Country]
                         ▦  'Sales Territory'[Sales Territory Group]
                         ▦  'Sales Territory'[Sales Territory Image]
                         ▦  'Sales Territory'[Sales Territory Key]
                         ▦  'Sales Territory'[Sales Territory Region]
                         ▦  'Sales Territory'[SalesTerritoryAlternateKey]
```

Figure 5.13: Temperature Key column

Now it's time to create a Temperature Key column in the Internet Sales table. Create a new column in the Internet Sales table and then type in the DAX formula seen in *Figure 5.14*:

```
1 Temperature Key =
2 RELATED('Sales Territory'[Sales Territory Region]) &  //Return the Region from Sales Territory table
3 RELATED('Date (Order)'[Month Number Of Year])          //Return the Month Number of Year from the Date table
```

Figure 5.14: Temperature Key column of the Internet Sales table

You may have observed that unlike a VLOOKUP in Excel or a join in SQL, we did not have to specify the join columns when using the RELATED function! This is because the built-in navigation functions automatically leverage the existing relationships in the model.

Now that the Temperature Key column has been created in the Internet Sales table, let's create the relationship. Click on **Manage Relationships** from the **Home** ribbon and then click on **New...** to open the **Relationship editor** window. Then, complete the following steps to create a new relationship:

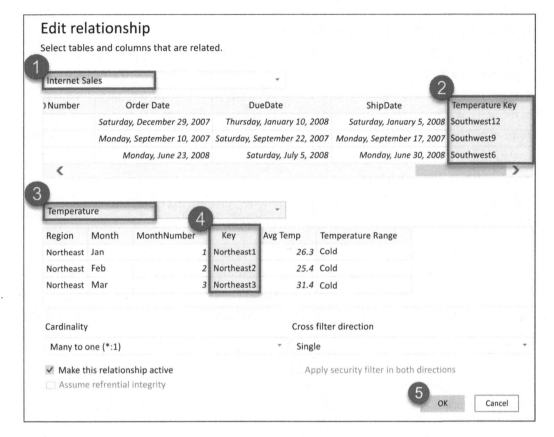

Figure 5.15: Creating a new relationship

See the numbered items in *Figure 5.15*:

1. Select **Internet Sales** from the first drop-down selection list.
2. Select **Temperature Key** from the list of columns (scroll right).
3. Select **Temperature** from the second drop-down selection list.
4. Select **Key** from the list of columns.
5. Click **OK** to save your new relationship.

So far in this chapter, you have learned how to create calculated columns in tables. These calculated columns increase the analytical capabilities of your data models by adding columns that can be leveraged to describe your metrics. You also learned how to create a concatenated key column in order to build a relationship between the Temperature and Internet Sales tables. In the next section, you are going to learn how to use DAX to create calculated measures.

Creating calculated measures

Calculated measures are very different than calculated columns. Calculated measures are not static, and operate within the current filter context of a report; therefore, calculated measures are dynamic and ever-changing as the filter context changes. You were introduced to filter context in the previous chapter when discussing many-to-many relationships. The concept of the filter context will be slightly expanded on later in this chapter. Calculated measures are powerful analytical tools, and because of the automatic way that measures work with filter context, they are surprisingly simple to author.

Before you start learning about creating measures, let's first discuss the difference between implicit and explicit measures.

Implicit aggregations occur automatically on columns with numeric data types. You saw this in the previous chapter when the month number column was incorrectly aggregated after being added to a report. There are some advantages to this default behavior—for example, if you simply drag the Sales Amount column into a report, the value will be automatically aggregated and you won't have to spend time creating a measure. As discussed in the next section, it is generally considered a best practice to create explicit measures in lieu of implicit measures.

An explicit measure allows a user to create a calculated measure, and there are several benefits to using explicit measures:

- Measures can be built from other measures
- Reusing measures makes the code easier to read
- They encapsulate code, making logic changes less time-consuming
- They centrally define number formatting, creating consistency

Calculated measures can do the following:

- They can be assigned to any table and further assigned to folders within that table
- They interact with all the relationships in the data model automatically, unlike calculated columns
- They are not materialized in a column, and therefore cannot be validated in the **Data View**

Now that you know what calculated measures are, let's take a look at how to create them.

Creating basic calculated measures

In this section, you are going to create four simple calculated measures. These calculated measures will create additional metrics that can be used in visualizations and reports to obtain deeper insights from your data:

- Total Sales
- Total Cost
- Profit
- Profit Margin

First, let's start by creating the Total Sales calculation.

Total Sales

To create your first measure, select the **Internet Sales** table and then click on **New measure** from the **Table tools** ribbon. Insert the following code in the formula bar:

```
Total Sales = SUM('Internet Sales'[Sales Amount])
```

See *Figure 5.16*:

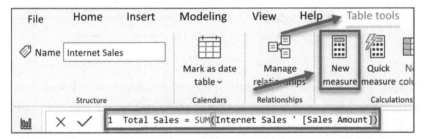

Figure 5.16: Create a Total Sales measure

One of the benefits of creating explicit measures is the ability to centralize formatting. Once the measure has been created, navigate to the **Measure tools** ribbon and change the formatting to **$ English (United States)**, as shown in *Figure 5.17*:

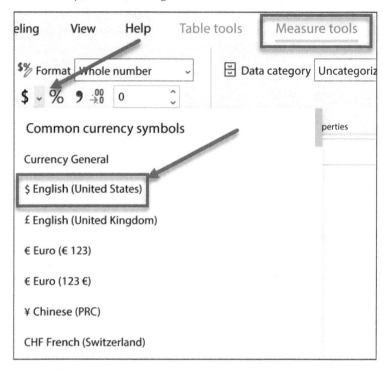

Figure 5.17: Change formatting to $ English (United States)

You just created your first calculated measure! It was simple and, as you will soon learn, extremely powerful. The total sales calculation is the sum of the sales amount, however, another way to read that calculation is the sum of the sales amount within the current filter context. You learned about filter context in the previous chapter and it will be further discussed later in this chapter, but for now, just know these seemingly simple calculations are very dynamic. Let's create some more calculated measures.

Total Cost

Now let's create the Total Cost measure. Once again, this is a simple SUM operation. Select the **Internet Sales** table, then click on **New measure** from the **Table tools** ribbon and type in the following DAX formula:

```
Total Cost = SUM('Internet Sales'[Total Product Cost])
```

Remember to apply formatting to this new measure; it is easy to miss this step when learning to create measures. The formatting should be **$ English (United States)**.

Profit

Profit is the next measure you will create. You may attempt to write something such as the following:

```
Profit = SUM('Internet Sales'[Sales Amount]) - SUM('Internet Sales'[Total
Product Cost])
```

This calculation would be technically correct; however, it is not the most efficient way to write code. In fact, another benefit of building explicit measures is that they can be built using measures you already created. Reusing existing calculated measures will make the code more readable and make code changes easier and less time-consuming. Imagine for a moment that you discovered that the Total Sales calculation is not correct. If you encapsulated all this logic in a single measure and reused that measure in your other measures, then you need only change the original measure, and any updates will be pushed to all other measure references.

Now it is time to create the Profit measure. Select your **Internet Sales** table and then click on **New measure** from the **Table tools** ribbon. Type the following into the formula bar—remember to apply formatting afterward:

```
Profit = [Total Sales] - [Total Cost]
```

This calculation returns the same results as the original attempt. The difference is that now you are reusing measures that were already created in the data model. You may have noticed that I referenced the name of the measure without the table name. When referencing explicit measures in your code, it is considered a best practice to exclude the table name.

Profit Margin

Now it's time to create the Profit Margin calculation (the profit margin is simply (profit/sales). For this measure, you are going to use the DIVIDE function. The DIVIDE function is recommended over the divide operator (/) because the DIVIDE function automatically handles divide-by-zero occurrences. In the case of divide-by-zero occurrences, the DIVIDE function returns blank.

Create a new measure in the Internet Sales table using the following code:

```
Profit Margin = DIVIDE([Profit], [Total Sales])
```

Next, set the formatting as a percentage. From the **Modeling** ribbon, click on the **%** icon, as shown in *Figure 5.18*:

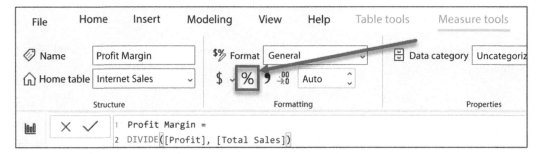

Figure 5.18: Setting formatting as a percentage

Functions in DAX have required and optional parameters. So far, you have only learned about required parameters. Let's take a look at optional parameters.

Optional parameters

You may have noticed that the DIVIDE function accepted three parameters and you only provided two. The third parameter allows you to set an alternative result for divide-by-zero occurrences. This alternate result is optional. Optional parameters are denoted by square brackets on both sides of the parameter. These optional parameters are prevalent in many DAX functions. Take a look at *Figure 5.19*:

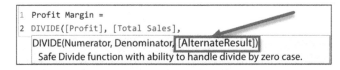

Figure 5.19: Optional parameters in DAX functions

Optional parameters are very often overlooked by developers, but as you will learn, there is a lot of functionality and value that can be achieved by leveraging these parameters. Now, let's take a look at how and where to assign calculated measures.

Assignment of calculated measures

Unlike calculated columns, measures do not need to be assigned to a specific table to function properly. Because of this, it is very easy and common to forget to make sure the proper table is selected prior to creating a measure. This results in measures being assigned to random tables during development.

Fortunately, you do not need to delete the measure and recreate it in the proper table; instead, you can simply move measures from one table to another by changing the **Home table**.

To move a calculated measure from one table to another, you will follow these steps, as you can see in *Figure 5.20*:

1. Select the measures.

2. Find the **Measure tools** ribbon.

3. Click on the **Home table** dropdown and select the correct table:

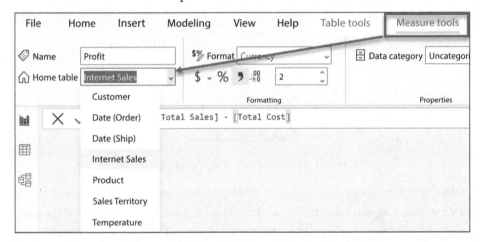

Figure 5.20: Moving a calculated measure to a new table

Calculated measures can be assigned to any table in your data model and will still function properly. However, measures should be assigned to the table where it logically makes the most sense. This way, the measure is easy to find and utilize in visualizations and reports. Let's take a look at how measures can be logically organized and grouped into folders.

Display folders

In Power BI, columns and measures can be assigned to folders. This is extremely useful for organizing related measures and improving the overall usability of the data model. By properly leveraging display folders, measures will be easier to find and similar measures, like time intelligence calculations, can be grouped in their own folder.

As you can see in *Figure 5.21*, the newly created measures are mixed in with the existing columns:

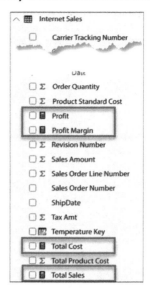

Figure 5.21: Calculated measures displayed in a table

At the time of writing, adding measures to display folders can only be accomplished from the **Model View**. Select **Model View** from the left navigation pane. Next, expand the **Internet Sales** table and select the **Profit** measure. Finally, in the **Properties** pane, find the **Display folder** property and type `Measures`. Take a look at *Figure 5.22*:

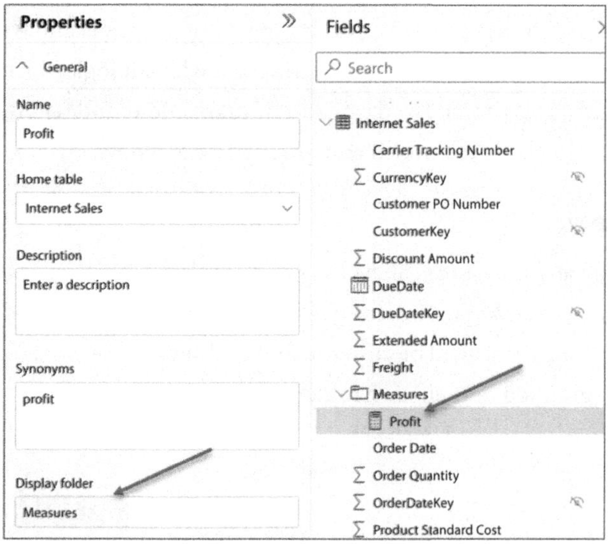

Figure 5.22: Calculated measures displayed in a table

All of your measures can be moved to a display folder at one time. Simply multi-select the measures to be moved by holding down the *Ctrl* key while selecting each measure and then enter the folder name. See the completed example in *Figure 5.23*:

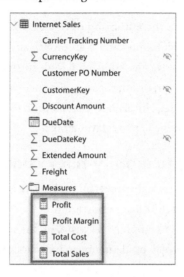

Figure 5.23: Displaying measures in a folder

Previously, we mentioned that these calculated measures are simple yet powerful. These measures are powerful because filtering in DAX occurs automatically. Let's take a deeper look at automatic filtering and filter context.

Understanding filter context

The automatic filtering that occurs in Power BI is a really awesome feature and is one of the reasons that so many companies are gravitating to this tool. The active relationships that are defined in the data model, and that you learned how to create in the previous chapter, are automatically used by DAX to perform the automatic filtering of calculated measures. This is directly tied to the concept of the filter context. You were introduced to the filter context in the previous chapter. I want to briefly expand on what was covered in the previous chapter here before discussing the CALCULATE function.

A simple definition of the filter context would be that it is simply anything in your report that is filtering a measure. There are quite a few items that make up the filter context. Let's take a look at a few of them:

- Any attributes on the rows; this includes the different axes in charts
- Any attributes on the columns

- Any filters applied by slicers (visual filters); slicers are discussed in the next chapter
- Any filters applied explicitly through the **Filters** pane
- Any filters explicitly added to a calculated measure

In short, the filter context makes the authoring of calculated measures a simple and intuitive process. A simple total sales calculation can be automatically filtered by all the tables in your data model without having to write any additional logic into your calculated measures. If you want to see total sales by customer, product name, product weight, country, or any other number of columns in your data model, simply add that column to your report and your measure is *auto-magically* filtered thanks to the active relationships!

Using CALCULATE() to modify filter context

The CALCULATE function is an extremely powerful tool in the arsenal of any DAX author. In fact, the CALCULATE function is one of the most important functions in all of DAX. This is because the CALCULATE function can be used to ignore, overwrite, or change the existing filter context. You may be asking yourself why—why would anyone want to ignore the default behavior of Power BI? Let's take a look at an example.

Let's assume you want to return the total sales of each country as a percentage of all countries. This is a very basic percentage of total calculation: Total Sales per country divided by Total Sales for all countries. However, how do you get the total sales of all the countries so that you can perform this calculation? This is where the CALCULATE function comes into the picture. Take a look at *Figure 5.24*:

Sales Territory Country	Total Sales	
Australia	$9,061,000.58	**$29,358,677.22**
Canada	$1,977,844.86	**$29,358,677.22**
France	$2,644,017.71	**$29,358,677.22**
Germany	$2,894,312.34	**$29,358,677.22**
United Kingdom	$3,391,712.21	**$29,358,677.22**
United States	$9,389,789.51	**$29,358,677.22**
Total	**$29,358,677.22**	

Figure 5.24: Calculating the total sales of all the countries

To do the percentage of total calculation, you first need Total Sales all Countries on the same row as Total Sales. Therefore, you need to create a new calculated measure that ignores any filters that come from the Country attribute. Create a new calculated measure in your Internet Sales table using the following DAX formula:

```
1 Total Sales all Countries =
2 CALCULATE(
3     [Total Sales],
4     ALL(
5         'Sales Territory'[Sales Territory Country]))
```

Figure 5.25: Use CALCULATE to ignore filters from Country

The calculation in *Figure 5.25* will return all sales for all countries, explicitly ignoring any filters that come from the Country column. Let's briefly discuss how and why this works.

The first parameter of the CALCULATE function is an expression, and you can think of this as an aggregation of some kind. In this example, the aggregation is simply Total Sales. The second parameter is a filter that allows the current filter context to be modified in some way. In the preceding example, the filter context is modified by *ignoring any filters* that come from the Country attribute. Let's take a look at the definition for the ALL function used in the second parameter of the CALCULATE function:

ALL: Returns all the rows in a table, or all the values in a column, *ignoring any filters* that may have been applied.

Alternatively, the REMOVEFILTERS function can be used instead of ALL to achieve the same results. For this example, these functions can be used interchangeably. I find that most developers new to DAX find REMOVEFILTERS a bit easier to understand. Modify the measure created in the last step, Total Sales all Countries, to use REMOVEFILTERS instead of the ALL function, as you can see in *Figure 5.26*:

```
1 Total Sales all Countries =
2 CALCULATE(
3     [Total Sales],
4     REMOVEFILTERS(
5         'Sales Territory'[Sales Territory Country]))
```

Figure 5.26: Replace the ALL function with REMOVEFILTERS

The most difficult challenge to creating our percentage of total calculation in DAX is creating the total sales for all countries. With this calculated measure completed, let's complete the percentage of the total calculation.

Calculating the percentage of total

Now, create another calculated measure in the Internet Sales table using the following code. Make sure that you format the measure as a percentage:

```
% of All Countries = DIVIDE([Total Sales], [Total Sales all Countries])
```

In *Figure 5.27*, you can see the completed example with both of the new measures created in this section. Without a basic understanding of the CALCULATE function, this type of percentage of total calculation would be nearly impossible:

Sales Territory Country	Total Sales	Total Sales all Countries	% of All Countries
Australia	$9,061,000.58	$29,358,677.22	30.86%
Canada	$1,977,844.86	$29,358,677.22	6.74%
France	$2,644,017.71	$29,358,677.22	9.01%
Germany	$2,894,312.34	$29,358,677.22	9.86%
NA		$29,358,677.22	
United Kingdom	$3,391,712.21	$29,358,677.22	11.55%
United States	$9,389,789.51	$29,358,677.22	31.98%
Total	**$29,358,677.22**	**$29,358,677.22**	**100.00%**

Figure 5.27: Completed example with new measures

In *Figure 5.27*, you may notice that a new row with the value of **NA** appeared in the column **Sales Territory Country**. Previously, this NA value was automatically hidden by the Power BI visual because **Total Sales** returned a blank value. However, **Total Sales all Countries** will ignore the NA filter and return total sales for all countries and therefore, the NA value now appears in the table visual.

In this section, you were introduced to the CALCULATE function in DAX. The default filters that are applied in Power BI are awesome, but sometimes you need the ability to evaluate an expression, like total sales, in a modified filter context, and the CALCULATE function is perfect for that.

Working with time intelligence functions

Another advantage of Power BI is how easily time intelligence can be added to your data model. DAX has a comprehensive list of built-in time intelligence functions that can be easily leveraged and add significant analytical value to your data model. In this section, you are going to learn how to use these built-in functions to create the following measures:

- Year to Date Sales
- Year to Date Sales (Fiscal Calendar)
- Prior Year Sales

 Take a look at the alternative methods for calculating time intelligence in the DAX cheat sheet at https://tinyurl.com/pbiqs-daxcheatsheet.

In order to leverage time intelligence functions in DAX, you must have a date table in your data model and that date table must have all available dates with no gaps. These are very important conditions that must be met. Oftentimes, developers try to use the date column from their transaction table (fact table). This can result in calculations that do not work and return incorrect results. In the previous chapter, you learned how to properly build a relationship from your date table to your fact table and multiple methods for marking your date table as a date table. Now that we have added some clarity here, let's create a year-to-date sales calculation.

Creating year-to-date calculations

Create a new calculated measure in your Internet Sales table using the following DAX formula. See the results in *Figure 5.28* below. Remember to format the measure as **$ English (United States)**:

```
YTD Sales = TOTALYTD([Total Sales], 'Date (Order)'[Date])
```

Maybe your requirement is slightly more complex, and you need to see the year-to-date sales based on your fiscal year end rather than the calendar year-end date. The TOTALYTD function has an optional parameter that allows you to change the default year-end date from 12/31 to a different date. Create a new calculated measure in your Internet Sales table using the following DAX formula:

```
Fiscal YTD Sales = TOTALYTD([Total Sales], 'Date (Order)'[Date], "03/31")
```

Now, let's take a look at both of these new measures in a table in Power BI:

Year	Month	Total Sales	YTD Sales	Year	Month	Total Sales	Fiscal YTD Sales
2005	July	$473,388.16	$473,388.16	2005	July	$473,388.16	$473,388.16
2005	August	$506,191.69	$979,579.85	2005	August	$506,191.69	$979,579.85
2005	September	$473,943.03	$1,453,522.89	2005	September	$473,943.03	$1,453,522.89
2005	October	$513,329.47	$1,966,852.36	2005	October	$513,329.47	$1,966,852.36
2005	November	$543,993.41	$2,510,845.77 ①	2005	November	$543,993.41	$2,510,845.77
2005	December	$755,527.89	$3,266,373.66	2005	December	$755,527.89	$3,266,373.66
2006	January	$596,746.56	$596,746.56	2006	January	$596,746.56	$3,863,120.21
2006	February	$550,816.69	$1,147,563.25 ②	2006	February	$550,816.69	$4,413,936.91 ③
2006	March	$644,135.20	$1,791,698.45	2006	March	$644,135.20	$5,058,072.11
2006	April	$663,692.29	$2,455,390.74	2006	April	$663,692.29	$663,692.29
2006	May	$673,556.20	$3,128,946.94	2006	May	$673,556.20	$1,337,248.48 ④

Figure 5.28: Comparing YTD Sales with Fiscal YTD Sales

The newly created measures YTD Sales and Fiscal YTD Sales have both been added to the preceding table. Let's take a closer look at how these two measures are different; the relevant sections in the table are annotated with the numbers one to four, corresponding to the following notes:

1. The amount displayed for December 2005 is $3,266,374.66 This is the cumulative total of all sales from January 1, 2005 to December 31, 2005.

2. As expected, the cumulative total starts over as the year switches from 2005 to 2006; therefore, the YTD Sales amount for January 2006 is $596,747.

3. In the Fiscal YTD Sales column, the cumulative total works slightly differently. The displayed amount of $5,058,072.11 is the cumulative total of all sales from April 1, 2005 to March 31, 2006.

4. Unlike the YTD Sales measure, the Fiscal YTD Sales measure does not start over until April 1. The amount displayed for April 2006 of $663,692.29 is the cumulative total for April. This number will grow each month until May 31, at which point, the number will reset again.

In this section, you learned about a built-in time intelligence function in DAX; there are many of these functions that make doing time series analysis much easier. Now let's take a look calculating a prior year sales calculation.

Creating prior year calculations with CALCULATE()

A lot of time series analysis consists of comparing current metrics to the previous month or the previous year. There are many functions in DAX that work in conjunction with the CALCULATE function to make these types of calculations possible. In this section, you are going to create a new measure to return the total sales for the prior year.

Using *Figure 5.29* as a reference, create a new calculated measure in your `Internet Sales` table for `Prior Year Sales`:

```
1  Prior Year Sales =
2  CALCULATE(
3      [Total Sales],              // SUM('Internet Sales'[Sales Amount]
4      SAMEPERIODLASTYEAR(         // Change the filter context to go back one year
5          'Date (Order)'[Date]))
```

Figure 5.29: Create a Prior Year Sales calculation

`CALCULATE` allows you to ignore or even change the current filter context. In the preceding formula, `CALCULATE` is used to take the current filter context and modify it to one year prior. This calculated measure also works at the day, month, quarter, and year levels of the hierarchy. For example, if you were looking at sales for `June 15, 2020`, then the `Prior Year Sales` measure would return sales for `June 15, 2019`. However, if you were simply analyzing your sales aggregated at the month level for `June 2020`, then the measure would return the sales for `June 2019`.

> For a comprehensive list of all the built-in time intelligence functions, please take a look at `https://tinyurl.com/pbiqs-timeintelligence`.

In this section, you learned how to add time series analysis to your data model, adding significant analytical value and allowing you to extract valuable insights from your data across time. In other programming languages, it would take significant amounts of code and an in-depth validation process to perform the same calculations that can be achieved in DAX with minimal effort.

Role-playing tables with DAX

In *Chapter 4*, *Building the Data Model*, you learned how to develop your data model to deal with role-playing tables, by importing a table multiple times. We mentioned then that there was an alternative method using DAX. In this section, we will explore this alternative method and the pros and cons of using DAX versus the method you have previously learned.

Since leveraging DAX does not require importing a table multiple times, you will immediately gain savings on storage and, unlike the other method, with DAX, you will not need to manage multiple tables in Power BI Desktop.

The DAX method requires that inactive relationships be created in order to work correctly. Inactive relationships are not often used in DAX because they are not used automatically like active relationships. Unlike active relationships, you can have more than one inactive relationship between two tables.

Let's create a new relationship between the Internet Sales table and the Date (Order) table. First, open the relationship editor by referring to *Figure 5.30* and the steps following:

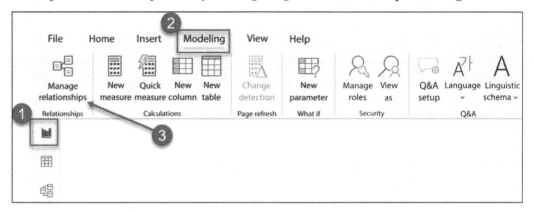

Figure 5.30: Launch the Manage relationships dialog box

1. Navigate to the **Report View**.
2. Select the **Modeling** ribbon across the top of Power BI Desktop.
3. Click on **Manage relationships**.

Once the **Manage relationships** box appears, click on **New...** to create a new relationship. Continue creating the relationship with the steps by referring to *Figure 5.31* and the steps following:

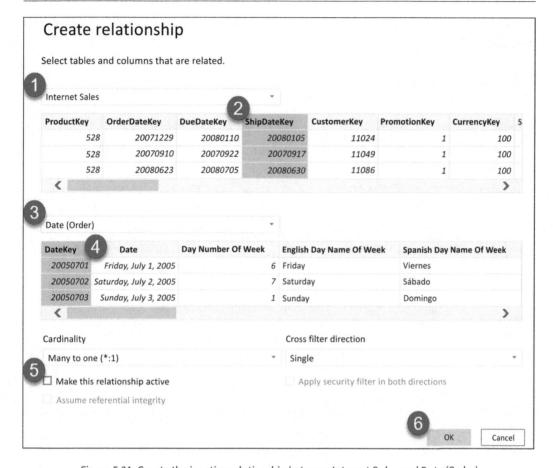

Figure 5.31: Create the inactive relationship between Internet Sales and Date (Order)

1. Select **Internet Sales** from the drop-down menu.

2. Select the **ShipDateKey** column from the list of columns.

3. Select **Date (Order)** from the drop-down menu.

4. Select the **DateKey** column from the list of columns.

5. Do not select **Make this relationship active**.

6. Click **OK**.

The new relationship can be observed in *Figure 5.32*, which is a screenshot of the **Manage relationships** dialog box:

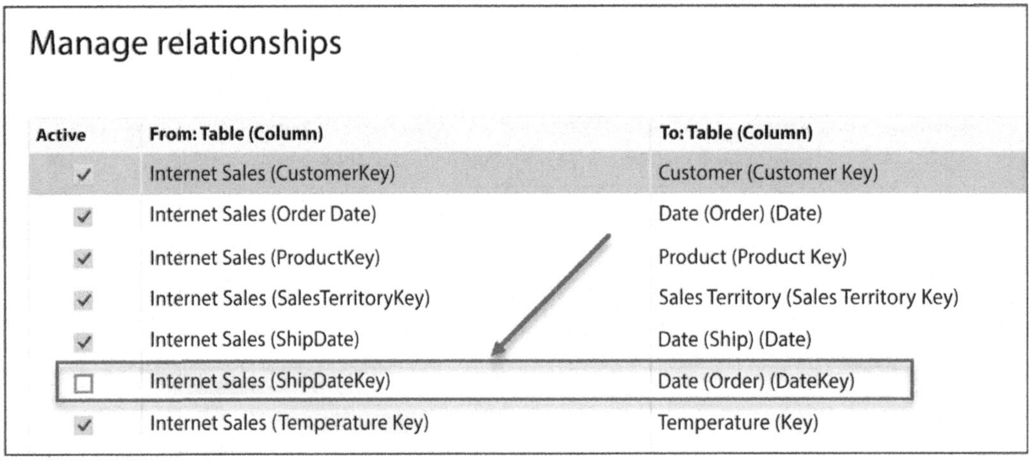

Manage relationships

Active	From: Table (Column)	To: Table (Column)
✓	Internet Sales (CustomerKey)	Customer (Customer Key)
✓	Internet Sales (Order Date)	Date (Order) (Date)
✓	Internet Sales (ProductKey)	Product (Product Key)
✓	Internet Sales (SalesTerritoryKey)	Sales Territory (Sales Territory Key)
✓	Internet Sales (ShipDate)	Date (Ship) (Date)
☐	Internet Sales (ShipDateKey)	Date (Order) (DateKey)
✓	Internet Sales (Temperature Key)	Temperature (Key)

Figure 5.32: New relationship between Internet Sales and Date (Order)

Now that the inactive relationship has been created, we can create the calculated measure to return Total Sales by Ship Date. The completed calculated measure can be seen in *Figure 5.33*:

```
1 Total Sales (by Ship Date) =
2 CALCULATE(
3     [Total Sales],
4     USERELATIONSHIP(
5         'Internet Sales'[ShipDateKey],
6         'Date (Order)'[DateKey] ) )
```

Figure 5.33: New calculated measure

This measure will make use of two functions in DAX. First, the CALCULATE function is used here because the filter context is going to be modified to use the inactive relationship rather than the active relationship. Second, the USERELATIONSHIP function specifies that the Internet Sales table should be filtered by ShipDateKey rather than the active relationship on OrderDateKey.

The completed measure can be seen in *Figure 5.34* along with the original Total Sales calculation:

Year	Total Sales	Total Sales (by Ship Date)
2005	3,266,373.66	$3,105,587.33
2006	6,530,343.53	$6,576,978.98
2007	9,791,060.30	$9,517,548.53
2008	9,770,899.74	$10,158,562.38
Total	**29,358,677.22**	**$29,358,677.22**

Figure 5.34: Validating the new calculated measure

In *Figure 5.34*, the Total Sales measure is returning the total sales based on the active relationship in the data model, which is on OrderDateKey, therefore $3,266,373 is returned for the year 2005. Alternatively, the Total Sales (by Ship Date) measure is returning $3,105,587.33 in sales.

This approach does not require importing additional tables and therefore is superior to the method you learned in *Chapter 4*, *Building the Data Model*, for optimizing space in your data model. However, with the DAX method, you would be required to create a new measure for every measure in your data model that you wanted to see by the Ship Date. Therefore, if you had 50 measures in your table, you would create a new version of each of those measures and would specify that the new measure should use the inactive relationship on ShipDateKey rather than the current active relationship. Because of this reason alone, the method you learned in *Chapter 4*, *Building the Data Model*, is the most common approach to handling role-playing tables.

 With the addition of external tools and calculation groups, you can now create one measure to support role-playing tables! This makes the DAX method significantly easier to implement than ever before. Want to learn more? Check out the following YouTube video on this implementation: https://tinyurl.com/RolePlayingTables.

In this section, you learned an alternative method to provide support for role-playing tables in Power BI Desktop. This method has historically required significantly more development effort and therefore has not been as popular as the method you learned previously.

As we bring this chapter to a close, I feel it's necessary to mention that there are several developer-friendly tools that can help the DAX developer gain better insights into their data models. These tools are outside the scope of this book, but as you continue your journey with DAX, you will want to learn more about DAX Studio and the Tabular Editor.

Summary

In this chapter, you learned that DAX allows you to significantly enhance your data model by improving the analytical capabilities with a relatively small amount of code. You also learned how to create calculated columns and measures and how to use DAX to perform useful time series analysis on your data.

This chapter merely scratched the surface of what is possible with DAX. As you further explore the DAX language on your own, you will quickly become a proficient author of DAX formulas. As with everyone who learns DAX, you will inevitably learn that there is a layer of complexity to DAX that will require further education to really master. When you get to this point, it would be advantageous to look for classes or books that will help you to take your skills to the next level and truly master DAX!

Join our community on Discord

Join our community's Discord space for discussions with the authors and other readers:

https://packt.link/ips2H

6

Visualizing Data

Power BI is best known for its impressive visualization capabilities. Up to this point, the focus has been on importing data and modeling it to your specifications. The goal of this chapter is to bring that data to life through impactful visuals. The number of visuals is vast, and the aim is to provide an overview of most of the included visuals. It is impossible to do an in-depth tour of all the options; instead, the focus will be on getting familiar with the basic configuration, appropriate use for each of the built-in visuals, and how to acquire custom visuals not included in Power BI by default. The topics detailed in this chapter include the following:

- Report view basics
- Creating new visuals
- Filtering visualizations and data
- Visualizing tabular data
- Visualizing categorical data
- Visualizing trend data
- Visualizing KPI data
- Visualizing data using cards
- Visualizing geographical data
- Natural language
- Visuals from analytics
- Power BI custom visuals
- Data visualization tips and tricks

At the time of this book's publication, there are 40 readily available visuals in Power BI Desktop including the **Metrics, Shape map,** and **Azure map** visuals that are in preview and must first manually be enabled to use. Let's get started with bringing the model you have worked on up to this point to life!

 With Power BI's rapid update cycle, there will be many visuals added to the application over time. If you would like to leverage these as soon as they are available, you can find them in the **Preview features** section of Power BI Desktop's options. *Figure 6.1* shows how to access the **Preview features** setting. Once you have enabled area preview visuals, it usually requires a restart of Power BI Desktop, so make sure to save your work!

To turn on **Preview features**, click **File | Options and settings | Options | Preview features** and check the box next to **Shape map visual, Azure map visual,** and **Metrics visual.**

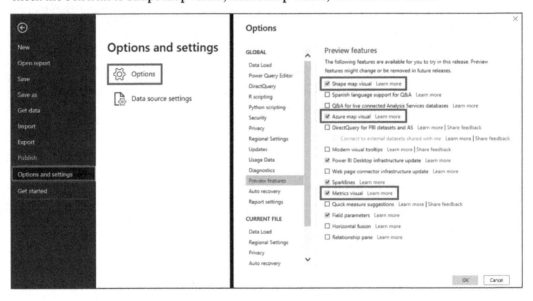

Figure 6.1: Enable Power BI preview features on the Options menu

As features are moved from preview to generally available, they will automatically fall off the preview features list and be automatically available upon loading Power BI Desktop. Other preview features are available but because they are not related to visualizations they will not be explored in this chapter.

Report view basics

As soon as you launch Power BI Desktop and close the **Getting Started** screen, you will find yourself in the **Report** view, which is where you will stay for the duration of this chapter. In the previous chapter, you explored the **Model** view as well as the **Data** view, but these areas are not necessary for the visualization work discussed in this chapter. There are many items of interest in this initial **Report** view area that need to be discussed so that you can work efficiently. Let's open the completed Power BI file from *Chapter 5, Leveraging DAX*, which includes all of the calculated columns and calculated measures that will be used in the upcoming visuals.

> For this chapter, you can build on top of the completed pbix file from *Chapter 5, Leveraging DAX*. If you would like to keep your work from each chapter separate, please open the completed pbix file called `Chapter 6 - Visualizing Data.pbix`. Then, under the **File** option, choose **Save As** and give this file a new name for the work you will be doing in *Chapter 6, Visualizing Data*.

Let's review the key areas of Power BI Desktop:

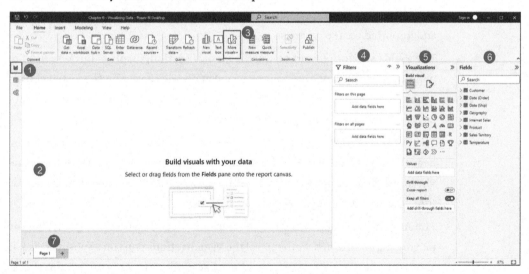

Figure 6.2: First view of Power BI Desktop

We can observe the following features:

1. **Report view**: Displays the report canvas, page navigation, and panes for customizing visualizations within the report. This is the default view that opens when Power BI Desktop is launched.

2. **Report canvas**: The main design area holding all report visuals.

3. **More visuals**: A menu with options to access custom visuals from AppSource or local files. After importing, these will appear in the **Visualizations** pane.

4. **Filters pane**: Apply filters to various scopes:

   - **Filters on this page** applies to every visual on the selected page.

   - **Filters on all pages** applies to every visual on every page in the report.

   - **Filters on this visual** only appears when a visual is selected, and only affects the selected visual.

5. **Visualizations pane**: Consists of four sections working together to customize the data and formatting of visualizations:

   - **The Visuals section** displays all available visualizations including enabled preview and imported custom visuals.

   - **The Fields section**, found below the visuals section, displays buckets used to populate the different areas on the visual and varies based on the visual chosen. For instance, a table will have a single **Columns** bucket, while a pie chart will have **Legend**, **Details**, **Values**, and **Tooltips** buckets.

   - **The Format section**, which can be accessed by clicking on the paintbrush icon near the top of the **Visualizations** pane, controls the look and feel of the visual. The formatting options will vary based on the visual selected but generally include title, font size and color, and data label settings.

   - **The Analytics section**, which is not shown but can be accessed by clicking the magnifying glass icon near the top of the **Visualizations** pane on a subset of visuals, allows for the addition of reference lines like minimum or maximum thresholds, the median line, and an average line. The options will vary based on the visual selected and often allow for both static and data-driven lines.

6. **Fields pane**: Displays all available fields to be added to visuals and filters. If a table or column is hidden in the data view, it will not appear in the **Fields** pane.

7. **Page navigation**: Select which report page to display on the canvas. Each page has a limited work area where visuals are displayed, so it is common to have more than one page in a Power BI report. Pages can be added by clicking the plus button at the end of the page list.

It is important to note that when working with visual filters, a visual must be selected. A visual is selected when you see the anchor points (small lines at each corner and halfway down each side) appear around the visual in question after clicking on it. This can be seen in *Figure 6.3*. Clicking on an anchor point will allow you to resize a visual, button, image, or other selected object in the report. Now that you are familiar with the **Report** view features and layout, it is time to start visualizing!

Creating new visuals

Before exploring the various visualizations available in Power BI, let's look at the three ways to add visuals to the report canvas. All these methods will result in the same final product. However, depending on the type of visualization needed, it may cut a few clicks off your workflow to use one method over another.

The first method for adding a visual is using the **New visual** button on the ribbon. This will add a blank stacked column chart to the **Report** canvas, at which point you can start to drag and drop fields or check the box next to a field to add it to the visual. If a stacked bar chart is not the desired visual, it can be changed by selecting a different visual from the **Visualizations** pane:

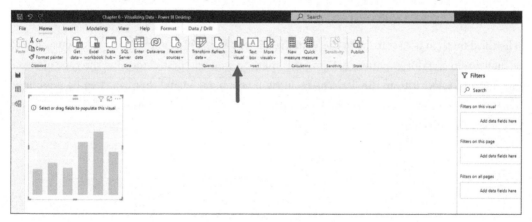

Figure 6.3: New visual button on the Home ribbon to add a blank visual

The second method for creating a new visual is starting from the **Fields** pane. To get started, ensure no visuals are selected by clicking anywhere in the blank area of the report canvas, then simply check the box next to a field or drag a field and drop it on the **Values** bucket in the **Visualizations** pane. A new visual will be created based on the data type of the field selected. The result is generally a clustered column chart for numeric fields and a table for non-numeric fields. You can then change to the desired visual if the correct type was not generated automatically.

Figure 6.4: Create a new visual by checking the box next to any item in the field list

The third method is to start from the **Visualizations** pane, which allows for a more customized visualization creation experience. Using this method, you will first determine the type of visual needed and select it from the list. The result will be a blank visual that can then be populated with the desired fields being checked off or dragged from the **Fields** pane to the field buckets in the **Visualizations** pane.

Figure 6.5: Create a blank visual of your choice by clicking on any item in the Visualizations pane

The final method for creating a visual is to double-click on any blank area of the canvas. This will create a Q&A visual, which is good for users that do not have a deep knowledge of the data model, would like to build visuals by typing out natural language queries, and have the option to turn the resulting visual into a standard visual. The Q&A visual will be covered in more detail later in the chapter.

Now that you have a good understanding of the various methods for creating new visualizations on the **Report** canvas, let's get to work building some high-impact visuals.

Filtering visualizations and data

Filtering the data that users will see within a Power BI report is the most effective way to answer very specific questions about that data, and there are many ways to accomplish this. One of Power BI's most useful features is its ability to allow users to interact with a visual, which will then apply the selection as a filter to the rest of the visuals on that page. This is known as cross-filtering. This behavior really puts the power into the user's hands, and they can decide how they want to filter the visuals. This makes a report much more robust because it can answer many more questions about the data without the need to create and maintain additional pages or visuals.

Along with this functionality, report developers can add more visible and explicit forms of filtering using the slicer visual that is available in the **Visualizations** pane. This provides the option to choose a very specific field from the data that you know end users will want to use to filter some or all of the visualizations on the page.

The default interaction between two visuals, when supported, is called cross-highlighting. If two visuals do not support cross-highlighting, the default interaction is cross-filtering. Consider a report with a bar chart showing sales by country and a pie chart showing profit by age. Under the **default behavior**, selecting **United States** in the bar chart would cause the pie chart to continue showing sales for all countries while highlighting the slicer that corresponds to **United States**. This is very useful for seeing how a subset of one visual is represented inside another. The interaction can be modified to cross-filter rather than highlight. With the cross-filter behavior, selecting **United States** in the bar chart would filter out all data except **United States** from the pie chart, reducing the overall cumulative profit value. This interaction is useful when looking to explore specific subsets of report data across all visualizations.

Now, let's dive in and get a better understanding of these two filtering options, as they will most definitely be elements in your finished reports. As you start to explore some of these examples, it is worth noting that the sample dataset only contains dates from the years 2005–2008. You may choose to eliminate all 2009 and 2010 dates from the **Date** table using the data transformation options learned in prior chapters, use slicers or filters to limit the dates, or take no action at all. Note though, that your visuals may look slightly different at times depending on your decision.

Cross-filtering and cross-highlighting

Almost every single visual that is readily available within Power BI has some sort of element that users can interact with. At the same time, every visual can be impacted by these very same elements. This provides a lot of flexibility when it comes to deciding which visuals to include on a report page. Cross-highlighting will be covered again later in this chapter, but it is important to understand how this feature works so it can be leveraged throughout the examples to come. Let's create two very simple visuals based on the current data model so you can see exactly how cross-highlighting works. For now, let's not worry about the details of these visuals as they will be fully described in later sections of this chapter.

Let's look at setting up the example:

1. From the **Visualizations** pane, select the **Stacked column chart**. Make sure the anchor points discussed earlier are visible. If necessary, click on the blank chart placeholder on the **Report** canvas so the anchor points will appear.

2. From the **Fields** pane, check the box next to **Total Sales** from the **Internet Sales** table. Notice that the field shows up under the **Y-axis** bucket of the **Fields** section.

3. From the **Fields** pane, drag **Sales Territory Country** from the **Sales Territory** table to the **X-axis** bucket in the **Fields** section. Resize the visual by using the visual's anchor points to make it easier to read the labels. Reference *Figure 6.6* to validate that everything is set correctly. While not used in this example, dragging a field to the **Legend** field well would create the stacked effect where the height of the bar represents the total for the X-axis category and each band represents a legend value inside that category.

Figure 6.6: Stacked column chart showing sales by country

 You may notice that some of the visual elements do not meet your standards. For example, the size of the text for various items in this visual is far too small to read. These are the types of changes that would be made in the **Format** area but we will not be doing so in this specific example. Common formatting options for each of the visuals will be discussed within their respective sections in this chapter.

4. You can already start to interact with any of the columns in the chart, but since this is the only visual, it really isn't that exciting. Add another visual to the **Report** canvas; make sure you left-click somewhere in the empty space so that no visual is currently selected.

5. Next, from the **Visualizations** pane, select the **Pie chart**, which will be added to the **Report** canvas. You may have to move the visual to a location more to your liking.

6. In the **Fields** pane, check the box next to **Age Breakdown** in the **Customer** table. If it does not go to the **Legend** bucket, drag it there.

7. Using either of the two methods described so far, add **Profit** from the **Internet Sales** table to the **Values** bucket. See *Figure 6.7* to verify the setup:

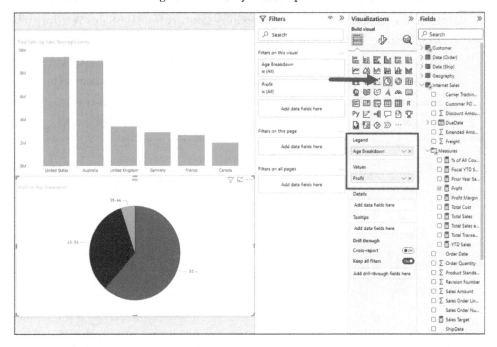

Figure 6.7: Pie chart showing profit by age breakdown

Now that the example is all set and there are two visuals in the **Report** canvas, you can really see how cross-highlighting works. Select (left-mouse-click) the column labeled **United States** in the stacked column chart. You will immediately see that the pie chart changes to having a much smaller highlighted area. By hovering over the **35-44** section of the pie chart, you can now see that the United States makes up $166,050.59 of the $558,724.98 total for that category. This same type of highlighting can be done by selecting a slice of the pie chart, which will then highlight a subset of the stacked column chart. Just with this simple example, you can see how effective cross-highlighting is in answering questions about the data. Keep this in mind as you move forward with the other examples so you can keep seeing the impact highlighting has.

Edit interactions

Throughout all the examples to come, you will have the capability of using cross-highlighting and cross-filtering. Almost everything seen inside a visual can be selected, and it will affect all the other visuals within that same report page. This behavior can be altered though, and there will be situations where you do not want a specific visual to be filtered by any others.

The way to control this is through an option called **Edit interactions**, which can be found on the **Format** ribbon when a visual is selected. When you select the **Edit interactions** button, you will see new icons next to all the other visuals on the current page, as seen in *Figure 6.8*. In this example, the **Pie chart** is selected and you can now decide if any of the other visuals will be affected by cross-highlighting or cross-filtering from the **Pie chart**. The two primary icons are a column chart with a funnel in the lower-right corner, which lets us know that the visual will be cross-filtered, and a circle with a line through it designating that the visual will not be affected at all; no filtering or highlighting will occur when interacting with the paired visual. Based on the visual type, there will be an icon that looks like a column chart but no funnel in the lower-right corner, which you can see on the stacked column chart. This means that the visual will be cross-highlighted rather than filtered, as shown in *Figure 6.8*. This option is something that you will have to do for each individual visual.

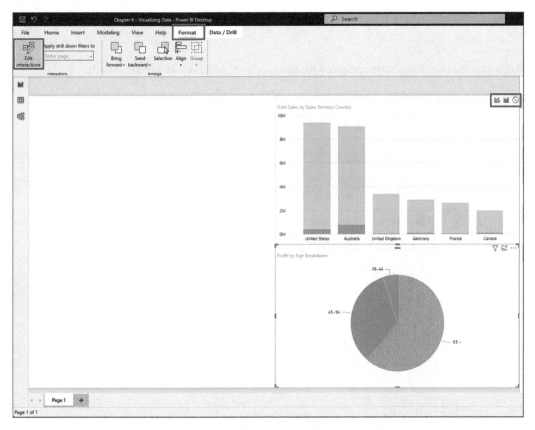

Figure 6.8: Change default cross-filtering and cross-highlighting behavior with Edit interactions

In general, all visuals allow the options for no interaction and filtering. Only a subset of visuals, like the bar, column, and pie charts, allow highlighting. The default interaction behavior is highlighting. If highlighting is not available for the visual pair, then the default behavior is filtering.

Slicer

Now that you know cross-filtering will always be an option for users, what do you do when end users want to filter by something that isn't used inside any of the visuals? This is where the **Slicer** visual comes into play. The **Slicer** visual only allows one field or hierarchy to be displayed but, depending on the data type of that field, different presentation options will be available.

The slicer has a different set of options based on the following types of data being displayed:

- String/text
- Numeric
- Date

Let's explore these different options with the visuals that have already been built.

String/text

Let's start by setting up a slicer with string or text values:

1. Ensure no other visuals are selected by clicking on any blank area on the **Report** canvas.
2. In the **Visualizations** pane, select the **Slicer**. Move it to someplace convenient within the **Report** canvas. You can use the anchor points to resize the visual as you see fit.
3. In the **Fields** pane, check the box next to **Temperature Range** from the **Temperature** table to add it to the selected slicer **Field** bucket.

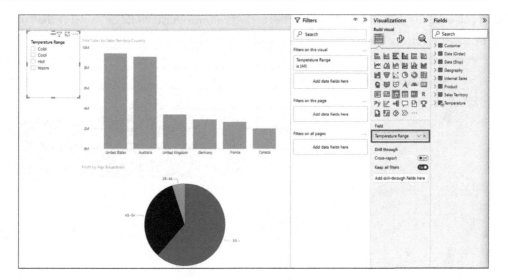

Figure 6.9: Slicer showing the Temperature Range field

The slicer will default to the **List** view. This allows users to see a distinct list of all the options they can now filter on from the specific field. You should see four temperature options in the list, each with a blank box to its left. Clicking in a box will single-select a member from the list resulting in other visuals being filtered. If you are looking to save space on the canvas but want all the functionality of the list view, then look at the drop - down view available from the down arrow in the top-right corner of the slicer.

If you were to select the **Cold** option, the stacked column chart would be showing the **Total Sales by Sales Territory Country** when the weather was cold.

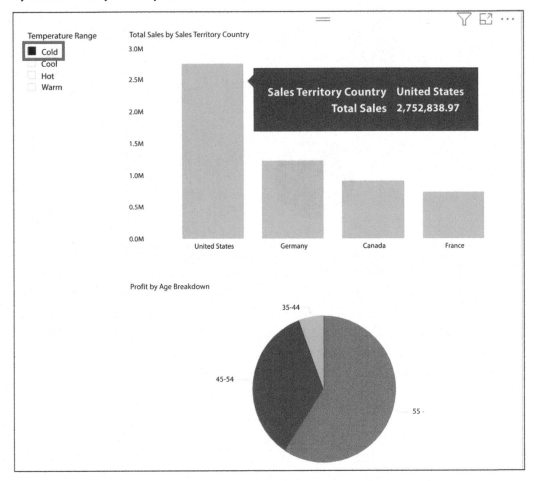

Figure 6.10: Stacked column chart filtered to the Cold Temperature Range

To multi-select, you have two options. The first is to hold down the *Ctrl* key on your keyboard while making your selections. The second option lies within the **Format** area under the **Visual section,** then **Slicer settings,** then **Selection** expandable menus. Here, you will find an option called **Multi-select with CTRL**, which is set to **On** by default, and by turning this off, you no longer need to hold the *Ctrl* key to multi-select.

If hierarchical data is used as a filter, multiple fields may be added to the slicer's **Field** bucket. When this happens, the slicer will display a stair-stepped list or drop-down set of values. The slicer behaves the same as described in this section but allows for a much more user-friendly display of data. By using hierarchies, it is possible to create much larger lists of values while keeping it easy for users to find the members by which to filter. The hierarchies used in a slicer can be explicitly defined in the data model, or they can instead be created by dragging multiple fields from the same table into the slicer, or even multiple fields from different tables if a relationship exists between the tables.

Let's set up a slicer with a hierarchy:

1. Ensure no other visuals are selected by clicking on any blank area on the **Report** canvas.
2. In the **Visualizations** pane, select the **Slicer**. Move it to someplace convenient within the **Report** canvas.
3. In the **Fields** pane, check the box next to **Sales Territory Drilldown** from the **Sales Territory** table to add it to the selected slicer **Field** bucket.

Figure 6.11: Slicer with the Sales Territory Drilldown hierarchy

Unique to slicers using string/text values is the ability to add the search functionality. Clicking the ellipses (**...**) in the top-right corner of the slicer header will reveal a menu of options, the first of which is **Search**.

Adding a search option greatly improves the user experience when working with large lists.

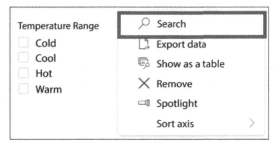

Figure 6.12: Enable search on slicers using a string/text field

Using hierarchies in slicers is an easy way to reduce the number of slicers on a report page, which in turn will free up valuable canvas real estate for storytelling through visuals.

Numeric

Now, add another slicer to the current report page, which uses a numeric field, to explore the numeric range slicer:

1. Ensure no other visuals are selected by clicking on any blank area on the **Report** canvas.
2. From the **Visualizations** pane, select the **Slicer**. Move and resize it as you see fit.
3. From the **Fields** pane, check the box next to **Year** from the **Date (Order)** table.

Immediately, you will see a very different presentation for the filter. A numeric field will result in a sliding bar that can be moved from either side to give a range of values, which will be used to filter the other visuals on the page. By moving the left end of the slider one value to the right, the year 2005 will be removed from the selected range and the data in the visuals will be changed. See *Figure 6.13*.

The slicer can also be set to use the **List** format that was seen in the temperature slicer example above. To change the display format, click the down arrow located in the upper-right corner of the slicer.

If the down arrow and eraser are not visible, simply hover the mouse over the slicer.

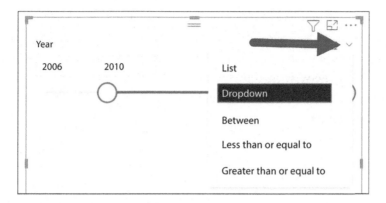

Figure 6.13: Display options for slicers using a numeric field

The format options from *Figure 6.13* are as follows:

- **List**: A distinct list of values from the selected field. Best used when there are a small number of options to choose from.

- **Dropdown**: Drop-down menu containing a distinct list of values from the selected field. Like the **List** option in functionality but choices are hidden until a user expands the drop-down. Also best used for a smaller set of values so users don't have to scroll through hundreds of choices.

- **Between**: This choice will only present itself for fields that are of the numeric and date data types. It allows users to specify a boundary-inclusive range of values. This means a range between 100 and 500 will include data points 100 and 500 rather than being filtered out.

- **Less than or equal to**: Like the **Between** option, but the sliding scale can only be adjusted from the right side, the upper boundary, which is included in the filter values.

- **Greater than or equal to**: This is the same as the previous option, except you can only adjust the sliding scale from the left side, the lower boundary, which is included in the filter values.

 When using the **List** option for a smaller set of filter choices, try changing the orientation from vertical to horizontal. If you add a background color to this setup, it gives the feeling of having buttons to filter with. To set this up, just go to the **Format** area of the slicer. From the **Visual** pane, navigate to **Slicer settings**, then **Options**, and change the value of the **Orientation** setting to **Horizontal**. Then, expand the **Items** area and select a font color and background color of your choice, and you will see the design feels like a set of buttons.

Be sure to consider the context in which a numeric filter will be used and decide the appropriate format. A dropdown or a list may be more suitable when filtering tire sizes as the user will likely be looking for a single or small range of values. However, when filtering based on price, one of the range options, such as **Between**, may be more applicable due to the vast variations in prices based on the manufacturer, size, mileage rating, and so on, and this would make searching through a list very time-consuming.

Date

Add a fourth slicer to the current **Report** page, which uses a **Date** field:

1. Ensure no other visuals are selected by clicking on any blank area on the **Report** canvas.
2. From the **Visualizations** pane, select the **Slicer**. Move and resize it as you see fit. From the **Fields** pane, check the box next to **Date** from the **Date (Order)** table.

At first glance, it appears Power BI has just generated another numeric range slicer. However, the lower and upper boundaries are dates. Clicking on either boundary will display a calendar to aid in selecting a date.

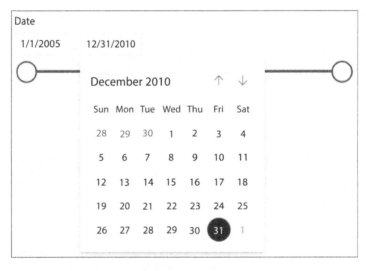

Figure 6.14: Calendar displayed when selecting a date on a slicer using a date field

In addition to the options available to the text and numeric slicers, the date slicer adds relative date and time formats. The relative filter, shown below, allows ranges to be set relative to the current date or time. It can be configured to look at the last, current, or next *N* number of units. The relative units can be days, weeks, months, or years for a relative date.

The relative units can be minutes or hours for a relative time.

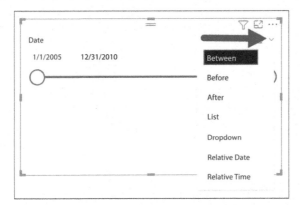

Figure 6.15: Display options for slicers using a date field

You have now seen a couple of different ways to allow users to filter the visuals that have been created for them. Cross-filtering will always be there for users, but you can take a more traditional route with the **Slicer** visual and present them with specific options they would find meaningful to filter the data.

The last step is to rename this report page from **Page 1** to **Slicers** by right-clicking the page name and selecting **Rename Page**.

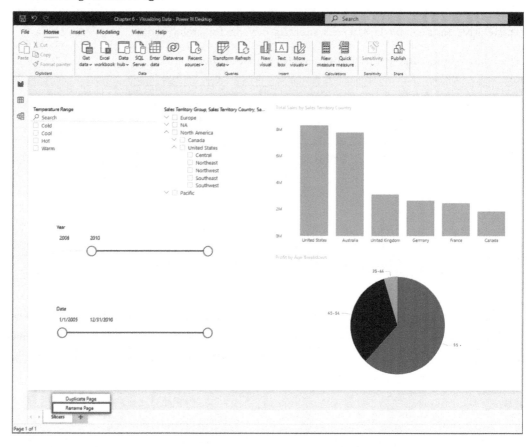

Figure 6.16: Options menu to duplicate or rename report pages

Report filters

There is one other way to filter data and that is through the **Filters** pane. Here you can select specific fields to filter a single visual, all the visuals on a specific page, or all the visuals on all pages. While this is a very useful option, it does come with some hidden effects. The **Filters** pane is not as easily visible as a filter sitting on the canvas. As such, it is easier for users to miss seeing which filters have been applied and therefore possibly miss some key context for a report or a report page. One way to avoid confusion is to place a callout in a textbox on the report stating filters are being used on specific pages, or create an overview page where users can be given a tour of the report configuration before diving into the data.

There are three main contexts for report filters available in the **Filters** pane:

1. **Filters on this visual** are only available when a visual is selected on the canvas. This will be pre-populated with fields that are already present in the visualization's field wells but with the default setting of **All**. These filters apply to this visual only and are applied in addition to any other slicer or interaction filtering.

2. **Filters on this page** are applied to all visuals on the current page. These filters can vary from page to page and are not specific to any one visualization.

3. **Filters on all pages** are applied to all visuals on all pages in the report. Changing from one page to another will show that these filters do not change. One thing you will notice about the dataset being used in all the examples is there are only valid dates in the years between 2005 and 2008. If you'd like to skip a few steps along the way through this chapter and apply a global filter to only include dates where there is data, you can optionally add the **Year** field from the **Date (Order)** table to the **Filters on all pages** and filter to only include the years 2005–2008.

With interaction behavior, slicers, and filters, there is no shortage of methods for filtering the data context for a visual, page, or even the entire report. We will explore even more about filtering in the next chapter when examining Power BI's drillthrough and tooltip functionalities.

With the slicers created, let's dive into the various ways to visualize data, starting with the most foundational of all visualizations: tables and matrices.

Visualizing tabular data

There are many options within Power BI to visually represent data, but sometimes users may want to see and compare detail-level data and exact values. In these scenarios, using the **Table** or **Matrix** visual is the most effective option. When leveraging either of these two visuals, it is important to take advantage of the **Format** section of the **Visualizations** pane to ensure that users can easily interpret the data that is being presented. One of the best ways to bring attention to values of importance with these visuals is by using **Conditional formatting**. This section will also take advantage of the hierarchies created in *Chapter 4, Building the Data Model*, to allow for drilldowns within the visuals.

Table

The table visual is perfect for looking at many values (measures) for a category. To really make the table shine, you will also want to take advantage of the **Conditional formatting** options.

In this example, you will be using the **Sales Territory Region** as the category and looking at four different values to analyze each region's performance.

Let's look at setting up a table:

1. Add a new page to the report by clicking the plus icon at the far right of the page list below the **Report** canvas.

2. Rename the new blank page from Page1 to Tabular Data.

3. From the **Visualizations** pane, select the **Table** visual. Resize it to take up a little less than half the **Report** canvas. Notice, like the slicer, that there is only one bucket in which to populate fields, called **Columns**.

4. Add the following fields by locating them in the **Fields** pane and clicking the checkbox next to each:

    *   **Sales Territory Region** from the **Sales Territory** table

    *   **Total Sales** from the **Internet Sales** table

    *   **Profit** from the **Internet Sales** table

    *   **Total Cost** from the **Internet Sales** table

    *   **Total Transactions** from the **Internet Sales** table

See *Figure 6.17* for reference:

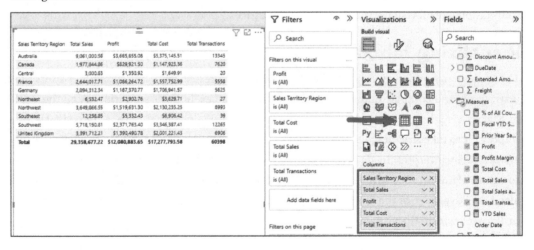

Figure 6.17: A table visual with Sales Territory Region and several measures

Already, you can see how this table provides great insights about the selected category, **Sales Territory Region**. While the default formatting effectively displays the data, there are many formatting options that can be adjusted to enhance the table's appearance. First, change the size of the text for the data, as well as the headers:

1. With the **Table** visual selected, go into the **Format** section (paintbrush over a column chart icon) of the **Visualizations** pane and expand the **Column headers** section.

    There are many options that can be adjusted, but for now, let's simply adjust the **Font size** option under the **Text** card to something larger, making it easier to read the headers.

2. Next, expand the **Values** section and make the same change here for the **Text Size** option under the **Values** card.

Sales Territory Region	Total Sales	Profit	Total Cost	Total T
Australia	9,061,000.58	$3,685,855.08	$5,375,145.51	
Canada	1,977,844.86	$829,921.50	$1,147,923.36	
Central	3,000.83	$1,350.92	$1,649.91	
France	2,644,017.71	$1,086,264.72	$1,557,752.99	
Germany	2,894,312.34	$1,187,370.77	$1,706,941.57	
Northeast	6,532.47	$2,902.76	$3,629.71	
Northwest	3,649,866.55	$1,519,631.30	$2,130,235.25	
Southeast	12,238.85	$5,332.43	$6,906.42	
Southwest	5,718,150.81	$2,371,763.40	$3,346,387.41	
United Kingdom	3,391,712.21	$1,390,490.78	$2,001,221.43	
Total	**29,358,677.22**	**$12.080,883.65**	**$17,277,793.58**	

Figure 6.18: The Format section of the Visualizations pane offers many options to customize visualizations

Now that the table is easier to read, let's explore the **Conditional formatting** options, which will provide customized text or background colors based on data values.

3. Return to the **Visualizations** pane's **Fields** section by clicking the **Build** icon where the five fields previously added can be seen under the **Values** bucket. Note the small drop-down arrow next to each field.

4. Select the arrow next to **Total Sales** and locate the option for **Conditional formatting**, as shown in *Figure 6.19*. With the mouse over the **Conditional formatting** option, you will be presented with several choices that are similar in functionality and setup.

Select the **Background color** option.

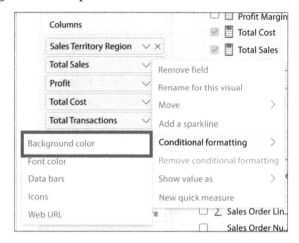

Figure 6.19: Conditional formatting options available from a field in the Visualizations pane

5. In the resulting menu, place a checkmark in the box that is in the bottom left labeled **Add a middle color**.

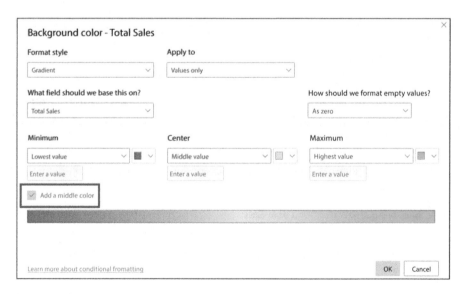

Figure 6.20: Background conditional formatting configuration screen

6. Click **OK**.

Notice that the **Total Sales** column is color-coded to easily identify the regions that are good (green) and bad (red) performers. This is something that can be applied to any columns you feel would be enhanced by conditional formatting. With the use of this table visual, you can gain a very quick and detailed understanding of performance for the **Sales Territory Region** category.

Sales Territory Region	Total Sales	Profit	Total Cost	Total Tra
Australia	9,061,000.58	$3,685,855.08	$5,375,145.51	
Canada	1,977,844.86	$829,921.50	$1,147,923.36	
Central	3,000.83	$1,350.92	$1,649.91	
France	2,644,017.71	$1,086,264.72	$1,557,752.99	
Germany	2,894,312.34	$1,187,370.77	$1,706,941.57	
Northeast	6,532.47	$2,902.76	$3,629.71	
Northwest	3,649,866.55	$1,519,631.30	$2,130,235.25	
Southeast	12,238.85	$5,332.43	$6,906.42	
Southwest	5,718,150.81	$2,371,763.40	$3,346,387.41	
United Kingdom	3,391,712.21	$1,390,490.78	$2,001,221.43	
Total	**29,358,677.22**	**$12,080,883.65**	**$17,277,793.58**	

Figure 6.21: Background conditional formatting applied to the Total Sales field in the table visual

It is important to remember cross-highlighting and cross-filtering with the table visual. Any of the rows that are present within the table can be selected and will apply a filter to all other visuals on the same page.

Often, the report consumers will need to see how data from multiple categories intersect. To do this, you will explore the matrix, which builds on the foundation created by the table visualization.

Matrix

Where a table does a great job of allowing users to consume tons of detailed data about a single category, the **Matrix** visual can accomplish this for more than one category. The **Matrix** visual allows users to select a category for the rows and columns allowing them to see detailed data at a cross-section of two categories. **Conditional formatting** is also available for use within the **Matrix** visual and is incorporated in the same fashion as accomplished in the previous example. Other than **Conditional formatting**, the matrix visual can take advantage of established hierarchies to give users the capability of drilling down into more granular data. Many of the other visuals can also take advantage of hierarchies, but for tabular data, the **Matrix** visual does a great job with this.

Let's look at setting up a **Matrix**:

1. Ensure no other visuals are selected by clicking on any blank area on the **Report** canvas.
2. From the **Visualizations** pane, select the **Matrix**.

3. From the **Fields** pane, drag **Sales Territory Drilldown** from the **Sales Territory** table to the **Rows** bucket.

4. From the **Fields** pane, drag **Date** (a natural hierarchy in Power BI) from the **Date (Order)** table to the **Columns** bucket. This will bring in the **Year**, **Quarter**, **Month**, and **Day** fields. If you do not see the hierarchy it may be an indicator that automatic time functionality is turned off. To enable this feature select **File** | **Options and settings** | **Options** | **Data Load** and enable the **Auto date/time for new files** setting.

5. Finally, from the **Fields** pane, drag **Total Sales** and **Profit** from the **Internet Sales** table to the **Values** bucket.

See *Figure 6.22* for reference. Move and resize the matrix as you see fit.

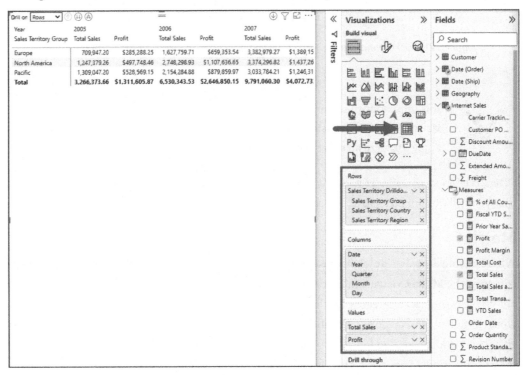

Figure 6.22: Field selection for the matrix visual

Now, you can see that the amount of insight available to report consumers is even greater than that of the **Table** visual. You should apply the same format changes to the header and value **Text size** as were applied to the **Table** at this point. The **Matrix** allows users to see detailed information about the different geographic regions, as well as a breakdown per year.

Also, you will see that there are some new icons in the upper left of the visual that relate to the drilldown feature referenced earlier in this chapter. Because hierarchies are present on both the rows and columns, you must decide which you would like to expand for further details from the **Drill on** drop-down menu.

Focus solely on the rows option and expand the geographical category. The first upward-pointing arrow, which should be currently grayed out, allows users to move up a level in the hierarchy. The button is unavailable because the highest level of the hierarchy is currently displayed.

The option just to the right of this, which is depicted by two disconnected downward arrows, will change the category to the next level of the hierarchy, which is the **Sales Territory Country** in this example. Select this option two times so the **Sales Territory Region** level of the hierarchy is displayed. Notice that the higher levels of the hierarchy are not displayed in the report. The third option, which is depicted by two connected downward arrows, will also go down one level at a time through the hierarchy, but results in the previous (higher) level continuing to be visible on the matrix. By having the **Matrix** and **Table** next to each other, you can see the difference in detail that can be achieved by each of them. Both, though, can benefit greatly from **Conditional formatting**.

Visualizing categorical data

Where the **Table** and **Matrix** visuals allow for a detailed look at multiple measures, the visuals in this section are best for displaying a data value across multiple categories. In the upcoming visuals, you will be displaying bars, columns, and other visual elements, which will be proportional to the data value. These visuals have a far less detailed view of the data, but it is very easy and quick to distinguish the differences in the values within the chosen categories. All of the visuals allow for cross-highlighting, cross-filtering, and the use of drilldowns, which will not be a focus since it was covered in the previous examples. This section will focus on how to understand and configure the following visuals:

- Bar and column charts
- Pie and donut charts
- Treemaps
- Scatter charts

Continue using the same Power BI report from the previous examples. Start by creating a new report page called Categorical Data.

Bar and column charts

Both the **Bar** and **Column** charts are very similar in setup and how they visualize data. The only difference here will be the orientation: the **Bar chart** uses rectangular bars horizontally where the length of the bar is proportional to the amount of data, while the **Column chart** displays the bars vertically, but both are used to compare two or more values. Both visualizations have three different formats: **Stacked**, **Clustered**, and **100% stacked**. For this example, you will focus on the **Bar chart**, but users can easily switch over to the **Column chart** with the click of a button.

 There are some situations where the **Bar chart** will better display data, and the same thing can be said of the **Column chart**. The biggest limitation of the **Column chart** would be the limited space on the **X-axis** where the category would go. So, if you have a lot of data labels or if they are very long, you may find that the **Bar chart** is the better option. An example where you might choose the **Column chart** over the **Bar chart** is if your dataset contains negative values. In a **Bar chart**, the negative values will show on the left side while in a **Column chart** they will display on the bottom. Users generally associate negative values with a downward direction.

Let's look at setting up a **Bar chart**:

1. From the **Visualizations** pane, select the **Stacked bar chart**. Move and resize the visual to take up a quarter of the **Report** canvas.

2. From the **Fields** pane, drag **Sales Territory Country** from the **Sales Territory** table to the **Y-axis** bucket.

3. Next, from the **Fields** pane, drag **Profit** from the **Internet Sales** table to the **X-axis** bucket. This forms the base of the visual and visualizes which countries make the most profit.

4. Extend this visual to break down each country's profit by age group. From the **Fields** pane, drag **Age Breakdown** from the **Customer** table to the **Legend** bucket.

5. Optionally, in the **Visualizations** pane, switch to the **Format** section and toggle the **Data labels** to **On**.

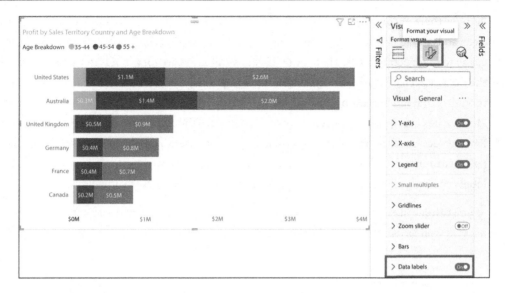

Figure 6.23: Data labels can be turned on from the Format section of the Visualizations pane

In regard to the other two options, **Clustered** and **100% stacked,** you can simply select those visuals to experience the different presentations. You will notice the **Data labels** remain and add great value regardless of the visual selection.

Pie and donut charts

Both the **Pie chart** and **Donut chart** are meant to visualize a particular section compared to the whole, rather than comparing individual values to each other. The only difference between the two is that the **Donut chart** has a hole in the middle, which could allow for some sort of label. Both visuals can be very effective in allowing cross-highlighting, but if there are too many categories, it can become difficult to read and interpret.

Let's look at setting up a **Donut chart:**

1. Ensure no visuals are selected by clicking on any blank area on the **Report** canvas.
2. From the **Visualizations** pane, select the **Donut chart**. Move and resize it to take up a quarter of the **Report** canvas, preferably above or below the **Bar chart**.
3. From the **Fields** pane, drag **Temperature Range** from the **Temperature** table to the **Legend** bucket.
4. From the **Fields** pane, drag **Total Sales** from the **Internet Sales** table to the **Values** bucket.

Because there are only four values within the **Temperature Range** category, this chart looks very clean and easy to understand. There is something, though, that can be added that will make it even easier to read: detail labels. This option is very similar to **category labels** in that you can display the data of each of the quadrants without having to use the tooltips. One thing that is different though is that it is already on, and all you need to do is decide how much detail to have displayed. More values being present can cause even more clutter though. To access these options, go to the **Format** section of the **Visualizations** pane, expand the **Detail labels** option, and manipulate the **Label contents** dropdown under the **Options** sub card. For this example, choose the **All detail labels** option and increase the font size if desired under the **Values** subheader.

As you can see in *Figure 6.24*, you now have a very nice and easy way to understand the presented data, as well as use it for cross-filtering and cross-highlighting:

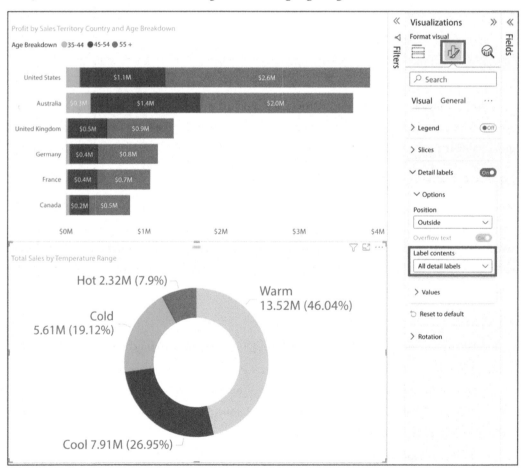

Figure 6.24: Label style settings for the donut chart

When creating pie and donut charts, consider how filtering the data may affect the readability of the chart. In addition to having too many slices that clutter the chart, having slices that are too narrow to easily identify, or slices that are very similar in size, can be detrimental to a consumer's ability to draw accurate conclusions from the chart.

Treemap

A fantastic visual for displaying hierarchies is the **Treemap** visual. It accomplishes this by nesting the data in rectangles, which are represented by color, which are commonly known as "branches." If you add a category into the **Details** bucket of the visual, you will note smaller rectangles within the "branches" and these are known as "leaves," hence the name **Treemap**. In order to maximize this visual, you will need to do a little extra setup and bring in a new table, and create a new hierarchy. Let's go through this process now:

> You need to bring in the **DimGeography** table from the AdventureWorksDW Excel workbook. Since you accomplished this during *Chapter 4, Building the Data Model*, you should be able to see this source under the **Recent Sources** option on the **Home** ribbon. If not, you can connect to this source by pointing to this location: Microsoft-Power-BI-Start-Guide-Second-Edition-main\Data Sources\AdventureWorksDW.xlsx.

1. Once the **Navigator** appears, place a checkmark next to the **DimGeography** table and click **Load**.

2. You will need to do a couple of quick fixes to this new table before you can leverage it. Navigate to the **Model** view and delete the inactive relationship between **Sales Territory** and **DimGeography**.

3. Next, rename the table **Geography** and hide the **FrenchCountryRegionName** and **SpanishCountryRegionName** fields.

4. Create a new hierarchy. Right-click on the **EnglishCountryRegionName** column and select **Create hierarchy** from the dropdown. Rename the new hierarchy Region Drilldown.

5. With the hierarchy selected, add **StateProvinceName** to the hierarchy by changing the **Select a column to add level...** option in the **Properties** pane to the **StateProvinceName** field.

6.   Repeat the previous step to add the **City** field to the hierarchy. Click **Apply Level Changes**.

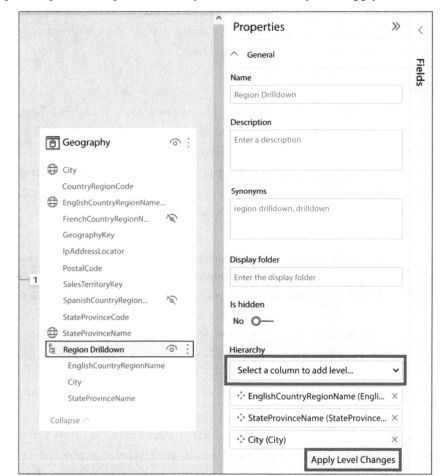

Figure 6.25: Apply fields and order to the Region Drilldown hierarchy

Now that you have a new geographical hierarchy that goes all the way down to the city level, you can see how this will display with the **Treemap** visual.

Let's look at setting up a **Treemap**:

1.   Navigate back to the **Report** view. Ensure no visuals are selected by clicking on any blank area on the **Report** canvas.

2.   From the **Visualizations** pane, select the **Treemap**. Move and resize this visual so that it takes up a quarter of the remaining report canvas.

3. From the **Fields** pane, drag **Region Drilldown** from the **Geography** table to the **Category** bucket.

4. Next, from the **Fields** pane, drag **Total Sales** from **Internet Sales** to the **Values** bucket.

5. Last, from the **Fields** pane, drag **Year** from the **Date (Order)** table to the **Details** bucket.

The size of each of the rectangles is determined by the value being measured, which in this case is **Total Sales**. The "leaves" in this visual are portrayed by the **Year** category, while the **Region Drilldown** creates the "branches." Because you are using a hierarchy, you have full access to the **Drilldown** capabilities shown earlier. You should also now be able to tell that the **Treemap** visual arranges the rectangles by size from top left (largest) to bottom right (smallest).

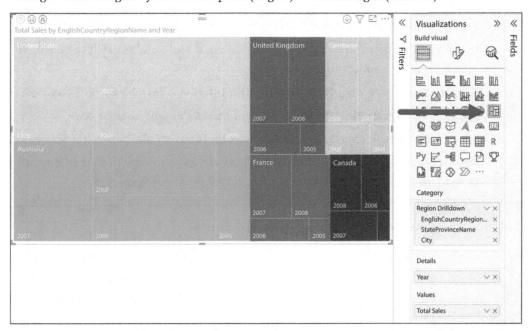

Figure 6.26: The treemap visual with group and detail levels displayed

Look to treemaps as an alternative when bar and column charts become too cluttered by the number of categories because it still allows the consumer to compare the size of one category to another.

Scatter chart

The last visual used for categorical data is the **Scatter chart**, sometimes referred to as the **Bubble chart**. This visual allows you to show the relationships between two or three numerical values. You are given the opportunity to place values on the X- and Y-axes, but what is different about this visual is the ability to add a third value for the size, and this is where the name **Bubble chart** comes from. There is also a very unique option available within the **Fields** section to really bring this data to life, and it is called the **Play Axis**. Let's create the **Scatter chart** first, and then discuss the **Play Axis**.

Let's look at setting up a **Scatter chart**:

1. Ensure no visuals are selected by clicking on any blank area on the **Report** canvas.
2. In the **Visualizations** pane, select the Scatter chart. Move and resize it to take up the remainder of the **Report** canvas.
3. From the **Fields** pane, drag **Total Sales** from the **Internet Sales** table to the **X-Axis** bucket.
4. From the **Fields** pane, drag **Profit** from the **Internet Sales** table to the **Y-Axis**.
5. From the **Fields** pane, drag **Order Quantity** from the **Internet Sales** table to the **Size** bucket.
6. Finally, from the **Fields** pane, drag **EnglishCountryRegionName** from the **Geography** table to the **Legend** bucket. The visual should look similar to *Figure 6.27*.

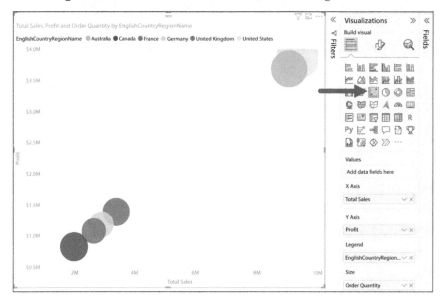

Figure 6.27: Scatter plot configured to show sales, profit, and order quantity by En-glishCountryRegionName

Now, the last part that you will configure on this visual will be the **Play Axis**, which is unique to the **Scatter chart**. By adding a component of time, you can bring a little animation to this visual. For our example, add the **English Month Name** field from the **Date (Orders)** table to the **Play Axis** bucket, and you will see a **play** button appear along with the 12 months. By pressing the play button, you will now be able to watch the bubbles move to display their values aggregated across all years, by month.

The **Scatter chart** uses a sampling algorithm when plotting larger sets of data to improve performance. The standard method used plots every 10th data point. In general, that sampling method is adequate. However, as datasets grow larger, high-density clusters of data can be oversampled, leaving some sparse data points to be completely omitted from the chart. To solve this issue, a setting is available in the **Format** section under the **General** options, then in the **Properties** option's **Advanced options** subheader, to enable a **high-density sampling** algorithm that takes proximity to nearby data points into account, thereby ensuring the data points outside the high-density cluster are represented on the chart rather than being missed simply because they were not the 1 in 10 selected for display. This setting prioritizes an accurate distribution over accurate density on the **Scatter chart**. When showing items with no data, adding a ratio line, or using the **Play Axis**, the high-density setting will be ignored and the scatter chart will revert back to the standard sampling described at the beginning of this section.

Visualizing trend data

The term **trend data** refers to displaying and comparing the change in value over time. Power BI provides many options in this category, each with its own focus. The idea for each of the visuals is to draw attention to the total value across a length of time. Create a new report page called Trend Data, and dive right in to see what the differences are between the following options:

- Line and area charts
- Combo charts
- Ribbon charts
- Waterfall charts
- Funnel charts

To begin, let's explore the line and area charts. These are the most commonly used charts for visualizing trend data, and the ones that the visualizations report consumers are likely most familiar with already.

Line and area charts

The **Line chart** is the most basic of the options when it comes to analyzing data over time. The **Area chart** and **Stacked area chart** are based on the **Line chart**; the difference is that the area between the axes and the line is filled in with colors to show volume. Because of this, the focus will be on the line chart for the next example.

Let's look at setting up a **Line chart**:

1. From the **Visualizations** pane, select the **Line chart**. Resize it to take up a quarter of the **Report** canvas.

2. From the **Fields** pane, drag the **Date** field from the **Date (Order)** table to the **X-axis** bucket.

3. Add two measures to compare over time. From the **Fields** pane, drag **Total Sales** and **Prior Year Sales** from the **Internet Sales** table to the **Y-axis** bucket.

4. Finally, click **Expand all down one level in the hierarchy** two times to display the quarter and month, as seen in *Figure 6.28*.

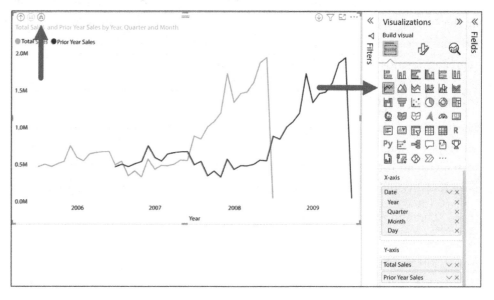

Figure 6.28: Total Sales and Prior Year Sales line chart with an indicator on how to drill down to quarter, month, and day levels

With this **Line chart**, you can clearly see there was a large growth in sales between **2007** and **2008**. Visuals that focus on trend data can very easily illustrate any outliers, which can allow users to further investigate the cause of the seen trend. This visual can also benefit from some of the formatting options such as data labels.

Combo charts

As the name states, a **Combo chart** combines the **Line chart** and **Column chart** together in one visual. Users can choose to have either the **Stacked column** format or the **Clustered column** format. By combining these two visuals, you can make a very quick comparison of the data. The main benefit of this type of chart is that you can have one or two Y-axes. Two measures can either share the same Y-axis, like **Total Sales** and **Profit**, which are both numeric values, or they could be based on completely different values, like **Order Quantity** and **Profit**, which are numeric and percentage, respectively. Let's use two different axes for this example:

1. Ensure no visuals are selected by clicking on any blank area on the **Report** canvas.

2. From the **Visualizations** pane, select the **Line and stacked column chart** visual. Resize it to take up a quarter of the **Report** canvas.

3. From the **Fields** pane, drag **Date** from the **Date (Order)** table to the **X-axis** bucket.

4. From the **Fields** pane, drag **Order Quantity** from the **Internet Sales** table to the **Column y-axis** bucket.

5. Finally, from the **Fields** pane, drag **Profit** from the **Internet Sales** table to the **Line y-axis** bucket.

In this example, you can see that there are two Y-axes; the left one relates to the **Order Quantity** while the right one corresponds with the **Profit**. Expand the hierarchy one level; this will give more data points to see the trending between the two measures, as seen in *Figure 6.29*:

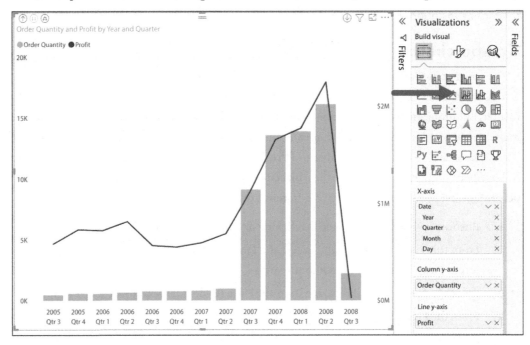

Figure 6.29: Combo chart with columns representing order quantity and a line representing profit

From this visual, it's fairly easy to validate that when more items are sold, more profit is made. This, like many other visuals, can also benefit from data labels.

Ribbon chart

The **Ribbon chart** is no different than the other visuals explored in this section; it is good at viewing data over time. What makes ribbon charts effective though is their ability to show rank change; the highest range or value is always displayed on the top for each of the time periods. The chart also does have a unique visual flowing appeal to it that is different than the other visuals.

Let's look at setting up a **Ribbon chart**:

1. Ensure no visuals are selected by clicking on any blank area on the **Report** canvas.
2. From the **Visualizations** pane, select the **Ribbon chart** visual. Resize it to take up a quarter of the **Report** canvas.

3. From the **Fields** pane, drag **Date** from the **Date (Order)** table to the **X-axis** bucket.

4. Next, from the **Fields** pane, drag **Total Sales** from the **Internet Sales** table to the **Y-axis** bucket. At this point, you will see that it looks like a **Column chart**.

5. Upon adding a category to the **Legend** bucket, the visual will display a flowing ribbon. For this exercise, drag **EnglishCountryRegionName** from the **Geography** table to the **Legend** bucket.

The first thing you may notice is the lighter areas between time periods; this is really one of the best parts of the **Ribbon chart**. This area shows the value for the category for the previous period and the upcoming one. Also, the tooltip gives each value a rank and shows any increases and decreases. This, like many other visuals, also gets a nice visibility improvement by adding data labels, as seen in *Figure 6.30*.

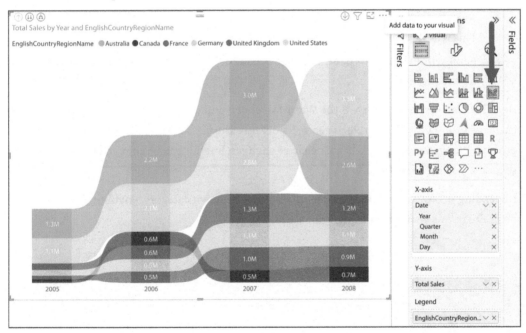

Figure 6.30: Ribbon chart showing total sales by country and year

The dynamic ranking feature of the ribbon visualization makes it unique but does come at the cost of making it more difficult to discern size in relation to prior periods or size in relation to other categories within the same period.

Waterfall chart

This next visual, the **Waterfall chart**, is very helpful in understanding the changes that occur from an initial value. It displays a running total in relation to values being added or subtracted. By populating a field in the **Breakdown** option of the visual, you can see if it has had a positive or negative impact from value to value.

Let's look at setting up a **Waterfall chart**:

1. Ensure no visuals are selected by clicking on any blank area on the **Report** canvas.
2. From the **Visualizations** pane, select the **Waterfall chart**. The current report page should have a quarter of the area still available. Use half of this for the **Waterfall chart**.
3. From the **Fields** pane, drag **Date** from the **Date (Order)** table to the **Category** bucket.
4. Next, from the **Fields** pane, drag **Profit** from the **Internet Sales** table to the **Y-axis** bucket. This will show how much each year has contributed to the total profit.
5. Finally, from the **Fields** pane, drag **Age Breakdown** from the **Customer** table to the **Breakdown** bucket.

Now, you can see the strength of the **Waterfall chart,** and you can see how much contribution each age group provided between years. By default, the visual uses the green color to indicate positive changes and red to indicate negative changes, but this can be changed from the **Format** section if you are so inclined.

Depending on how many values are within your breakdown category, enabling data labels can be useful in this visual, as seen in *Figure 6.31*:

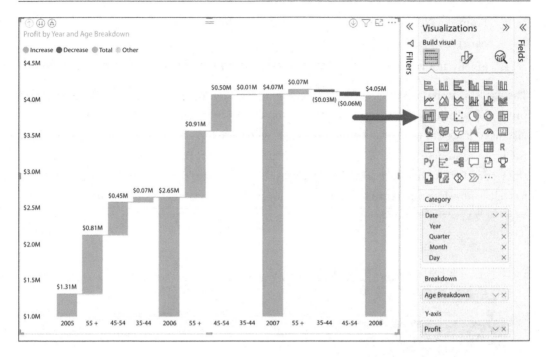

Figure 6.31: Waterfall chart showing profit by age breakdown and year

The **Waterfall chart** is particularly useful when searching for how much a particular category (represented by the breakdown field) contributes to the overall gain/loss between two periods.

Funnel chart

The **Funnel chart** allows users to see the percentage difference between values. Normally, the highest value is at the top and the lowest is at the bottom, which gives the look of a funnel. Each stage of the funnel will tell the percentage difference between itself and the previous stage, as well as compared to the highest stage. With this type of design, it makes sense that the **Funnel chart** is very effective when visualizing a linear process with at least three or four stages. The sample dataset does not have a process with multiple stages, but there is data that will still create something that gives value.

Let's look at setting up a **Funnel chart**:

1. Ensure no visuals are selected by clicking on any blank area on the **Report** canvas.

2. From the **Visualizations** pane, select the **Funnel chart**. It should fill in the final remaining space on the **Report** canvas.

3.   From the **Fields** pane, drag **CountryRegionCode** from the **Geography** table to the **Category** bucket.

4.   Finally, from the **Fields** pane, drag **Profit** from the **Internet Sales** table to the **Values** bucket.

The way this visual is set up allows you to very easily identify which countries make the most profit and which make the least, but this is something that can be achieved with many other visuals. What gives the **Funnel chart** an edge is when you hover over one of the sections within the funnel and note the items that appear within the tooltip. You will see, when hovering over the section for **FR**, that the tooltip lets you know how it compares to the section directly above it, as well as how it compares to the highest section, which is represented by the **US**.

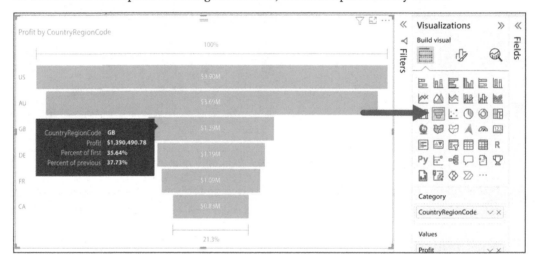

Figure 6.32: Funnel chart showing profit by country and as a percent of the largest profit winner

There is no shortage of ways to visualize trend data in Power BI. Next, let's look at calling out important data points using KPIs.

Visualizing KPI data

KPIs, or **Key Performance Indicators**, are measurable values that demonstrate how well a company is achieving a certain objective. Power BI has several options to measure the progress being made toward a goal for operational processes. The strength of a KPI visual lies in its simplicity. It displays a single value and its progress toward a specific goal.

Create a new report page called KPI Data and take a closer look at the gauge and KPI visuals.

Gauge

The **Gauge** visual displays a single value within a circular arc and its progress toward a specified goal or target value. The **Target value** is represented by a line within the arc. With the current dataset, there is no measure that can be used to illustrate an accurate business goal, so one will have to be created. Before setting up this visual, a new calculated measure will need to be created.

The gauge will be using the **Total Sales** field as the **Value** field. The target will be 10% more than the previous year's total sales, so a DAX calculation is needed to create this measure:

1. In the **Fields** pane, right-click the **Internet Sales** table and select the **New Measure** option. This brings the focus to the formula bar.

2. Name the measure **Sales Target**, and use the following DAX formula to get our target:

    ```
    Sales Target = [Prior Year Sales] * 1.1
    ```

    Now that all the necessary measures have been created, let's set up the **Gauge** visual and create the first KPI.

3. From the **Visualizations** pane, select the **Gauge**. Move and resize it as you see fit.

4. From the **Fields** pane, drag **Total Sales** from the **Internet Sales** table to the **Value** bucket.

5. From the **Fields** pane, drag **Sales Target** from the **Internet Sales** table to the **Target Value** bucket.

Using a **slicer** visual alongside this KPI will be helpful with this dataset. Add the **slicer** visual using the **Year** field from the **Date (Order)** table for the **Value**. If you choose the year **2008**, you will see that the value changes along with the target, as seen in *Figure 6.33*. With this dataset, the year 2008 has the most recent transactions, and because of this visual, you can see that the goal has still not been met.

If you look at any of the other previous years, you can validate that the total sales surpass the target every year.

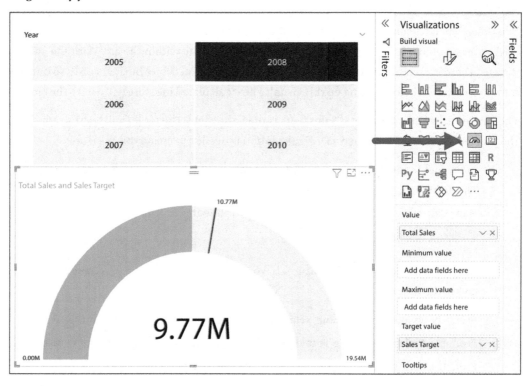

Figure 6.33: Gauge showing sales vs. target sales for the year 2008

The **Gauge** does not require a target, maximum, or minimum field but they each help create a more user-friendly visual. The minimum and maximum values can be set manually on the Gauge axis formatting options for the visual if a dynamic range is not required.

KPI

Where the **Gauge** visual uses the circular arc to show the current progress, the **KPI** visual takes a more explicit approach and just shows the value in plain text, along with the goal. The only real visual elements that are in play with this visual occur when the indicator value is lower than the goal and the text is shown in red, and when it has surpassed the goal and the text is in green. This is one of the more direct visuals and perfectly exemplifies what users look for in a **KPI**.

Let's look at setting up a **KPI**:

1. Ensure no other visuals are selected by clicking on any blank area on the **Report** canvas.

2. From the **Visualizations** pane, select the **KPI**. Move and resize it as you see fit.

3. From the **Fields** pane, drag **Total Sales** from **Internet Sales** to the **Value** bucket.

4. Next, from the **Fields** pane, drag **Prior Year Sales** from the **Internet Sales** table to the **Trend** bucket.

5. Finally, from the **Fields** pane, drag **Year** from the **Date (Order)** table to the **Trend Axis**.

If, after following the preceding steps, the visual displays a value of **Blank** for the indicator, do not worry. This is because it is trying to show the Total Sales for the year 2010, the most recent value in the dataset. If you did not apply the report level filter for **Date (Order) Year** at the beginning of this chapter, you will notice there are no sales for **2009** or **2010**, so to have this visual display correctly simply choose any other year from the slicer that was added in the previous section. Once you have accomplished this, you will now be able to view the **KPI** visual, and it should look like *Figure 6.34*.

Figure 6.34: KPI showing sales vs. the prior year sales for 2008

Be sure to look at the formatting options for the **KPI** visual to set the appropriate color coding for the indicator. The default settings have higher values as "good" but this is not always the case. Imagine a scenario where the **KPI** is visualizing shipping delays; in that case, a lower number would be better and the **KPI** can be configured as such.

Visualizing data using cards

The ways for Power BI to get detailed data into the hands of a user are vast. Tables, matrices, bar charts, and combo charts all provide large quantities of data to users in a single visual. Sometimes, like with a **KPI**, users just need to see a number. When the trend or target components of a **KPI** are not required, turn to the **Card** visualization. The **Card** is the most basic of visuals displaying only a single value. If slightly more detail is necessary but required at a group level, look to the **Multi-row card**.

Before moving on, create a new report page called Card Data.

Card

The **Card** is useful for highlighting a series of related metrics in a dashboard, displaying the most recent or oldest date in a dataset, and calling out important numbers for a detailed report. Some formatting options are available to change the font size or color, but at its core, the card visual just displays a single value.

Let's look at setting up a **Card**:

1. Ensure no other visuals are selected by clicking on any blank area on the **Report** canvas.
2. From the **Visualizations** pane, select the **Card**. Move and resize it as you see fit.
3. From the **Fields** pane, drag **Sales Amount** from the **Internet Sales** table to the **Fields** bucket.
4. Explore the **Format** section to change the category text and title text, or switch the display units from millions to thousands.

Figure 6.35: Card showing the aggregate total sales amount

It is important to ensure the report provides context for what is being displayed on the **Card** because it lacks categories. Consider using slicers on report pages with cards rather than report- or page-level filters to ensure users are fully aware of the filters being applied to the card.

Multi-row card

The **Multi-row card** allows for slightly more data to be displayed than the card. It accepts multiple fields and automatically groups all non-summarized fields. For instance, adding the **Sales Territory Country** and **Total Sales** would result in one row per country. Adding the **Color** field from the **Product** table would automatically group the **Total Sales** by both **Sales Territory Country** and **Color**. This behavior sounds similar to a **Table** or **Matrix**, but the **Multi-row card** does not display data in a tabular format; instead, it creates separate sections in the visual for each group.

Let's look at setting up a **Multi-row card**:

1. Ensure no other visuals are selected by clicking on any blank area on the **Report** canvas.
2. From the **Visualizations** pane, select the **Multi-row card**. Move and resize it as you see fit.
3. From the **Fields** pane, add the following fields to the **Fields** bucket:

    -   **Sales Territory Country** from the **Sales Territory table**
    -   **Total Sales** from the **Internet Sales** table
    -   **Profit** from the **Internet Sales** table
    -   **Profit Margin** from the **Internet Sales** table

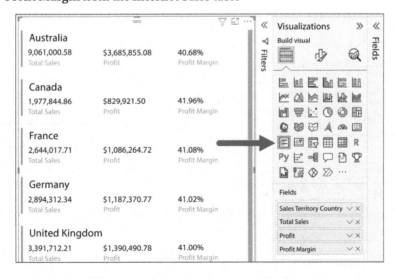

Figure 6.36: Multi-row card showing sales and profit measures by country

While the **Multi-row card** can display more fields compared to the card, it comes at the cost of customization. There is little to no control over how the data is displayed outside some basic font size and color options.

Visualizing geographical data

One of the most exciting ways to visualize data in Power BI is through the various maps. All the maps serve the same purpose, to illustrate data in relation to locations around the world, but there are some small differences between each of them. All of the maps, except the **Shape map**, have the option to visualize latitude and longitude coordinates, which will be the best way to ensure the appropriate location is displayed. The reason for this is that the information provided to the visual will be sent to **Azure Maps** or **Bing Maps** to verify the positioning on the map. If you do not provide enough detail, then **Azure** may not return the desired results.

For example, if you were to provide the map visual with a field that contains only the city name, that could result in some confusion because there may be multiple cities with that name in multiple states, provinces, or even countries. In these scenarios, you will either want to supply some sort of geo-hierarchy to give a better definition, or create new columns with more detailed information. Power BI also has a built-in feature when dealing with geographic data that allows users to help identify the type of data that is being provided: this is called the data category. Let's go ahead and take advantage of this for our dataset to make the map visuals more accurate:

1. From the **Fields** pane, expand the **Geography** table. Select the **City** field by clicking the name of the field rather than the checkbox to its left.

2. On the **Column Tools** ribbon, change the **Data category** to **City**. Once here, you will see the **Data category** option.

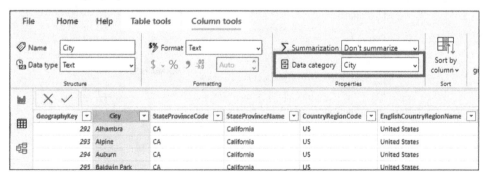

Figure 6.37: Change the data category for a field on the Column tools tab of the ribbon while on the Report view

3. Repeat the steps above for the **StateProvinceName** field, selecting the **State** or **Province** data category.

4. Repeat the steps above for the **EnglishCountryRegionName**, selecting the **Country** data category.

Now that you have defined the geographical data for Power BI, you can proceed with using the various map visuals. One thing of note is that using any of these visuals does require internet access because data will be sent to **Azure Maps** or **ESRI** depending on the visual chosen.

Before you begin, create a new report page called `Geographical Data`.

Map

The first visual to illustrate geographical data is simply called the **Map** visual. This visual is also referred to as the **bubble map** because it plots the points of data with circles that can be set to change in size based on a supplied measure. With this visual, if you have the latitude and longitude coordinates in your dataset, then nothing needs to be sent to **Azure Maps**. Such detailed data is unavailable, so you will need to supply the necessary information through the **Location** bucket, which will be sent to **Azure Maps**.

Let's look at setting up a map:

1. From the **Visualizations** pane, select the **Map** visual. Move and resize it to take up a quarter of the **Report** canvas.

2. To ensure there is no confusion about the locations to be mapped, use the geo-hierarchy, which has been created within the **Geography** table. From the **Fields** pane, drag the **Region Drilldown** from the **Geography** table to the **Location** bucket. Six countries will be represented by a bubble.

3. Next, from the **Fields** pane, drag **Total Sales** from the **Internet Sales** table to the **Bubble size** bucket. This value will dictate the size of the bubbles displayed for each city on the map. Larger bubbles indicate countries with higher sales amounts.

4. Finally, from the **Fields** pane, drag **Age Breakdown** from the **Customer** table to the **Legend** bucket. With this, the bubbles start to look like little pie charts, as seen in *Figure 6.38*.

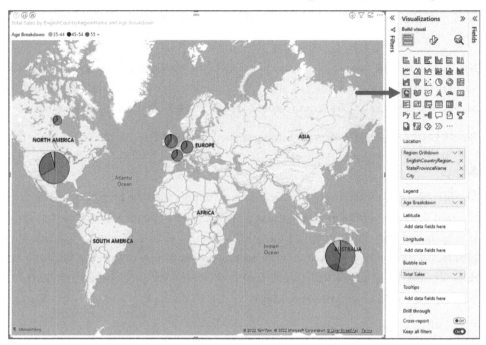

Figure 6.38: A map showing sales by country by age breakdown

When using a geo-hierarchy with a map, enable the **Drill** mode, which is signified by the down arrow in the upper right. Remember this for any visual where you have a hierarchy selected; you should explore the different views it gives you.

Filled map

Unlike the traditional map visual, which uses a bubble to indicate locations, the **Filled map** visual uses shading to display the geographic data. So, the lighter an area looks, the lower the representative value. For this visual, it is recommended to visit the **Format** section and dictate the range of colors for the shading so it will appear more apparent.

Let's look at setting up a **Filled map**:

1. Ensure no visuals are selected by clicking on any blank area on the **Report** canvas.

2. From the **Visualizations** pane, select the **Filled map**. Move and resize it to take up a quarter of the **Report** canvas.

3. From the **Fields** pane, drag **Region Drilldown** from the **Geography** table to the **Location** bucket.

4. From the **Visualizations** pane, switch to the **Format** section. Expand the **Fill colors** header and the **Colors** subheader. Click the **conditional formatting** button next to the color selector.

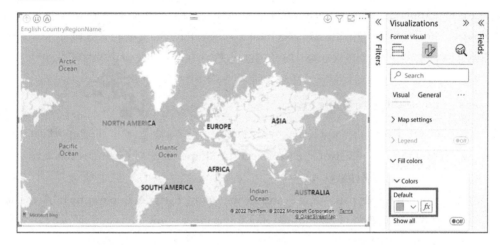

Figure 6.39: Filled map highlighting each country in the Region Drilldown hierarchy

5. Change the **What field should we base this on?** setting to the **Profit** field from the **Internet Sales** table.

6. Check the box next to the **Add a middle color** option. Click **OK**.

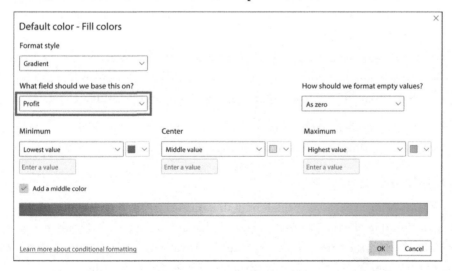

Figure 6.40: Configuration to set colors on the filled map based on profit

The base layer on the filled map can be changed to a variety of themes including road, dark, light, and aerial, which shows satellite imagery.

Shape map

Similar to the **Filled map**, the **Shape map** visual uses shading/saturation to show the geographic data. One thing that makes the **Shape map** unique is that it allows users to upload their own maps to be illustrated. In order to accomplish this, you must have a JSON file that contains all the necessary information required by Power BI. By default, the visual does offer some standard maps but currently does not have an option to show the entire world.

Let's look at setting up a **Shape map**:

1. Ensure no visuals are selected by clicking on any blank area on the **Report** canvas.
2. From the **Visualizations** pane, select the **Shape map**. Move and resize it to take up a quarter of the **Report** canvas.
3. From the **Fields** pane, drag **StateProvinceName** from the **Geography** table to the **Location** bucket. Do not be alarmed if nothing appears initially; you still need to tell Power BI which map to use.
4. From the **Fields** pane, drag **Profit** from the **Internet Sales** table to the **Color saturation** bucket.
5. From the **Format** section of the **Visualizations** pane, expand the **Map settings** section, where there will be a subheading also labeled **Map settings** that contains a drop-down selection for the **Map** category. For this example, select **USA: states**, which Power BI may have detected on its own.
6. This is another example where taking control of what colors will be used for the shading can be helpful. Apply the same middle color by turning the **Gradient** setting **on** from the **Filled map** under the **Fill colors** heading then the **Colors** subheading.

In addition to simple geographical mapping, the **Shape map** provides the ultimate flexibility, allowing you to bring more detailed mapping, such as census tracts, to Power BI.

ArcGIS Map

The **ArcGIS Map** visual is very different in that there is an option to pay for additional features. Also, the location where you can make visual changes to the map is different as well. Normally, you would access the **Format** section of the **Visualizations** pane but, for this map, you must hit the ellipsis in the upper-right corner of the visual and choose the **Edit** option.

You will be focused on a couple of key areas, but there are a lot of options that are worth exploring.

Let's look at setting up an **ArcGIS Map**:

1. Ensure no visuals are selected by clicking on any blank area on the **Report** canvas.
2. From the **Visualizations** pane, select **ArcGIS Maps for Power BI**. Move and resize it to take up the final quarter of the report canvas.
3. From the **Fields** pane, drag **StateProvinceName** from the **Geography** table to the **Location** bucket.
4. From the **Fields** pane, drag the **Total Sales** measure from the **Internet Sales** table to the **Color** bucket.

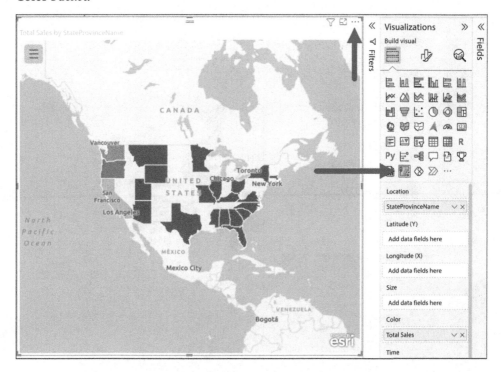

Figure 6.41: ArcGIS map showing total sales by state

This visual is ready to go with the current configuration, but if you want to change how things look, you must take a new route that is unique to this visual. In the upper left-hand corner, you will see an icon containing three horizontal lines; left-click this and choose the **Edit** option highlighted in *Figure 6.41*. This brings up a few icons where various settings can be changed. Choosing the fourth icon from the top and then selecting the **StateProvinceName** layer will allow you to modify the symbols and settings for this layer, as seen in *Figure 6.42*.

The first area to visit to make a slight change will be the **Symbology** option. Here, you can select a symbol type and by using the **Style options**, control the level of transparency as well as the color palette being used.

Explore the various color and symbol options and choose whatever selection you find most effective.

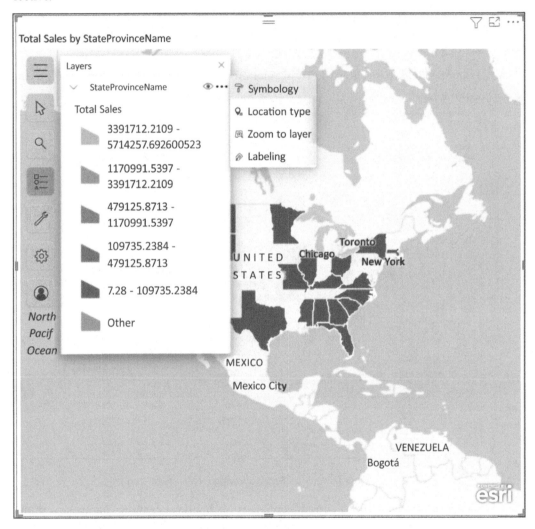

Figure 6.42: Options menu in the ArcGIS map, which provides vast customizations

This is the only change you will be making for this example, but you should take the time and examine all the other options available to you.

Azure maps

The newest member of the Power BI mapping family is the **Azure maps** visual. Unlike some of the other options, this map requires latitude and longitude. It does not accept generic locations like city or state, or even more specific locations like ZIP code. The map style can be changed between several options including satellite, hybrid, grayscale, and terrain. A powerful feature of this map is the ability to add reference layers that can be uploaded in GeoJSON form. Other notable functionality includes overlaying a bar chart on the map and displaying real-time traffic.

Due to the latitude and longitude data point requirement, there is no sample data available in the lab, but a screenshot has been included for reference. In *Figure 6.43*, you will notice buckets for **Latitude**, **Longitude**, **Legend** (used for color coding groups), **Size**, and **Tooltips**.

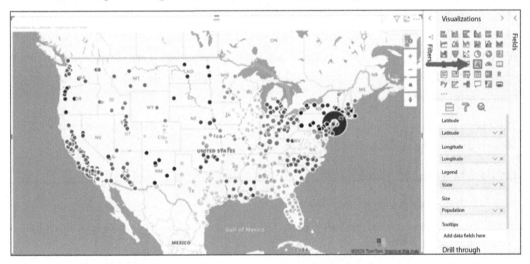

Figure 6.43: Azure map showing population by location

All the maps described in this chapter are very similar, but each has specific functionality that does not exist in the others. The traditional map and **Filled map** visuals are the most used, but you will need to decide when one might illustrate your dataset better than the other.

Advanced visualizations

Power BI contains a robust set of visuals for analyzing data, from tables and charts to immersive mapping. Sometimes, you want to go beyond a standard set of visuals. Thankfully, Power BI also provides a set of visualizations that go far beyond just displaying data points in interesting ways. Let's explore some unique and interesting ways Power BI allows you to interact with data and build unique reporting solutions.

Natural language with Q&A

Not all data is as straightforward as showing the sales amount by month. Often, when a report is being developed, you may not know all the different visualizations a user would like to see. While Power BI has great flexibility thanks to built-in cross-filtering, drilldown, and the ability to see data behind a visual, it will never be able to cover all possible reporting scenarios. One of the most powerful ways to enable self-service functionality in Power BI is using the **Q&A** visual. The **Q&A** feature is often described as a search engine for your data.

The **Q&A** visual allows users to simply ask a question in natural language and receive an answer in the form of a pre-built visual. This is great for data exploration as well thanks to search suggestions and autocomplete functionality. The suggestions are only as good as the data model you have built. Without specific domain knowledge, Power BI makes suggestions for additional terms people may search for. In the case of the model in the examples, Power BI has suggested a few additional terms that could be used in place of customer, which are client, consumer, user, or buyer. Adding these as synonyms in the data model will provide added flexibility to users searching for answers.

This visual is unique in that it does not have a **Field** section in the **Visualizations** pane. All the setup is done in the visual itself on the **Report** canvas.

Let's look at setting up a **Q&A** visual:

1. Create a new report page called Q&A.

2. From the **Visualizations** pane, select **Q&A**. Move and resize it to take up the left half of the canvas.

3. In the **Ask a question about your data box**, type the following query: total sales, and press *Enter*. Notice the visual creates a card showing total sales of **29.36 M.**

4. Continue typing the following in the **Ask a question about your data box**: total sales by sales territory. Choose the suggested result, **total sales by sales territory country.** The visual has now switched to a **Bar chart** showing sales by country.

5. Continue typing the following in the **Ask a question about your data box**: total sales by sales territory country and age breakdown. The visual now shows a **Clustered bar chart**.

6. Complete the query as total sales by sales territory country and age breakdown as stacked bar chart.

7. Finally, click the **Turn this Q&A result into a standard visual** button to the right of the query box as indicated in *Figure 6.44*.

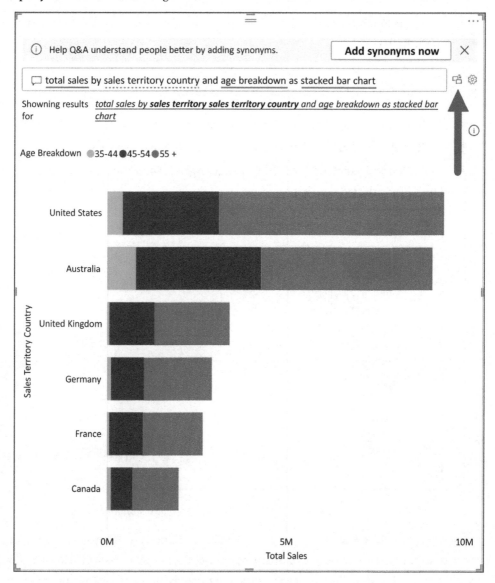

Figure 6.44: Use the Turn this Q&A result into a standard visual button to keep the visual built by the Q&A result

Let's create one additional **Q&A** visual to see how visual interactions work:

1. Ensure no other visuals are selected by clicking on any blank area on the **Report** canvas.

2. From the **Visualizations** pane, select **Q&A**. Move and resize it to take up the right half of the canvas.

3. In the **Ask a question about your data box**, type the following query:

    ```
    profit by date (order) month as column chart
    ```

4. In the column chart, click the **February** column. Notice the change in the **Stacked bar chart**.

5. In the **Column chart**, click the **February** column again to reset the selection.

6. In the **Stacked bar chart**, click **United States Age 45-54**. Notice the change in the column chart inside the **Q&A** visual.

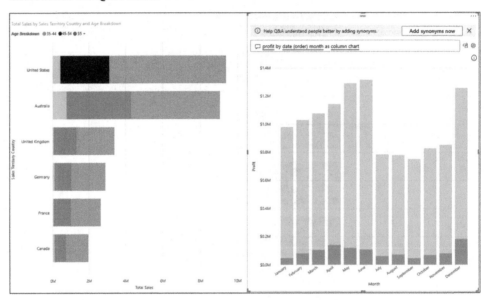

Figure 6.45: Q&A visual being filtered by a standard visual

As you have seen, the **Q&A** visual is not only capable of aiding in the creation of new visuals, it is also a powerful tool for users to explore the data, create their own custom visuals, and interact with other visuals. The ability to interact with other visuals provides a great amount of flexibility to any report.

Visuals from analytics

Up to this point, all the visuals have been focused on visualizing the data in the data model. There are a couple of visuals that go one step further and provide information about the data that are not easily gained by a human looking at a report. These visuals leverage machine learning to provide actionable insight and allow the use of additional programming languages in Power BI.

Two of the most common programming languages in use today are R and Python. Power BI offers a built-in visual for each of these languages with an easy interface for bridging the gap between the Power BI data model and the programming language surface. Each of these requires a local installation for Power BI to use for processing. Simply add the fields you would like to use in your code to the **Values** bucket for the visual and reference them by name in your code. A few lines of sample code are generated to show the proper way to reference the fields as well. Adding the R or Python visual unlocks dozens of additional visualization possibilities including boxplots, stem plots, 3D scatterplots, and contour plots.

The final visualization is the **key influencers** visual. If you have ever wanted to understand what impact different fields have on one another, this visual will help. Define the field to be analyzed and then simply add all the fields you wish to analyze as influencers. The result will show how each field influenced the metric being analyzed, a rank showing which had the largest influence, and to what extent the field was influenced. For instance, you can determine what influence, if any, the month of the year, the latitude, the elevation, and the number of days of sun had on the temperature in a particular city ranked and quantified. Visual interactions are maintained as well, meaning you could filter the key influencers visualization with data from a slicer or bar chart, and as the user changes the slicer to select bars in the chart, the key influencers would reevaluate based on the new filtered dataset.

There are many other analytical visualizations to fit various needs. The decomposition tree provides a visual drilldown across multiple dimensions and in any order the user chooses. The paginated report visual will, as the name suggests, display a paginated report that has been deployed to the Power BI service. The metrics visual can be used to create scorecards. Finally, run an automated flow with the Power Automate visual or embed a Power Apps app right inside the report with the Power Apps visual.

These visuals provide a great deal of additional value to a Power BI report if the built-in visualizations do not provide the insights or functionality required.

Power BI custom visuals

Throughout this chapter, you have seen many different visuals and how they work with specific types of data. Although there are many options readily available with Power BI, you have access to hundreds of additional visuals from Microsoft AppSource right at your fingertips. Users can either navigate to AppSource via any web browser or, while inside of Power BI Desktop, you can select the **From AppSource** option in the **Home** ribbon's **More Visuals** menu.

Once you select this option, a menu will appear where you can simply search the entire collection of custom visuals available. Once you have found a visual that you would like to use, just click on the **Add** button shown in yellow. Users can also download the visualization file, which can be imported into Power BI by using the **From my files** option, which is also in the **Home** ribbon's **More Visuals** menu. It is important to understand that when you select a custom visual, it saves as part of the Power BI report file and doesn't remain inside the application. So, if you just downloaded a custom visual and then closed down Power BI, when you restart the application, you will not see that custom visual unless you open the report to which you saved the custom visual. This is a fantastic feature and it only continues to grow, so it is worthwhile to check out AppSource.

Data visualization tips and tricks

You have created eight different report pages filled with different visuals and investigated different configuration options for each of them. That being said, you have barely scratched the surface of all the features that are available to you, and with the very quick update cycle that Power BI has, that list of features will keep growing. This final section will explore a couple of features that are not exclusive to just one visual but can really help out when designing a report. It is highly recommended to watch the monthly videos that the Power BI team embeds in the product update announcements each month, which are published at https://powerbi.microsoft.com/blog/. This way, you can know exactly what is new and how to use it.

Changing visuals

Throughout this chapter, the workflow has been the same: add a blank visual then add fields. Often, this will work in a real-world development environment as well. However, there are times when you will not know what the best visual is for your data. It is not uncommon to create a bar chart only to realize you need to use a date that would be better served as a column chart. Maybe the requirements change, and the table needs to have an additional category added to the row groups causing the visual to switch to a matrix. It is entirely possible to rebuild the visual; however, the more useful option is to simply change an existing visual.

To change between visuals, simply select an existing visual on the **Report** canvas and select the desired visual from the **Visualizations** pane.

Be sure to note that when changing between visualizations, the field buckets are often different, which may cause some fields to be dropped from the visual. For instance, switching from a **Column chart** to a **Treemap** generally works well. The axis on the **Column chart** becomes the group on the treemap.

However, switching to a gauge will cause Power BI to pick a single field for the value and all other fields will be dropped. Power BI does maintain the metadata from your visual choices and, as long as no other major changes have been made, you can often switch between visuals and your prior settings will be restored. The prior visual metadata is cleared when Power BI Desktop is closed.

Formatting visuals

Many references have been made in this chapter to conditional formatting and visual formatting. These options can help enhance the look of a report and help users gain an understanding of the data more quickly by drawing their eye to specific elements or making certain key information stand out. It is highly recommended to explore the **Format** section of the **Visualizations** pane for each of the visuals created in this chapter to see the options that are available. Some options, like the title text, background, and visual header toggle, are nearly universal. In general, visuals from the same family will share the same, or very similar, options. For instance, a table and matrix will both have options for formatting the headers, values, and grid lines, while the trend charts will have options for axis scales, data labels, and plot surface. It is often useful to work on formatting a single visual to the desired look and then use the **Format painter** to apply the same settings to other visuals.

Figure 6.46: Format painter is found on the Home tab of the ribbon

Not all options will transfer (for instance, no grid lines on a pie chart) but the overlap will transfer even to visuals of a completely visualization different type.

The Analytics section

For every visual, you worked with the **Fields** section and the **Format** section of the **Visualizations** pane, but there is an option you may have noticed that is called **Analytics**. This option is available for most visuals; for our example, look at the **Line chart** example created earlier in this chapter. Once you have that visual selected, you can navigate to the **Analytics** section and see that you are presented with eight different line types that can be added to the visual. All you must do is decide which one to be displayed and turn it on. For this visual, add an **Average line** by expanding that section and selecting the **Add line** option. Once the line has been added, you can change the color, name, transparency, style, and position from this same area, as seen in *Figure 6.47*. Users can add as many of these lines as they choose, but remember, more is not necessarily better.

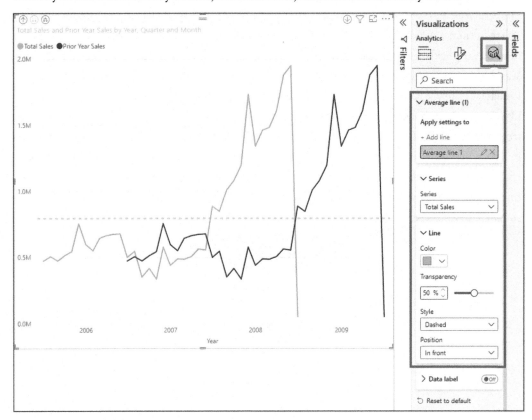

Figure 6.47: Reference lines being added from the Analytics section of the Visualizations pane

Additionally, if the visualization is based on a time data source, a forecast option will appear in the **Analytics** section. Specify the necessary input information such as forecast length and confidence interval and a forecast line will be added to the visual.

The Top N filter

At the very beginning of this chapter, there was a brief explanation about the **Filters** pane and how filters can be applied to different scopes. There are a couple of choices available to users for the filter fields, but the focus here will be on the **Top N** option. Even though it is called the **Top N** filter, this option allows a filter that will show either the top or bottom number of values. For example, if you look at the **Ribbon chart** created earlier in this chapter, you can see that there are six countries that appear in the visual. With this filter, you can set it so that it only displays the top four countries based on a chosen measure. So, in this situation, you could have that measure be **Total Sales**, which is what the visual is showing, or anything you want. Let's go ahead and click the dropdown next to the **EnglishCountryRegion** field in the **Filters on this visual** section. If **Top N** isn't showing by default in the **Filter type** section, select it from the dropdown. For the **Show items** section, leave the value of **Top** and manually input the number **4**, as shown in *Figure 6.48*. The last thing that needs to be done is to decide what measure will be used to determine the top four countries; keep things simple and drag in the **Total Sales** measure, and click **Apply filter**. The most important thing to remember is that you can use any measure you want for this filter.

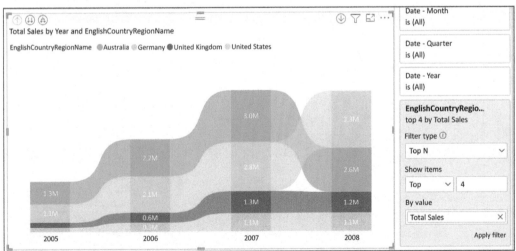

Figure 6.48: Ribbon chart filtered to the top 4 countries by total sales

The **Top N** option can also be changed to advanced filtering, which allows for string search, blank, include/exclude, and range filtering.

Show value as

Earlier in this chapter, you went through an example to take advantage of conditional formatting. This option can be found by clicking the downward arrow next to a field that is being used in a visual. Within this area is where you will find another option, which is labeled **Show value as**. This option will only be available for numeric data types and allows values to be displayed as a percentage of the grand total. The best way to take advantage of this is to place an identical column side by side and then use this option to display one of them as a percentage. For our example, revisit the **Matrix** visual you created for the **Tabular data** section. Locate the **Profit** measure in the **Fields** pane and drag it into the **Values** bucket for the visual, placing it directly after the **Profit** measure that is already in place, referencing *Figure 6.49*. The visual looks a little odd since there is a duplicated column, but now change the new field to show a percentage. Within the dropdown for the second representation of **Profit**, choose the **Show value as** option and select **Percent of grand total**.

Figure 6.49: Change the value displayed from dollars to a percent of grand total

The matrix was already a great visual to quickly see a lot of metric information about the sales territory regions, but now you have a firm understanding of what percentage each country is contributing to the grand total.

Summary

In this chapter, the focus was on how to configure visuals and what data they best illustrate. You also saw a couple of the most common formatting options that are used with these visuals. In the next chapter, you will look into the concept of digital storytelling. Power BI has a strong set of options that can be leveraged to allow users to experience and navigate through the data in an adventurous and exploratory manner.

Join our community on Discord

Join our community's Discord space for discussions with the authors and other readers:

https://packt.link/ips2H

7

Digital Storytelling with Power BI

In the previous chapter, you learned how to explore many of the readily available visuals within Power BI and how they can showcase your data. With the assistance of cross-highlighting and cross-filtering, you can also make the visuals work with each other—but there is so much more than just simple drag-and-drop reporting within Power BI. Power BI has several useful storytelling features. Alongside the different visuals, Power BI has a set of features that can tie together not only individual charts and graphs, but that can also allow users to navigate through multiple pages to discover exactly the level of detail they want from the data. Using these features, you can weave together the data in a way that allows interactivity far beyond what has already been seen. This allows users to take control of how they will view your Power BI report. If they just want to take a quick glance at a summary view of the data, they can; but if they wish to dive deeper, you can offer multiple paths to take. This chapter will investigate the following digital storytelling features:

- Configuring drill through
- Capturing report views with bookmarks
- Combining object visibility with bookmarks
- Report pages as tooltips
- Page navigation

When using these features, there are many different approaches that can be taken. You will be looking at them in their most basic forms, but they can flourish when you use your imagination. The idea of digital storytelling has become extremely popular, which will more than likely foster even more features for the future of Power BI, so keep an eye out!

 For this chapter, you will be using the completed Power BI file from *Chapter 6, Visualizing Data*. If you have not completed this on your own, you can open a completed version, located at `Microsoft-Power-BI-Start-Guide-Third-Edition-main\Completed Examples\Chapter 6 - Visualizing Data.pbix`. It is recommended that, upon opening this file, you immediately use the **Save As** option and name the report `Chapter 7 - Digital Storytelling with Power BI`. By doing this, you can preserve your work from chapter to chapter.

Possibly the most fundamental method for empowering digital storytelling is providing report consumers with the ability to tie multiple report pages to the same context; in Power BI, this is accomplished by using drill through.

Configuring drill through

In *Chapter 6, Visualizing Data*, you saw the power of filtering to allow a single visual to provide many different views of the data. For instance, a **bar chart** showing all sales could also show sales by year if cross-filtered by a date **slicer**. You also saw how the filter pane could be applied to visuals on a single page or across the entire report. Up to this point, those were the only two options available. The **drill through** feature allows users to navigate from one report visual to another report page while maintaining the filter context of the visual.

A common example of the use of **drill through** is going from a summary to a detail page. A summary page may contain several visualizations for sales data all aggregated at the country level. One of those could be a **pie chart** showing total sales broken down by country. While this can be useful, many users will want access to more detailed information, such as all the sales that happened in a particular country. A **drill through** filter will allow users to right-click on a slice of the **pie chart**, possibly representing the United States, and drill through to a detail report showing a table of sales that are now filtered to the United States.

While right-click drill through is effective, it is not obvious to the user that it's available. An alternative would be to configure a button for drill though which adds a very clear, visible drill through path. This allows users to quickly move from summary to detail and back to summary without ever needing to open the **Filters** pane. With the right configuration, **drill through** is a powerful data exploration tool.

Drill through filters are applied at the page level only and are configured in the **Fields** section of the **Visualizations** pane; they cannot be applied at the visualization or report level. The **Drill through** section has three options to configure:

- **Cross-report**: Drill through to another report in the same Power BI workspace or app when deployed to the Power BI service. There are a few special considerations with this scenario, like the drill through table and column names matching in both reports and the data in each field being case-sensitive.

- **Keep all filters**: When enabled, all filter context from the source visual in addition to the fields listed in the field bucket will be applied. When disabled, only fields listed in the **Drill through** field bucket will be applied as filters.

- **Add drill-through fields here**: Fields added to this bucket will automatically be enabled for drill through any time they are present in a visualization on any other page within the same report.

Figure 7.1: Drill through settings on the Visualizations pane

Let's explore an example by copying some of the visuals created previously, in *Chapter 6, Visualizing Data*, and moving them into new pages, leveraging the **Drill through** filter option.

Let's look at setting up an example. Note that the **Cross-report** and **Keep all filters** options should be set to **Off** and **On** respectively, as shown in *Figure 7.1*, then take the following steps:

1. Create two new report pages: the first one should be called **Summary** and the second **Drill Through**.

2. Navigate to the **Summary** report page and add a **Stacked column chart** visual. Move and resize the visual to take up the right half of the **Report** canvas.

3. From the **Fields** pane, drag the **Profit** measure from the **Internet Sales** table to the **Y-axis** bucket.

4. From the **Fields** pane, drag **Region Drilldown** from the **Geography** table to the **X-axis** bucket.

5. From the **Fields** pane, drag **Year** from the **Date (Order)** table to the **Legend** bucket:

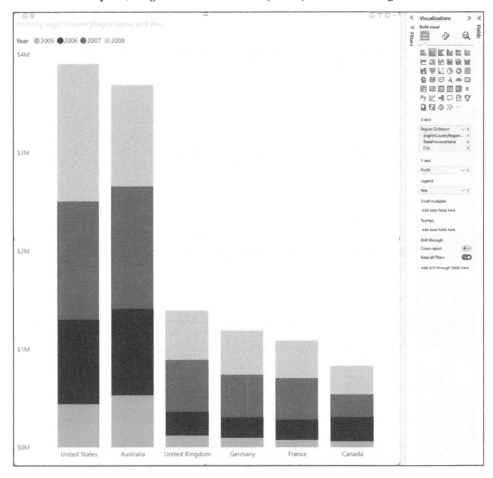

Figure 7.2: Bar chart displaying profit by country and year

6. Next, navigate to the **Drill Through** page. Add a **Table** visual. Move and resize the visual to take up the left third of the **Report** page, but leave a small amount of space above the visual, approximately 1/16 the height of the report page.

7. From the **Fields** pane, drag the following fields to the **Columns** bucket:

   • **StateProvinceName** from the **Geography** table

   • **City** from the **Geography** table

   • **Year** from the **Date (Order)** table

   • **Profit** from the **Internet Sales** table

8. Next, add a **Map** visual to take up the right two-thirds of the **Report** page.

9. From the **Fields** pane, drag **City** from the **Geography** table to the **Location** bucket.

10. From the **Fields** pane, drag the **Profit** measure from the **Internet Sales** table to the **Bubble size** bucket.

11. Finally, populate the **Drill through** fields by dragging **EnglishCountryRegionName** from the **Geography** table to the **Drill through** fields bucket:

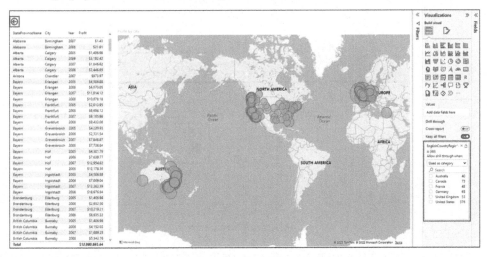

Figure 7.3: Map with a country on the drill through fields enabling the back button

When placing a field into the **Drill through** bucket, you will notice that a backward arrow image is automatically added to the page in the upper left-hand corner. This is simply an image that has been set with an action to go back to the previous page. By selecting the image, you will find that there are quite a few familiar format settings available in the **Format** section.

One of the more common settings to change is the **Line color** option under **Icon**, which will allow the selection of a color to make the back arrow more visible:

Figure 7.4: Back arrow with line color set to black

Everything is set for this example to demonstrate how **Drill through** works. Proceed by taking the following steps:

1. Navigate to the **Summary** page. Right-click the **2008** section for **United States**. There is now an option called **Drill through**. Hovering the mouse over this new option will present a list of available drill through reports. In this scenario, only one option exists. It is important to note that you can have as many drill through reports as you desire. Click the **Drill through** option:

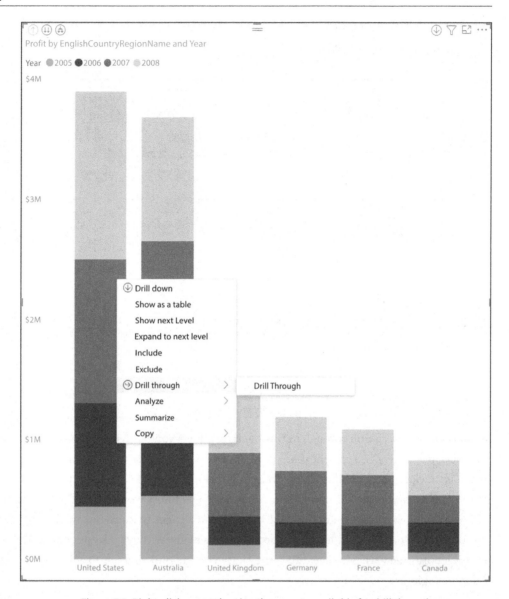

Figure 7.5: Right-click menu showing the reports available for drill through

2. Upon left-clicking the **Drill through** option, you will be taken to the corresponding **Drill Through** page. Notice both visuals have been filtered by the value of **United States**, and because the **Keep all filters** option is turned on, they are also filtered to the context of only **2008**.

Had the **Keep all filters** option been turned off, the visuals would be displaying only the **United States**, but all years:

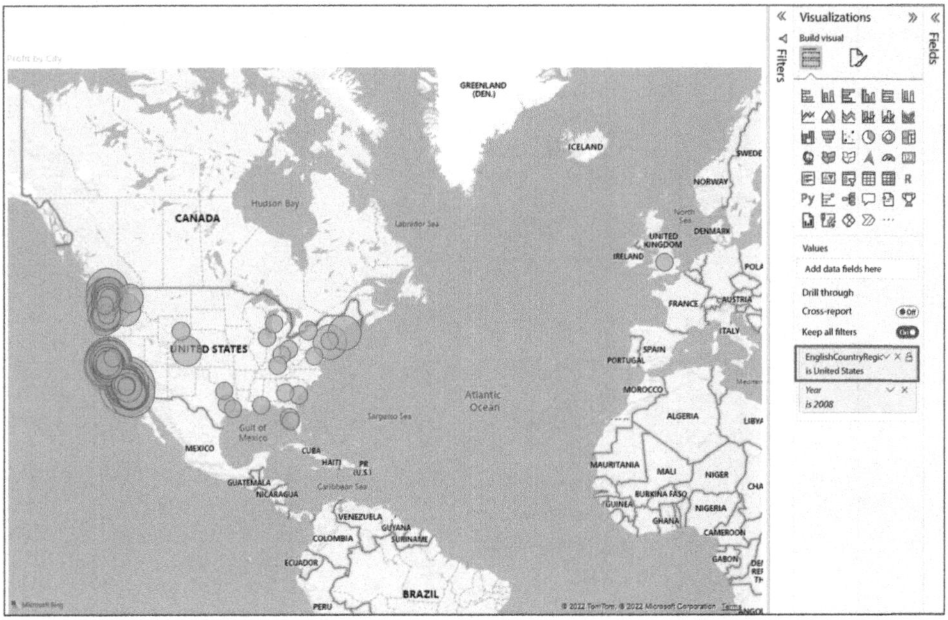

Figure 7.6: United States filter applied after performing drill through from the bar chart on the Summary page

As you can see, using drill through in this scenario allows you to dive deeper into sales records for a specific country, in a specific year. If you were to navigate back to the **Summary** page (using the page navigation or holding down *Ctrl* while clicking the back button in the top-left corner of the canvas) and make a different selection, those new filters would take effect on these two visuals. Thus, you can see that now you have two report pages that interact with each other. As more and more pages are added to the report, users will always have the option to drill through to this report page with whatever filters they have chosen, provided the visual uses the **English-CountryRegionName** field.

Drill through provides users with an ad hoc path to data exploration, allowing them to choose when and where to go deeper. There will be times when a more curated storytelling experience is required, and that is accomplished using bookmarks.

Capturing report views with bookmarks

Cross-filtering, cross-highlighting, and drill through filters make a big impact on how users consume data in Power BI reports. Sometimes, though, you may want to ensure that users see the data in a very specific way that will truly show its impact, satisfy report requirements, or simply provide alternative views of the data.

You can guide report consumers in a very interactive way using **bookmarks** and showing or hiding visualizations in the **Selection** pane. Using these options, you can make better use of the available canvas on each report page and still make it feel as if users have many choices as to how they will view the data.

The **Bookmarks** feature allows report creators to capture the view of a **Report** page. **Bookmarks** will save the current state of all filters, slicers, in-focus items, sorting, and spotlight visuals (more on that feature later in this section) on a page at the time when the bookmark is created. This allows users to return to the captured state by simply selecting the bookmark in question.

To begin working with bookmarks, navigate to the **View** ribbon and select **Bookmarks** from the **Show panes** section. You will see a new pane present itself to the left of the **Visualizations** pane:

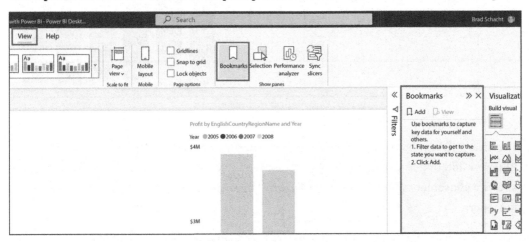

Figure 7.7: Showing the Bookmarks pane

Because you have not created any bookmarks, the only option available is **Add**. First, let's bring in a couple more visuals to the **Summary** page:

1. First, copy an existing visual to the **Summary** page. Navigate to the **Trend Data** report page. Select **Line chart**, which shows **Total Sales** and **Prior Year Sales**. Press *Ctrl + C* on the keyboard or click the **Copy** button from the **Home** ribbon.

2. Navigate to the **Summary** page. Press *Ctrl + V* on the keyboard or click the **Paste** button from the **Home** ribbon. Move and resize the visual as you see fit, leaving a small amount of space to add a filter.

3. Next, add a **Slicer** to the **Summary** page using the **Age Breakdown** field from the Customer table. Optionally, display the slicer as a series of buttons by navigating to the **Format** area for the slicer and changing the **Orientation** property to **Horizontal** within the **Slicer settings** on the **Visual** sub-pane section:

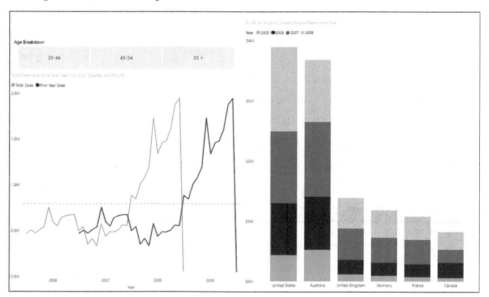

Figure 7.8: Summary page with line chart and slicer added

The slicer will filter both the **Bar** and **Line chart** without any additional work by leveraging Power BI's cross-filtering functionality. While it's not required, setting the filter to a series of buttons allows a consumer to more easily identify what filter context has been applied to this page of the report.

With the visuals in place, you can start to create bookmarks. There are a couple of different approaches that can be adopted. The first option you will look at is simply filtering the data to a specific state and then selecting the **Add** option inside the **Bookmarks** pane. Select the **35-44** option from the slicer to filter the **Summary** page. Creating a bookmark for this really isn't impactful because this is something that users can do by themselves with a visual slicer, but you can use some of the other features in combination with this to create a specialized view of the data—for instance, the **Spotlight** option.

Select the ellipsis in the upper right-hand corner of the **Stacked column chart** visual and choose the **Spotlight** option, which will fade all other visuals on the page. **Spotlight** is useful for drawing attention and focus to a single visual while keeping the remainder of the report page visible, so users can gather context for the data.

Now select the **Add** option inside of the **Bookmarks** pane and rename the bookmark as **Spotlight Column 35-44**. To rename the bookmark, select the ellipsis to the right of the newly created bookmark. You will see the **Rename** option, along with many others, as shown in *Figure 7.9*:

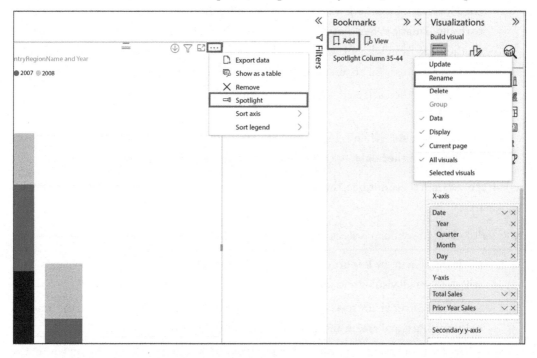

Figure 7.9: Spotlight option on the bar chart visual in addition to the Add and Rename bookmark options

Below is a short description of how each of the options on the options menu affects the bookmark:

- **Update**: Overwrite the bookmark settings with the current state of the page. To update a bookmark, do not click the name of the bookmark as Power BI will switch to that bookmark, resetting the state of the report. Set the report to the desired state and only then click the ellipsis next to the desired bookmark, and select **Update**.
- **Rename**: Change the name of the bookmark.

- **Delete**: Remove a bookmark.

- **Data**: When enabled, the bookmark retains the current state of the **Filters** pane and the selection of any visuals (slicer selection, visual highlighting, the selection of a section on a bar chart, and so on).

- **Display**: When enabled, the bookmark retains visual properties, such as the spotlight feature and the visibility.

- **Current page**: When enabled, selecting a bookmark automatically takes the user to the page where the bookmark was created and applies the data and display settings according to the bookmark. When disabled, a bookmark will only function when the user is already on the page from which the bookmark was created. This option effectively disables a bookmark unless you are on the page the bookmark references.

- **All visuals**: When selected, all visuals on the page, both visible and hidden, are part of the bookmark.

- **Selected visuals**: When selected, only the visuals that are selected, whether visible or hidden, when the bookmark is created or updated will be stored.

As you can see from these options, there are many different behaviors that can be controlled with bookmarks.

Now let's look at how bookmarks can be used:

1. Click any area in the **Report** canvas or surrounding area where there are no visuals. This will deselect all visuals and the bookmark.

2. Switch the **Slicer** visual to **45-54** and once again use the **Spotlight** feature on the **Stacked column chart**, and create another bookmark called **Spotlight Column 45-54**.

3. Add a third bookmark following the same steps but pointing to the **55+** option within the **Slicer**. This one should be called **Spotlight Column 55+**.

Users can now open the **Bookmark** pane and choose to view whichever bookmark they would like very easily.

An additional way to view bookmarks is in a slideshow style. Just to the right of the **Add** button is an option labeled **View** that will bring up some new icons at the bottom of the **Report** page. A forward and back arrow allows you to move through all the available bookmarks and tell a tailored story about the data. Also, while in this mode, all of the visuals are still completely available to be interacted with. To exit, simply choose the **X** icon next to the arrows at the bottom or the **Exit** option within the **Bookmarks** pane. The order of bookmarks can be very important when using the slideshow view. The order can be changed by simply dragging and dropping the bookmarks into the desired order:

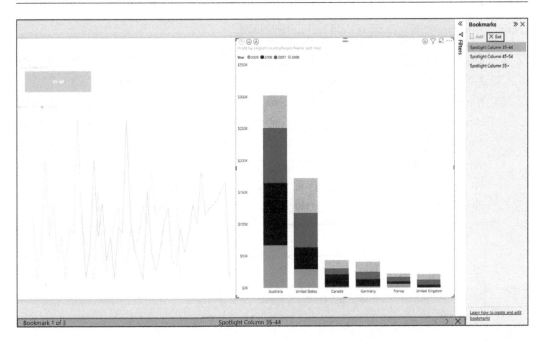

Figure 7.10: Options for exiting the Bookmarks view

You have already seen many ways to use bookmarks, but there are still more. Another fantastic way to guide your audience to these tailored views of the data is by using images or buttons to link to bookmarks. To get a better understanding of how to accomplish this, let's look at the **Selection** pane.

Combining object visibility with bookmarks

The **Selection** pane provides a list of all objects on the current page and allows you to show or hide visuals. This is useful if a slicer or visual is needed for cross-filtering but is not needed for analysis. It is also useful to reuse the same **Report** page for the same data but use different visuals when you are pressed for space. The following section will demonstrate how to maximize your use of space when visualizing data in different ways.

Bookmarking alternate views of the same data

Some users may want to see sales by country figures as a **bar chart**, and others may want to see them as a **table**. If there is not enough room for both visuals, the default answer may be to create a new page. However, it can be cumbersome to recreate and maintain the same exact filters on multiple pages. An alternative solution would be to put both visuals on the same page and dynamically show or hide them based on a user selection of "chart" or "table."

Let's look at how this scenario could be implemented:

1. On the **View** ribbon, click the **Selection** option in the **Show Panes** section. The **Selection** pane appears adjacent to the **Bookmarks** pane.

2. Navigate to the **Summary** page and create a duplicate of the **Stacked column chart**. This can be done by selecting the chart and pressing *Ctrl + C* then *Ctrl + V*, or using the **Copy** and **Paste** buttons on the **Home** ribbon.

3. With the duplicate visual selected, change it to a **Table** visual. Move it so that it lies directly on top of the column chart. Initially, it will look a little chaotic. You will see that this new visual is showing up in the **Selection** pane. In my example, it is called **Table**:

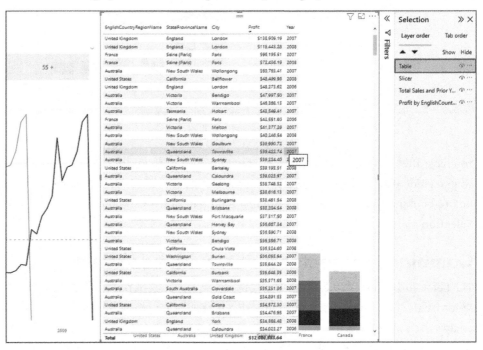

Figure 7.11: Table and bar chart displayed on top of each other

4. Just to the right of this object, inside of the **Selection** pane, you will see an eye icon.

5. Click the eye icon. You will see that the table visual disappears from the canvas—it is still part of the **Report** page but has been hidden.

6. Add a new bookmark and name it **Chart View**. Also, for this new **Chart View** bookmark, ensure that the **Data** option is not selected. The goal is to bookmark only the visual selection, not the data selection:

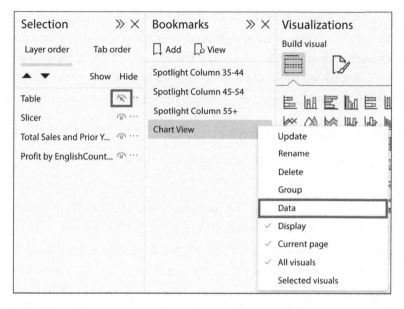

Figure 7.12: Chart View bookmark with data selection settings removed from the bookmark

Using the knowledge from the example you just completed, create one final bookmark that shows the table but hides the **Stacked column chart**. Call this bookmark **Table View** and be sure to remove the data selection from the bookmark options:

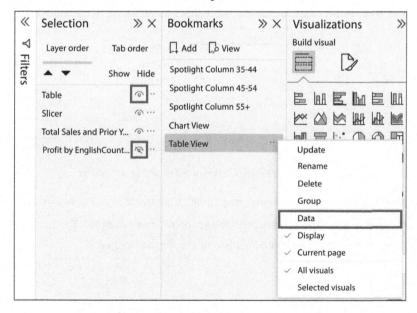

Figure 7.13: Table View bookmark settings

You can now see two different ways of displaying the same data within the same **Report** page, making efficient use of the available space. With the current report configuration, users need to open the **Bookmarks** pane to move between the **Table View** and **Chart View** bookmarks. While this is functional, it is not user-friendly. Adding a button to the report that automatically selects the appropriate bookmark is a great way to make the bookmark experience more approachable.

Using buttons to select bookmarks

Buttons can provide users with an even easier method for switching between bookmarks. To add buttons to your report, take the following steps:

1. While on the **Summary** page of the report, navigate to the **Insert** ribbon and click the **Image** button in the **Elements** section. This will launch a file browser to select an image file.

2. Navigate to the directory `Power-BI-Start-Guide-Third-Edition-main\Data Sources` and select the `Chart.png` image to add it to the canvas. In the **Format** section of the **Visualizations** pane, turn the **Title** property **On**, name the image **Chart Button**, then turn the **Title** property **Off**. This will help distinguish between the buttons in the **Selection** pane but not display the title on the image in the report:

Figure 7.14: Title disabled on the Chart Button

3. Repeat this process to add `Table.png` and change the title to **Table Button**.

4. To the best of your ability, stack the images on top of each other. You may need to reduce the size of other visualizations to allow space for the images.

Now it's time to turn these images into buttons the user can press to toggle between the **Chart View** and **Table View** bookmarks. This requires a couple of quick updates to the **Chart View** and **Table View** bookmarks.

5. Begin by selecting the **Chart View** bookmark and then hiding the **Table Button** image in the **Selection** pane. Select the ellipsis for the **Chart View** bookmark and choose the **Update** option. Now make the same change on the **Table View** bookmark, selecting the **Table View** bookmark, hiding the **Chart Button** image, and choosing the **Update** option from the bookmark's ellipsis.

The last piece that will tie all this together is to assign an action to the appropriate image within the bookmarks. An action will allow users to click on the **Chart Button** image, visible on the **Chart View** bookmark, and be taken to the **Table View** bookmark, giving the appearance of a toggle switch. Similarly, the **Table Button** image, visible on the **Table View** bookmark, will take the user to the **Chart View** bookmark again, giving the appearance of toggling to the other view.

6. While the **Table View** bookmark is selected, highlight the **Table Button** image in the **Selection** pane. The **Visualizations** pane will change to **Format**. Locate and expand the **Action** properties. Change the toggle to **On**, select **Bookmark** from the **Type** dropdown, and select **Chart View** from the **Bookmark** dropdown, as shown in *Figure 7.15*:

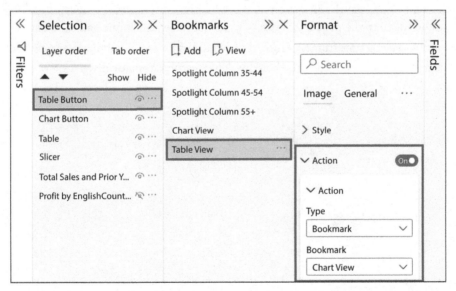

Figure 7.15: Turning an image into a button by creating an action that navigates to the Chart View bookmark

Now, when a user clicks on the **Table Button** image they will be taken to the **Chart View** book-mark, making a static image feel like an interactive button. In order to experience this behavior while developing the report, just hold the *Ctrl* key on the keyboard and left-click the image, and you will be taken to the **Chart View** bookmark. When the report is deployed to the Power BI service, users will not need to hold *Ctrl* while clicking the button to interact with it. They will simply left-click the image.

To finish this example, make the same changes to the **Chart View** bookmark and set the **Chart Button** image to have an **Action** that will navigate back to the **Table View** bookmark.

Using the Bookmark navigator

Creating buttons to navigate between bookmarks provides a great amount of flexibility to a report developer but comes at the cost of development time and complexity. Imagine needing to add additional bookmarks to this page. A stacked button approach would no longer work as it does with the chart/table toggle. This would require an update to the report to separate the existing buttons, create the new bookmark, create a new button, then size and space the buttons appropriately. This would need to be repeated each time an additional bookmark is required. Thankfully, there is a better way!

From the **Insert** tab on the ribbon, press the **Buttons** dropdown located in the **Elements** section. At the bottom of the list, expand **Navigator** and select **Bookmark navigator**. The bookmark nav-igator is added to the page and looks very similar to a slicer. Notice all the existing bookmarks are visible, saving time from having to set up buttons for each bookmark. As new bookmarks are created, they will be added to the bookmark navigator automatically.

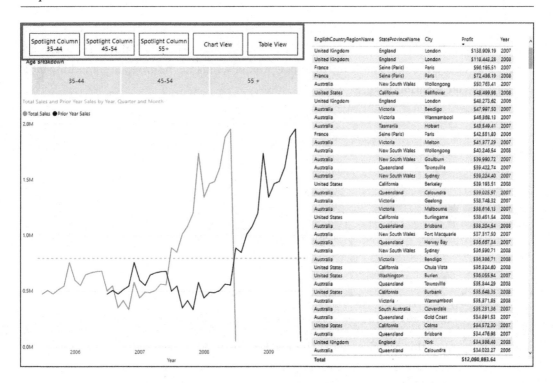

Figure 7.16: Report containing the bookmark navigator

Thinking back to the navigation buttons we created earlier in this chapter, you will recall there were only two. One for the chart view and one for the table view. However, by default, all the bookmarks are shown. To limit the bookmarks displayed you will first need to create bookmark groups.

From the **Bookmarks** pane select both the **Chart View** and **Table View** bookmarks by selecting the **Chart View** bookmark, and then, while holding the *Ctrl* key, click the **Table View** bookmark. Next, right-click and select the **Group** option. Optionally, rename the group to something more useful, like **Visualization Toggle**.

Figure 7.17: The newly created Visualization Toggle bookmark group

For the purpose of this exercise there is no need to create additional groups for the spotlight bookmarks, but those could be grouped together as well for a more clean and consistent report. So far, there is nothing special about the group other than to help organize the development environment and possibly aid a user who is navigating bookmarks using the **Bookmarks** pane. These groups do serve one additional purpose with the bookmark navigator.

Select the bookmark navigator on the report canvas. Locate the **Bookmarks** setting in the **Format** pane and choose the **Visualization Toggle** group from the dropdown. Notice now that the bookmark navigator only displays the bookmarks included in the **Visualization Toggle** group. By renaming, reordering, adding, or removing bookmarks from this group the navigator will automatically be updated.

As with many items in Power BI, there are a variety of visual formatting options, including changing the shape from rectangles, modifying the button font, switching from a horizontal to vertical grid layout, and many more. This is an incredibly useful feature that will no doubt save time and aid in creating well organized reports.

Hopefully, with these examples you can start to see the depth of what can be achieved by using the **Selection** and **Bookmarks** panes for digital storytelling.

Guiding report consumers through visualizations is helpful, but sometimes switching to a different report page with a completely different view of the data removes the user from their workflow. In cases where more detail is required but you would like to keep users in their workflow, you can enhance the built-in tooltips by displaying a report page as a tooltip.

Report pages as tooltips

Tooltips are another useful feature that allows a user to see precise information about a piece of a visual while moving the mouse around the **Report** canvas. While the formatting options discussed in the previous chapter can display value labels on a visual, sometimes that can cause a report to become too cluttered or a visual may just be too small to display a label. Tooltips solve this problem by allowing a user to see the label information for only the data point they hover the mouse over. But what if those tooltips could display even more information and provide even greater insight? Thankfully, Power BI comes through on this front by allowing you to specify a report page as a tooltip for a visual.

Power BI includes a few different important options for tooltip visuals. First, to use a visual for a tooltip, you must create a report page and tell Power BI that the page will be used as a tooltip. While any page can be a tooltip, report pages are large and are often too big to be an effective tooltip, so Power BI has a special canvas size specifically for use in tooltips. Finally, you can set a specific **report page** to display as the tooltip for each visual or allow Power BI to intelligently choose the appropriate page (if multiple pages are defined as tooltips).

Let's continue using the **Summary** page and build a visual tooltip to see how this functionality works:

1. Add a new page to the report and name the page **Tooltip**. Right-click on the page name and select **Hide page** since users will not be navigating to this page directly.
2. From the **Visualizations** pane, change to the **Format** section. Expand the **Page information** properties and change the **Allow use as tooltip** toggle setting to **On**.

Expand the **Canvas settings** properties and change **Type** to **Tooltip** if it did not change automatically:

Figure 7.18: Format options to turn the report page into a tooltip and change the size to tooltip dimensions

3. Power BI may scale the canvas to fit the screen. When we change **Type** to **Tooltip** it may not look like the canvas is much smaller if the scaling is set to **Fit to page**. To change the size of the canvas, navigate to the **View** ribbon, then locate the **Page view** option in the **Scale to fit** section and change it to **Actual size** or **Fit to page** as you desire.

4. On the top half of the canvas, create a **Card** visual using the `Profit` measure from the `Internet Sales` table.

5. On the bottom half of the canvas, create a **Pie chart** visual using `Temperature Range` from the `Temperature` table as the **Legend** and the `Profit` measure from the `Internet Sales` table as the **Values**.

6. To make the visual filter based on location, click anywhere on the blank canvas to deselect any visuals, and add **EnglishCountryRegionName** to the tooltip fields bucket on the **Visualizations** pane. Setting **Keep all filters** to **On** will operate similar to drill through filters, thereby retaining and applying all the source filters to the tooltip.

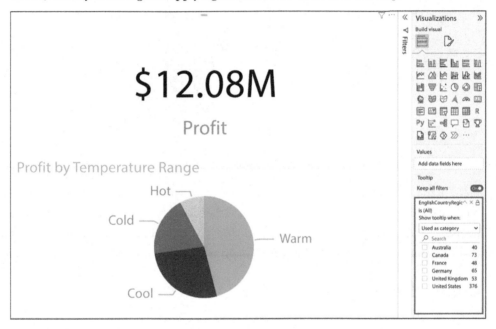

Figure 7.19: Enabling the tooltip page as an option any time the EnglishCountryRegionName field is used in a visualization

7. Next, return to the **Summary** page of the report. Select **Stacked column chart**. In the **Visualizations** pane, navigate to the **General** section. Locate the **Tooltips** properties and select **Report page** for the **Type** property and **Tooltip** for the **Page** property.

Now, when hovering the mouse over a column in the chart, the visual tooltip we just created should appear and the country will be passed in as a filter to the tooltip:

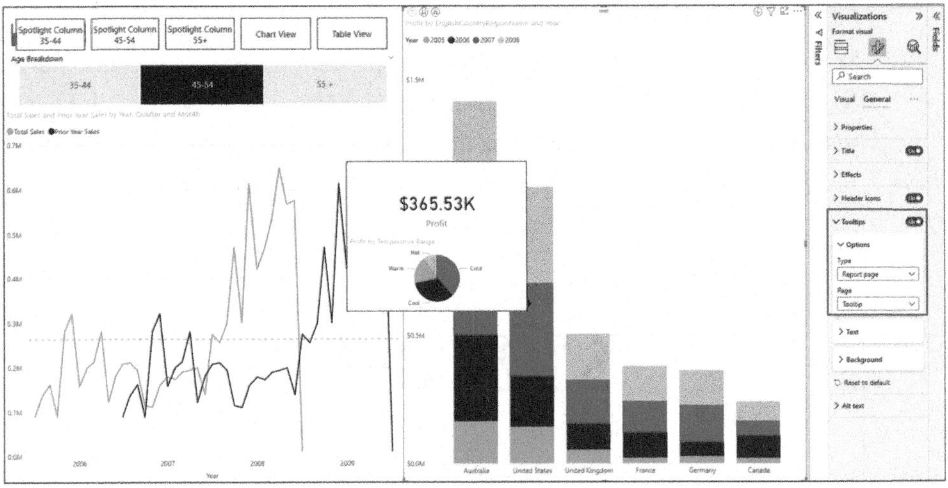

Figure 7.20: Setting the tooltip on a visualization to a report page

Many of the settings on a tooltip can be changed to provide more relevant information to users, but visual tooltips offer a powerful way to extend the tooltip functionality. By creating small pages of visuals and leveraging filters, you can provide a vast amount of additional data and insight that just cannot be matched by the default tooltips.

Using the Page navigator

So far, we have seen how to navigate between pages using drill through, weave through a report with bookmarks, and see additional details using tooltips. Now, let's explore how you can enhance the most common and basic method for navigating a report: pages. In Power BI Desktop, the pages display lines the bottom of the report canvas. In the Power BI service, pages are displayed in a list on the left side of the screen. What if a user's eyes never had to leave the report canvas? They could focus on the report, navigation to the relevant pages would be on each page, and in the case of Power BI Desktop, there would be no hidden pages to confuse the user. Of course, this can be accomplished using buttons, but the same issue arises that we saw with bookmarks earlier in this chapter. Creating additional pages means a lot of manual work to keep things updated and organized. This is where the page navigator comes into the picture.

The page navigator operates almost exactly like the bookmark navigator except it displays pages as the name suggests. To see this in action, navigate to one of the existing report pages, such as the **Slicers** page. From the **Insert** tab of the ribbon, select the **Buttons** dropdown in the **Elements** section. Expand the **Navigator** option and select **Page navigator**. Make some space for the page navigator by moving the **Temperature Range** and **Sales Territory Drilldown** slicers down and reducing the width of the page navigator.

Many of the same formatting options from the slicer visual and bookmark navigator are available on the page navigator. These include, but are not limited to, the shape of the buttons, the layout (which has been changed to a two-row grid as seen in *Figure 7.21* below for better readability), and font style. Two important settings are found in the **Pages** section. The first, **Show hidden pages**, determines if hidden pages are displayed in the navigation. By default, this option is set to **On**. The second, **Show tooltip pages**, determines if pages marked as tooltips are shown in the navigation. By default, this option is set to **Off**, which makes sense as tooltips generally need another visual to set their context. Note that when switching pages using the page navigator, a button to navigate back to the prior page is not added automatically. However, with a small amount of work you can easily add a back button or replicate the page navigator on each page.

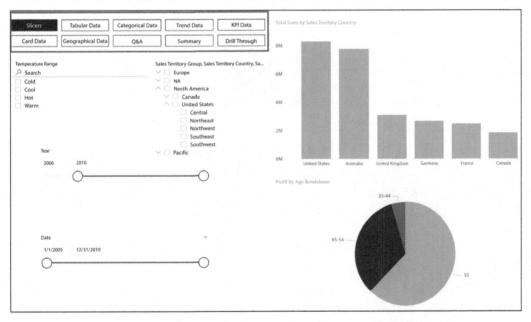

Figure 7.21: The Slicers page with the newly added page navigator in a two-row grid

With the page navigator in place, users now have an easily accessible, curated way to move between report pages. This allows developers to tell a better story by showing report consumers exactly which pages they should consider next rather than looking through a list of pages, some of which may be hidden or irrelevant to the current page's context.

Summary

Being able to use the features discussed in this chapter effectively will turn interactive reports into dynamic digital storytelling tools. Report developers have a wide variety of tools at their disposal to tell exciting stories from using space more efficiently by creating toggles, empowering users to drill through to gain detail-level insights, adding value by enhancing the built-in tooltips, or calling out important views with bookmarks. In the next chapter, you will see how to take this completed Power BI report and share it with others.

Join our community on Discord

Join our community's Discord space for discussions with the authors and other readers:

https://packt.link/ips2H

8

Using a Cloud Deployment with the Power BI Service

You've spent the course of this book creating amazing reports using the Power BI Desktop client. Hopefully, you feel more confident in your skills and ready to take the next steps. Now, it's time to share those reports with your team, company, or customers. In this chapter, you're going to learn about the Power BI service and will be doing the following:

- Exploring the Power BI service
- Creating workspaces
- Deploying reports to the Power BI service
- Creating and interacting with dashboards
- Sharing your reports and dashboards
- Maintaining dashboards

The Power BI service begins with a **freemium** model. You can get many of the features using the free model, but when you want to share data with others and use team development, it will need to be upgraded to the Pro or Premium edition. Other features requiring the Pro edition are the ability to store larger datasets and refresh more frequently, to name a couple.

 Before you begin this chapter, if you haven't already done so, make sure you sign up for a free trial premium account at Power BI (https://powerbi.microsoft.com/en-us/get-started/). Some sections will require a Pro license, such as the section dealing with workspaces.

Now, let's get started and begin exploring how to deploy reports to the Power BI service.

Exploring the Power BI service

In this section, we will explore the layout and organization of the Power BI service. We will review key digital assets and how they function:

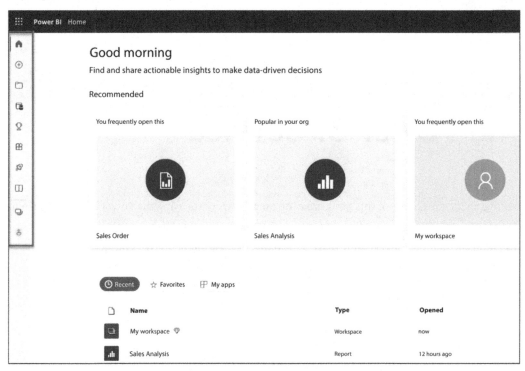

Figure 8.1: Exploring a workspace in the Power BI service

As shown in *Figure 8.1*, there are multiple key areas that you can interact with:

- **Dashboards**: You can pin the best elements from multiple reports into a unified set of dashboards. These dashboards are the first thing most of your casual users will interact with.

- **Reports**: This area refers to the projects that you have built in Power BI Desktop or in the service. These reports can be explored, modified, or downloaded in this section.

- **Workbooks**: You can upload Excel workbooks into this area. These Excel workbooks can be used as datasets or to form pieces of the workbook that can be pinned to a dashboard.

- **Datasets**: This is the raw data that you have built in Power BI Desktop. When you click a given dataset, you can build new reports from it. You can also build a new dataset by clicking **Get data** in the bottom-left corner of your browser.

- **Dataflows:** This feature in Power BI offers online self-service **Extract, Transform, Load (ETL)** and data preparation. This allows organizations to unify data from various sources, prepare the data for consumption, and ultimately publish it as a shared, central data source for users to view in Power BI.

- **Metrics:** This Pro feature allows users to capture, curate, and consolidate their metrics and track them against key business objectives, depending on the levels of permissions granted by the Power BI administrator. The goal is to align teams with key organizational goals transparently and strengthen an organization's data culture.

- **Scorecards:** This visual display serves as a graphical representation of key metrics in the **Metrics** section. It's a specific measurement created and displayed for an organization to track its progress. Creating scorecards requires an Admin, Member, or Contributor role in a workspace, in addition to build permission for a dataset.

- **Apps:** Power BI designers share the various components—such as reports, dashboards, and so on—with their intended broader audience through apps. It's the ideal way to bundle all the information assets in an easy-to-navigate way for their stakeholders. Designers can manage distribution lists, permissions, schedules, and more through apps.

- **Deployment Pipelines:** This feature allows creators to manage the life cycle for content such as reports, paginated reports, dashboards, datasets, and dataflows more effectively. It's available for an enterprise with Premium capacity, and allows the staged synchronizing and cloning of content, typically from development to test, and then test to production.

- **Data Hub:** This central repository provides an easy way to locate and manage datasets and data marts. Information like refresh status, usage metrics, related reports, and lineage is transparent. It helps reduce redundancy and increase the quality of use.

Now that we've reviewed the Power BI service at a high level, let's interact with the service's capabilities, starting with creating a workspace in the Power BI service, and then deploying a report from Power BI Desktop.

Creating workspaces

Workspaces are areas where groups of users can collaborate on datasets, reports, and dashboards. You can create a workspace if you have a Pro license for the Power BI service. This is the main way that your BI developers will be able to co-develop the same sets of data and reports. Typically, you'll create a workspace for each department in your company for the teams to store their items and data.

To create one, simply expand the **Workspaces** section in the left navigation menu and click **Create a workspace** at the bottom. Name the workspace that you wish to create and define which members are in the contact list.

Assigning roles will determine the level of permissions, such as who can edit the content or just view the content. The following table describes the roles. It is advisable to always check the Microsoft documentation for any special notes or updates.

Capability	Admin	Member	Contributor	Viewer
Update and delete the workspace	✓			
Add/remove people, including other admins	✓			
Allow Contributors to update the app for the workspace	✓			
Add members or others with lower permissions	✓	✓		
Publish, unpublish, and change permissions for an app	✓	✓		
Update an app	✓	✓		
Share an item or share an app[2]	✓	✓		
Allow others to reshare items[2]	✓	✓		
Feature apps on colleagues' Home	✓	✓		
Manage dataset permissions[3]	✓	✓		
Feature dashboards and reports on colleagues' Home	✓	✓	✓	
Create, edit, and delete content, such as reports, in the workspace	✓	✓	✓	
Publish reports to the workspace, delete content	✓	✓	✓	
Create a report in another workspace based on a dataset in this workspace[3]	✓	✓	✓	
Copy a report[3]	✓	✓	✓	
Create metrics based on a dataset in the workspace[3]	✓	✓	✓	
Schedule data refreshes via the on-premises gateway[4]	✓	✓	✓	
Modify gateway connection settings[4]	✓	✓	✓	
View and interact with an item[5]	✓	✓	✓	✓

Capability	Admin	Member	Contributor	Viewer
Read data stored in workspace dataflows	✓	✓	✓	✓
Notes: 1. Contributors can update the app associated with the workspace if the workspace Admin delegates this permission to them. However, they can't publish a new app or change who has permission to it. 2. Contributors and Viewers can also share items in a workspace if they have reshare permissions. 3. To copy a report to another workspace, and to create a report in another workspace based on a dataset in this workspace, you need build permission for the dataset. For datasets in the original workspace, if you have at least the Contributor role you automatically have build permission through your workspace role. 4. Keep in mind that you also need permissions on the gateway. Those permissions are managed elsewhere, independent of workspace roles and permissions. 5. Even if you don't have a Power BI Pro license, you can view and interact with items in the Power BI service if the items are in a workspace in a Premium capacity.				

You can also define whether users will be able to see the content of what's inside the workspace without being a member. This doesn't mean they'll be able to see the reports, but they will be able to see the metadata.

To determine the mode for the workspace, expand the **Advanced** settings and select what individual licensing or enterprise settings make the most sense. Some businesses require their IT to manage enterprise settings for Power BI, so please contact the right person in your organization to determine the best setting. Premium features and other settings allow for additional storage, which is handy for those executive reports that must always return their visuals in a few seconds.

 At any time, you can change the permissions or add users by editing the workspace if you have permission to do so. To do this, select the ellipsis button next to the workspace name on the main **Workspace** menu and click **Workspace Access**.

Setting up a workspace, its roles, and permissions covers the most basic access and security issues by defining who can access the report and other objects. Now let's dive into further access and security options.

Deploying reports to the Power BI service

There are numerous ways to publish a report to the PowerBI.com service, but the easiest way is by using Power BI Desktop. To do this, you'll need to simply open the report you want to deploy to the Power BI service, then click the **Publish** button on the **Home** tab in the desktop application, as shown in the following screenshot. If you have not previously signed in with your free PowerBI.com account, you will be prompted to create one or sign in with an existing account:

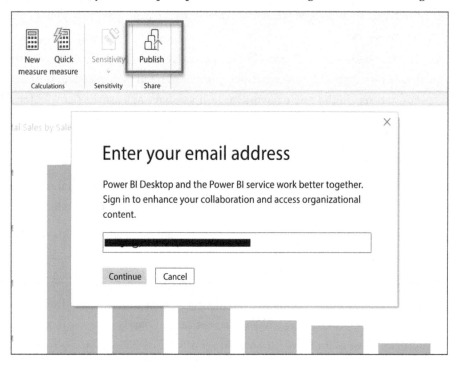

Figure 8.2: Power BI sign-in window that links your account from Desktop to the service

You'll then be asked which workspace you want to deploy to. At this point, take the following steps:

1. Select an existing workspace, or **My Workspace**, which will send the report and its data to your personal workspace. The report will then deploy to the Power BI service. The amount of time this takes will depend on how large your dataset is.

2. You'll then be presented with two options: **Open** or **Get Quick Insights**:

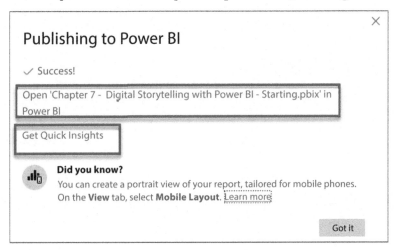

Figure 8.3: Power BI options

Quick Insights is an amazing feature in Power BI that will try to find additional interesting insights about your data that you may not have noticed initially. You'll notice that it not only provides a graphic of the data, but also a narrative to the right of the graphic. With the **Quick Insights** option, if you find any of the insights especially interesting, you can click the pushpin at the top right of the graphic to save it into a dashboard.

We'll cover dashboards in the next section of this chapter.

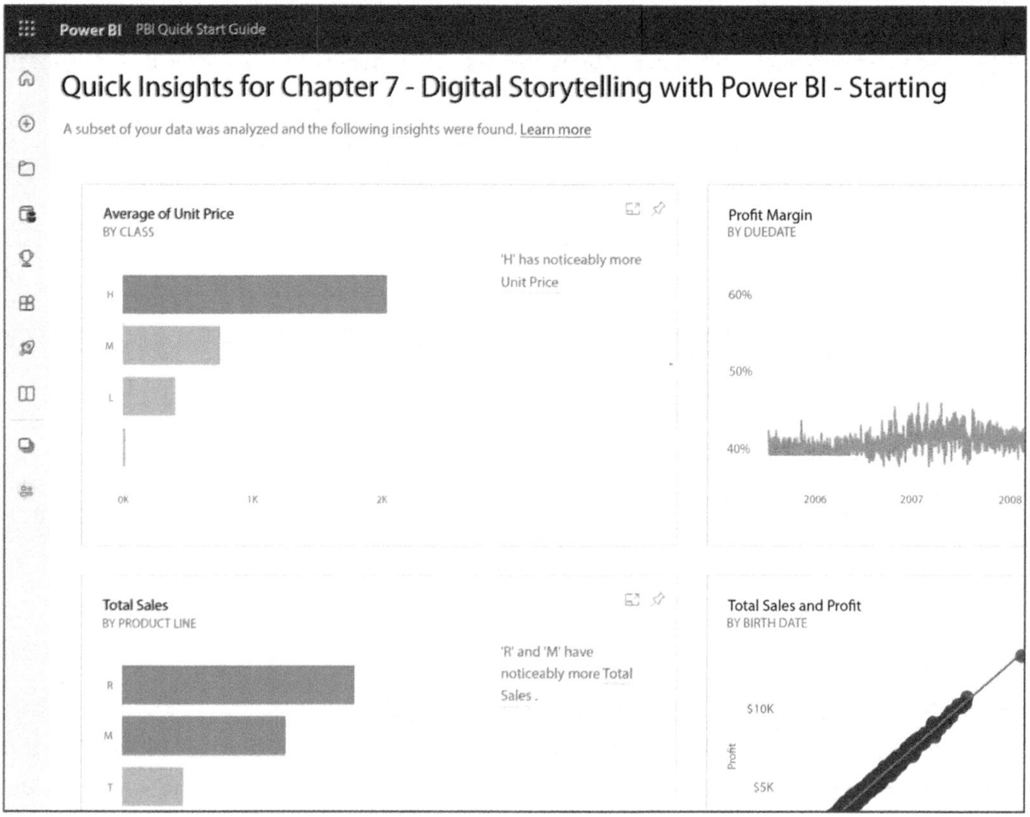

Figure 8.4: Quick Insights in the Power BI service

The value of this feature lies in the fact that Power BI has designed algorithms to review the data without human input, which avoids bias and may introduce trends and insights not previously considered. Leaders and teams can benefit from reviewing and discussing these new perspectives, and then decide if there's value in adding the information to their published reports and dashboards.

The Power BI service has expanded the Insights feature set so that you can also analyze pages in your published reports when you open them in the service. The **Get Insights** button is located on the top ribbon and will launch a description of **Trends** found in the data. The report we just published didn't have any additional insights, but *Figure 8.5* below shows what the feature looks like where there are additional insights and trends.

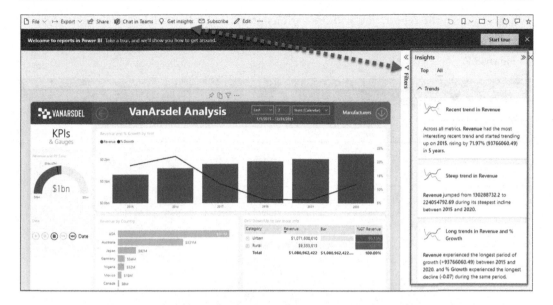

Figure 8.5: Get insights pane in an opened report

When you click on the **Trends** shown in the panel, you will launch a more detailed explanation, as shown in *Figure 8.6* below. To return to the main panel, simply click the back area in the top-left corner.

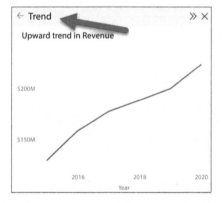

Figure 8.6: Quick Insights results in the Power BI service

If you choose to open the report upon publishing, PowerBI.com will launch in any web browser and show you the same report that you were viewing on the desktop. You'll also be able to immediately see the report in the Power BI mobile app from your Android, iPhone, or Windows phone.

When you open the report, you will see various powerful tools available, such as **Analyze in Excel**, **View Lineage**, **Sharing**, and more. These options are available in the top ribbon, as seen in *Figure 8.7*:

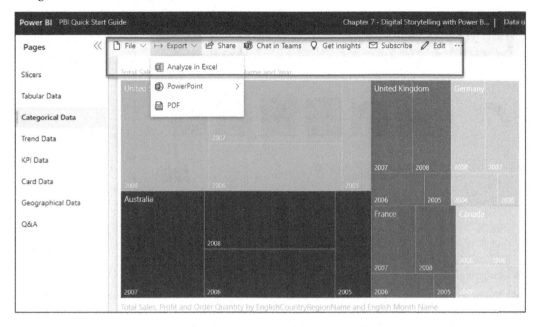

Figure 8.7: Many features are found along the top ribbon of the report page

It's also worth noting that hovering over reports and datasets will reveal ellipses that allow for some of the same options. There is usually more than one way to engage these powerful features in the Power BI service.

Now, let's explore the underlying features of the reports in the Power BI service, as well as the other main features.

Datasets

The **Datasets** area of Power BI holds the raw data that makes up your reports. When you hover over the dataset, as shown in *Figure 8.8* below, an ellipsis will appear, which you can click to reveal many options to manage and analyze your data:

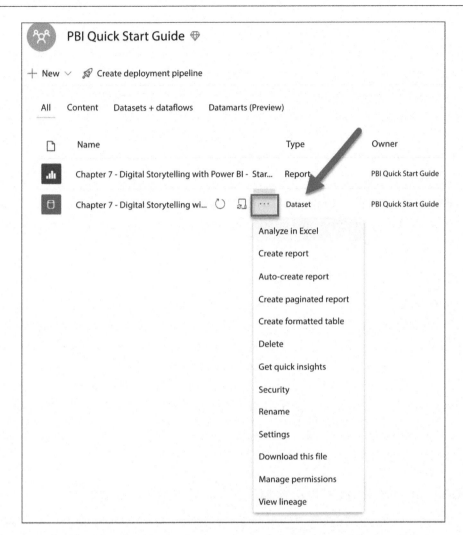

Figure 8.8: Key management and creation features found on the dataset

Some options are as follows:

- Analyze in Excel
- Create new reports, paginated reports, and tables
- Refresh or schedule refreshes (via **Settings**)
- Download as a Power BI Desktop file (.pbix)
- Manage permissions

When you start with a dataset, users can create new reports from your data if they have the right permissions, even when accessing it through the web. The entire user interface will feel nearly identical to Power BI Desktop, but you will be lacking the ability to modify the model, query, and relationships, as well as lacking the ability to create measures or calculated columns. The best part of building reports using the online Power BI framework is that you have a central dataset that your organization's central IT team can own, modify, and make human-readable for use by the entire organization.

While those benefits exist, it's very important to follow the best practices set by your organization's data governance. Doing report development from an online portal would not typically be a best practice when the reports are stored on version control systems, as "online" changes would fall outside of a standard development process.

Workbooks

The **Workbooks** section gives you the ability to upload Excel workbooks, which can be used as datasets for a report or to pin selected parts of that workbook to a dashboard. Workbooks can be updated by either reuploading the workbook, using the database management gateway, or using OneDrive. OneDrive is Microsoft's cloud-hosted hard drive system. With OneDrive, you can simply share or save your Excel workbooks, and if you're using a workbook in a Power BI report, it can also refresh manually or on a schedule.

Now we have explored some of the fundamental elements of Power BI's online service, let's use it to create and interact with our own projects.

Creating and interacting with dashboards

Once you have deployed your datasets and are using them in reports, you're ready to bring together the many elements into a single dashboard. Often, your management team is going to want a unified executive dashboard that combines elements such as sales numbers, bank balances, customer satisfaction scores, and more into a single dashboard. The amazing thing about dashboards in Power BI is that data is actionable and consumers can quickly respond. You can strategically display the most important information your viewers need to see from multiple reports and pages. For a deeper dive, you can click on any dashboard element and be immediately taken to the report that is the source of that information. You can also subscribe to the dashboard and create mobile alerts when certain numbers on the dashboard reach a milestone.

Now, let's jump in and apply this knowledge.

Creating your first dashboard

To create your first dashboard, follow these steps:

1. Start by opening the report from *Chapter 7, Digital Storytelling with Power BI*, here: `https://github.com/PacktPublishing/Microsoft-Power-BI-Quick-Start-Guide-Third-Edition`.

2. On each of the charts, tiles, and other elements, you'll see a pin icon at the top-right of that object. After you click on the pin, it will ask you which dashboard you wish to pin that report element to. You can, at that point, create a **New dashboard** or choose an **Existing dashboard** to add the element to, as shown in the following screenshot. This is what makes Power BI so magical—you're able to append data from your accounting department next to data from your sales and customer service teams, giving your executives one place to look:

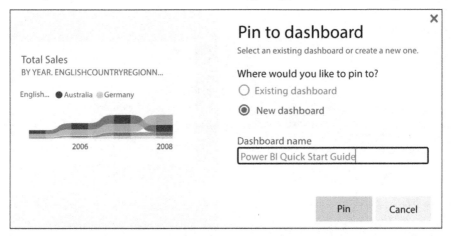

Figure 8.9: Pin a visual to a dashboard

3. If you have an existing dashboard, then select **Existing dashboard** and choose which one you want to use. If you don't have a dashboard yet, select **New dashboard**, give it a name, and then click **Pin**.

4. Once you pin the first item to the dashboard, you'll be prompted with a link to the dashboard. The newly created dashboard will allow you to resize elements and add additional tiles of information.

You have the option to click on **Edit** in the upper ribbon and **Add a tile** to add additional inter-esting data, such as web content, images (such as logos), text data, and videos to the dashboard, as seen in *Figures 8.10* and *8.11*. Many people use this in the line-manager dashboard to insert a company logo or even a short video from the executive team talking about the initiative that relates to the dashboard.

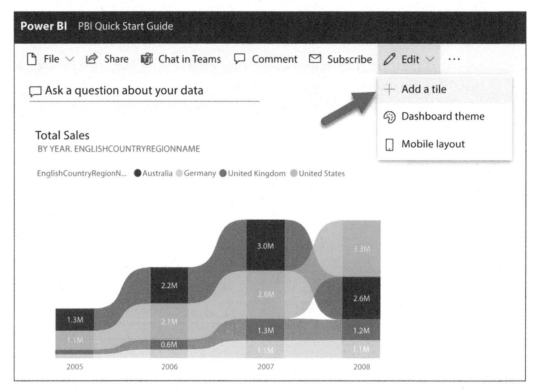

Figure 8.10: Dashboard pinned visual and option to add a tile in the ribbon

You can also pin real-time data as a tile, using custom streaming data. Under **Edit**, you would choose **Add a tile**. Once you click **Custom Streaming Dataset**, as seen in *Figure 8.11* below, you have the option to add a new dataset from **Azure Stream Analytics** or **PubNub**, or a developer can use an API to push data directly into the dashboard.

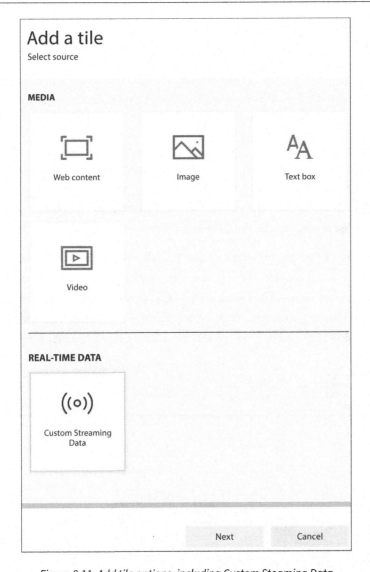

Figure 8.11: Add tile options, including Custom Steaming Data

Azure Stream Analytics is the most common of these live data streams. In this mechanism, devices can stream data through Azure Event Hubs, for example, which then gets aggregated with **Azure Stream Analytics**.

Imagine the power of a smart power grid sending thousands of records in a second to the cloud, and then **Azure Stream Analytics** aggregating this to a single record every five seconds, the status shown by a moving needle on a gauge or line graph in Power BI.

Another valuable feature is the ability to add Excel workbooks to your dashboard. This can be very helpful for both designers and end consumers of the information, because Excel is still a very common and robust tool in the world of business.

In a world of increased information availability, it's worth noting that a good way to view Power BI is from a phone, either in web view or in the native Power BI client, which is downloadable from the App Store for Android or iPhone.

There are going to be some dashboard elements that you will likely want to exclude from a phone device because the surface area is too small. By the very nature of the device, most people sign into Power BI on their phone to get a quick look at the numbers. For those consumers, you can create a specialized phone view of the dashboard.

In *Figure 8.10*, you can see that the **Edit** option also allows you to view the **Mobile layout**. The default phone view will contain every element from **Web View**. If you want to remove items, hover over each report element and click the pushpin to move it to the **Unpinned Tiles** section, as shown in the following screenshot. Once you're done, you can click the phone icon (or click on **Mobile layout**, based on your resolution) and flip it back to **Web layout** again:

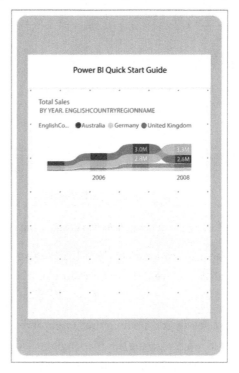

Figure 8.12: Power BI Mobile view

There are some really neat dashboard features we can explore, too. Let's return to the dashboard and explore.

Asking your dashboard a question

Once the dashboard is complete, you're able to ask questions about your data. Right above the dashboard data, you'll see the area where you can **Ask a question about your data**, a feature that may be turned off or on for your dashboard. For example, you enter a request to "*Show me the total stores by state*," and Power BI will typically produce a geographical response.

If you'd prefer to see your answer as a bar chart instead of a map, you can explicitly ask for it as a graph element—for example, "*Show me the total stores by state in a bar chart.*"

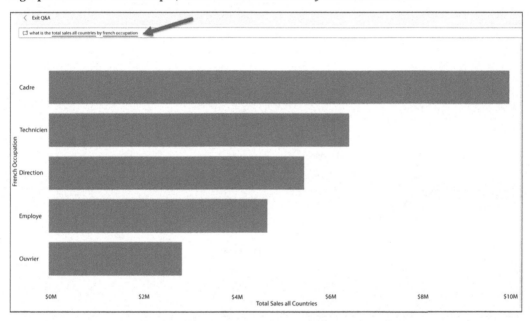

Figure 8.13: Q&A feature in the Power BI service

If you like the answer that comes back, you can click **Pin visual** in the top-right corner to pin the report item to a dashboard. You can also expand the **Filters** and **Visualizations** on the right to be very precise with your report item. For example, you may only want to see stores with sales above a certain level. While Power BI is great at answering questions with filters, it sometimes needs fine-tuning. If you're curious as to where Power BI pulled this data from, below your newly created report, you'll see the source of the data from which the report was derived.

A great way to encourage your users to utilize this feature is to provide Power BI with some sample questions. To do this, you would just select the gear icon at the top right, and then go to **Settings**.

Once there, click the dataset that you wish to create sample questions for in the **Datasets** tab, as shown in the following screenshot. Expand the **Featured Q&A questions** section, click **Add a question**, and add several questions that might interest your user:

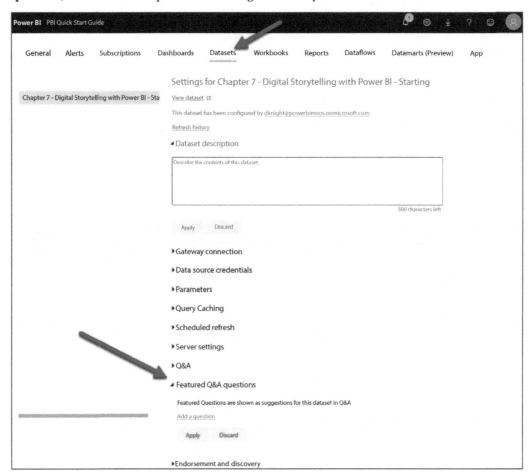

Figure 8.14: Q&A setting in the Power BI service

Creating featured questions will help your users to start to use the vocabulary of the report. For example, your sales team may be used to calling someone a "client," but your marketing team uses the term "customer." Featured questions will encourage all users to refer to customers as clients. If you want to use a variety of terms interchangeably, you can create synonyms inside Power BI Desktop. You can do this in the **Modeling** tab in Power BI Desktop when looking at your relationships. You can also create more advanced linguistic models in Power BI Desktop by importing linguistic models if you've developed them.

This can help with questions that you think users might ask, such as *"Who is my best customer in New York?"* or *"Show me the worst employees by office."* The linguistic model would translate what *"best"* and *"worst"* means to the company.

We've covered developer options in the Power BI service; now let's learn optimal ways to share with report consumers.

Sharing your reports and dashboards

The easiest way to share a dashboard or report is to simply click **Share** on the ribbon of any report or dashboard. Simply type the email address of the user that you want to share with and what type of access you want to give them.

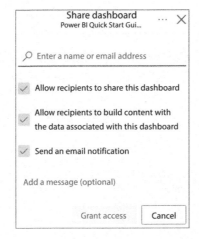

Figure 8.15: Sharing your dashboard popup

While you can't allow them to edit the report or dashboard, they will be able to view and reshare the report themselves. At any time, you can also see what assets are shared with you by going to **Browse** and **Shared with Me** from the left menu of the **Service** page. Then, you will see a list of users that have shared items with you. You can click on this list to filter the report lists that are shared with you.

As you can see, sharing in Power BI is quite simple, but you'll want to consider what your goal is first. If your goal is simply to share a view-only version of a report or dashboard that users could engage with, the basic sharing mechanism can do that. Conversely, if your goal is to allow users to also edit the report, you will want to use a workspace and assign roles to users in the workspace settings, as we discussed earlier in the chapter. To discourage users from printing reports and dashboards, you can have them subscribe to the reports and dashboards.

Lastly, if you want to logically package reports and dashboards together, and have the ability to have fine control over which reports can be seen by default, it is a best practice to use Power BI apps, as described in the first overview section. We will discuss these two methods in the following sections.

Subscribing to reports

Subscribing to dashboards is an important topic. This will email the report or dashboard to the user when the data changes on the report, typically daily or weekly.

This can be done by selecting **Subscribe** in the upper ribbon. Power BI will read the account you're signed in with and subscribe you using that email address. When subscribing to reports, you must select the report page that you wish to be emailed to you. With dashboards, the entire dashboard will be emailed.

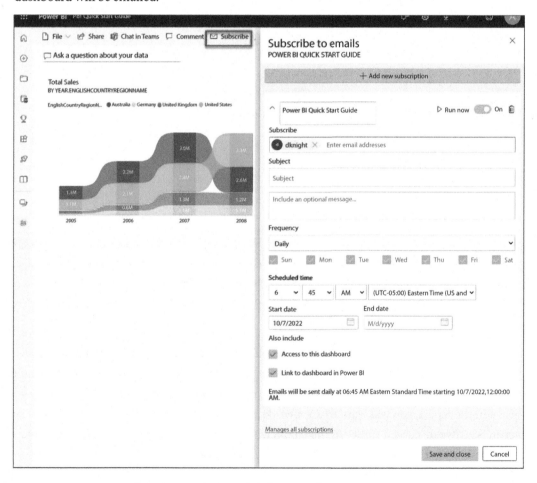

Figure 8.16: Setting up subscriptions in the Power BI service

You can also set up alerts from your mobile device to alert you when a critical number changes on a report. While looking at a dashboard, you can click the three vertical dots and then **Manage alerts** to create an alert. This will monitor the data on the report, and upon that number hitting a certain specified threshold based on the rule that you set, it will send you a phone alert and, optionally, an additional email. Alerts are great mechanisms to let you know if a given critical number, such as a profit margin, has fallen.

By default, the frequency of subscriptions will be whenever the data is updated, but this happens typically no more than once per day (although this can be altered).

Power BI apps

Power BI apps are the official and most convenient way for designers to share content with their consumers. You can bundle all types of reports, dashboards, spreadsheets, and more. Apps are designed to be published and distributed to a wide audience. Designers may customize permissions, notifications, navigation, and more to share full business stories with their organization.

To view and access an app, a user must have either a Power BI Pro or **Premium Per User (PPU)** license. Alternately, if an organization leverages Premium capacity, anyone with permissions may view the content.

Setting up an app is very straightforward. In your workspace, you will see **Create an App** in the upper right corner. Click this button to launch the setup process:

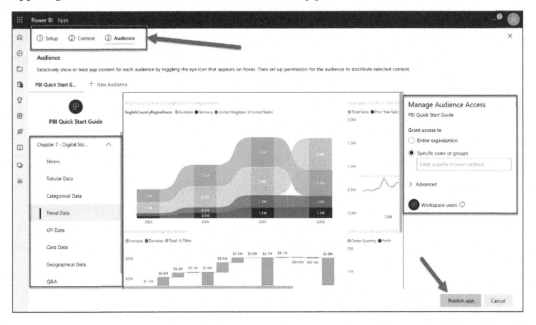

Figure 8.17: Setting up an app in the Power BI service

At the top there are three tabs: **Setup**, **Content**, and **Audience**:

- You fill out information like **Title** and **Description** in the **Setup** tab. You can also add a small logo to the icon.

- Under **Content**, you can arrange the order of the items included according to how your consumer will need to see it. You can also hide pages.

- Under **Audience**, you choose who gets permission to access the app and its contents. You can add individual emails, Azure Active Directory groups, or even share with the entire organization.

When you are happy with the setup, click **Publish app**. You will then see a pop up saying it may take a few minutes to create, and then another popup that allows you to copy the link for the app as well as go to the app. When you open the app, you will see the content on the left side of the page in the order specified. You will also see a ribbon at the top with options for exporting, subscribing, and more.

Setting up **Subscriptions** is very straightforward. Select **Subscribe** in the top ribbon and will see a new pane on the right side:

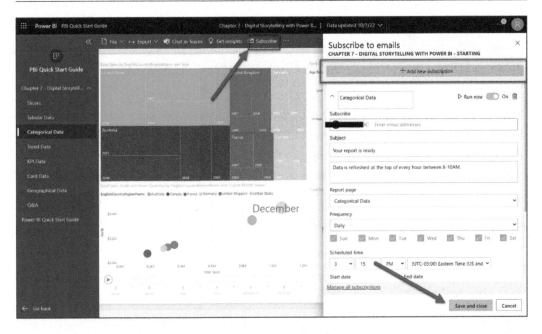

Figure 8.18: Setting up your app subscriptions

There you can customize the audience, the time of the email(s) sent out, the message the audience sees, and how that message will appear. Once you **Save and close**, that subscription will save. You can have multiple subscriptions and turn them off or on at any point.

Now that we've covered apps, which allow us to determine our content bundling and audience distribution, let's review dashboards and how we control the quality of data and who sees it.

Maintaining dashboards

After setting up dashboards, two important considerations are ensuring the data is up to date, and that it is only viewed by the people approved to view it. This is managed through refreshing and row-level security, which we will review in the next sections.

Setting up row-level security

In most organizations, security is not just a report-level decision. Organizations want more granular decisions, such as whether a sales executive can only see their own data. Another example is the ability for a teacher to see their own students, the school's principal to see all the teachers at their school, and the school board members to see all of the school's data. This level of granularity is quite possible in Power BI, but will require some thought ahead of time on how to lay out the data.

To show an example of this, we'll need to go back to Power BI Desktop and open `Chapter 6 - Visualizing Data.pbix`; this file can be downloaded from this book's GitHub repository at `https://github.com/PacktPublishing/Microsoft-Power-BI-Quick-Start-Guide-Third-Edition`.

The goal of this example is to ensure that United States sales managers can only see US sales, and likewise for Australian sales managers and Australian sales. We'll only use two countries in our example, but the same example can apply to the entire world, and can be expanded to be made more dynamic. To create this type of automated filter based on your user credentials, you'll need to use DAX language snippets.

Open Power BI Desktop and click **Manage roles** from the **Modeling** ribbon in the report:

1. Click **Create** to make a new role called **US**.

2. Then, select **Sales Territory** as your table to filter on and click **Add filter...** | **[Sales Territory Country]**, as shown in the following screenshot, *Figure 8.17*.

3. This will create a stub of code in the **Table filter DAX expression** box that shows `[Sales Territory Country]` = `"Value"`. Simply replace `Value` with **"Australia"**, keeping the quotations.

4. Your first role is created when you click **Save**. Do the same for **US** to complete the example:

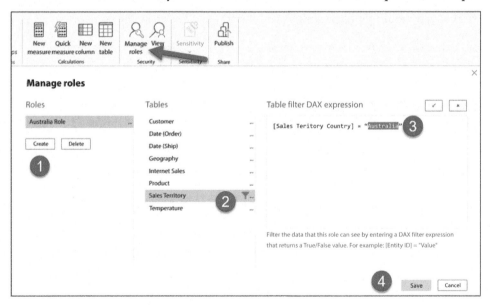

Figure 8.19: Setting up row-level security

Now that we've created the two rules, let's test them out. The Power BI desktop will not automatically filter the data for you, since you have access to the underlying data anyway, but it can be used to test it.

Start by clicking **View as roles** from the **Modeling** tab and selecting the role you wish to test. You'll notice after you click on **Australia**, for example, that every report element on each report page filters at that point to only show Australian data. Power BI Desktop also warns you that you're filtering the data, and that you can click **Stop viewing** to stop viewing as the role. Once you're ready to see what you've done on the Power BI service, publish the report to your Power BI account and open the report there. Then, take the following steps:

1. Navigate to the dataset matching your report and click on the ellipsis to select **Security**. You can then select the role. You could add **Azure Active Directory Security Groups** (such as your **Australian Employee group**) to this role if you have one created already in **Azure Active Directory**.

2. Type the email address of each member of that role. Click **Add**.

3. Click **Save** to start using the role, as shown in the following screenshot, *Figure 8.18*:

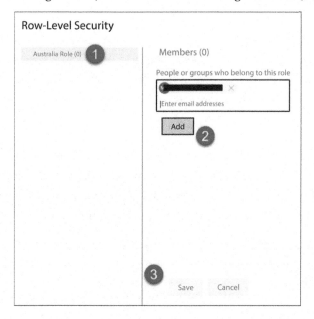

Figure 8.20: Assigning row-level security in the Power BI service

After clicking **Save**, members of that role will only see their own data in dashboards, reports, and any new reports that they build from the dataset. If your user has edit rights to the workspace or dataset, then these roles will not work since they already have the ability to see the underlying data. Admin, Member, and Contributor roles are exempt from row-level security rules but the Viewer role is not. It is important to note that simply configuring row-level security does not grant users the ability to see the report; it must be shared with them or they must be assigned the Viewer role for the workspace.

However, roles do work if the user is connecting to Power BI Desktop to see the data through Excel. Make sure the members of the workspace only have view rights selected if this feature is important to you. Now, let's learn about another important facet of reporting: scheduling refreshes.

Scheduling data refreshes

Once you have a report that everyone depends on, you're not going to want to refresh it manually each day. The Power BI service has the ability to refresh your datasets up to every half an hour — at the top and bottom of each hour — up to eight times a day for the Power BI Pro edition when you're not doing real-time analysis.

 Don't forget that if you want to see data in real time, you have the option to perform a direct query, where clicks run queries against your source system. Doing this will slow your reports down by large factors. You can also do real-time analysis of your data by using Azure services, such as Stream Analytics, where elements in your dashboards refresh every second.

If all of your data lives in the cloud, refreshing is very simple. You simply find the dataset in your workspace and will see the options **Refresh now** and **Schedule refresh**. You can also click on the ellipsis and select **Settings** to find the **Schedule refresh** options. When you expand that section, you are able to set your times at the bottom and top of the hour.

However, if you have some data or files on-premises, you must install the on-premises gateway. The table below shows the main differences between a personal and a standard gateway.

	On-premises data gateway	**On-premises data gateway (personal mode)**
Cloud services supported	Power BI, Power Apps, Azure Logic Apps, Power Automate, Azure Analysis Services, and dataflows	None

	On-premises data gateway	On-premises data gateway (personal mode)
Runs	As configured by users who have access to the gateway	As you for Windows authentication and as configured by you for other authentication types
Can install only as computer admin	Yes	No
Centralized gateway and data source management	Yes	No
Import data and schedule refresh	Yes	Yes
DirectQuery support	Yes	No
LiveConnect support for Analysis Services	Yes	No

For our purposes, let's use a personal gateway. The personal gateway is exclusively used for Power BI and single-user instances, often for the specific purposes of refreshing. In contrast, the standard on-premises gateways can be used across multiple cloud services, such as Power BI, Power Apps, Logic Apps, and Power Automate.

In the Power BI service, you can download the free gateway from the top-right arrow pointing down icon on `PowerBI.com`, as shown in *Figure 8.19*.

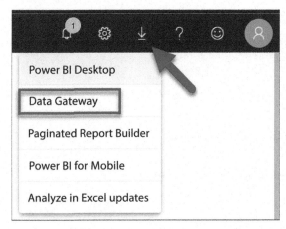

Figure 8.21: Option to download the data gateway

The first question that will be asked during the installation is whether you want to install the data gateway in personal mode or on-premises standard mode. Choose personal mode:

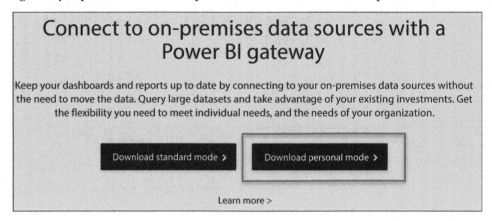

Figure 8.22: Download options for the Power BI data gateway

One main difference between the on-premises data gateway and the on-premises data gateway in personal mode is that personal mode runs as a local application compared to a Windows service in on-premises mode. By installing in personal mode, you could risk your data becoming stale if the application is not open when your PC starts, because the data is not available for refresh while the local machine is off. It is handy for those users who may not have admin access to their machine, or users who want easier data refreshes.

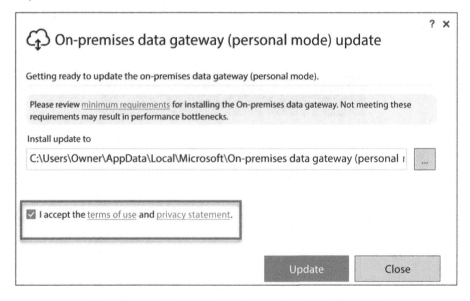

Figure 8.23: Agree to the terms of use and conditions to install

Once you install the gateway and assign your email, you will see it linked to your service account under **Dataset settings**. You will also see that confirmation when you check the status on your local machine. Sign in to connect the personal gateway to your service account.

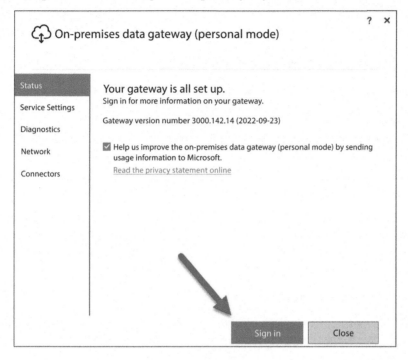

Figure 8.24: Confirmation of a successful install ready for sign-in

If you wish to just refresh the data immediately, there are two icons next to the dataset. You could select **Refresh Now**, or to schedule a refresh, click **Schedule Refresh**. This will take you to the dataset configuration screen. Expand the **Gateway Connection** section, select **Use an On-Prem Data Gateway**, and click **Apply**. You should see your gateway name in this section, with a status reading **Online**. If you don't see **Online**, check whether there are any proxy settings or firewall issues preventing Power BI from seeing your machine.

Next, expand the **Scheduled Refresh** section in the **Datasets** tab and switch the **Keep Your Data Up to Date** setting to **On**. You can then schedule the refresh to occur as often as every half an hour. Once you test the refresh, you can see **Refresh History** in this same tab to see whether the data was successfully refreshed. You can also get email notifications when refreshing fails.

If your data is already in Azure or OneDrive, then the on-premises gateway is not required. You just need to make sure the firewall will allow you to communicate with the Power BI service.

Using Metrics to track progress

One newer feature in the Power BI service that we covered in the overview, but will explore more in depth here, is called Metrics. It was first known as Goals, but the name changed in spring 2022.

The table below outlines the permission and requirements structure provided by Microsoft.

Permission	Minimum requirements
Author and share scorecards and metrics, and perform check-ins	Power BI Pro license
View scorecards and metrics	Power BI Premium capacity + Free user OR Power BI Pro license
View scorecard samples and author scorecards in **My Workspace**	Free user

To track a metric, take the following steps:

1. On the left navigation page, select the **Metrics** icon.
2. Select **Create your own scorecard**, as shown in *Figure 8.23*.

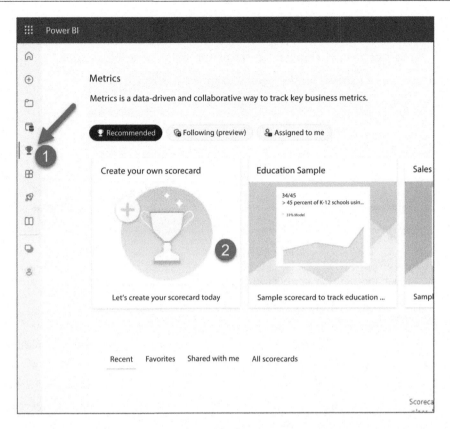

Figure 8.25: Create a new scorecard on the Metrics tab

Now, add a single metric you'd like to track individually or on a team. Power BI allows you to connect with underlying datasets or create unique goals ad hoc.

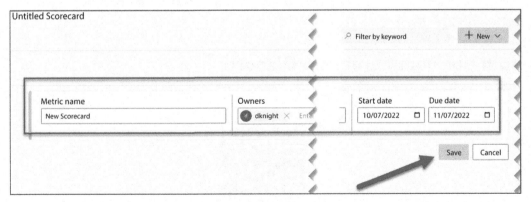

Figure 8.26: Add metric details to measure individual or team goals

Once this information is added, it is displayed with other metrics to track progress toward goals:

1. To update or modify, simply select the metric and edit the information.

2. You will need to hover for that option to appear as a pencil icon.

3. Once selected, you can change the details as needed.

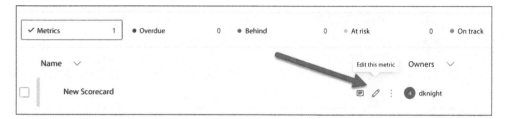

Figure 8.27: Update metric details

This feature is yet another way people can collaborate and measure success easily together.

Summary

The Power BI service allows your users to see the same reports on a web or mobile platform with the same type of interactivity as they experience in Power BI Desktop. It also allows users to build reports quickly and straight from a web platform. Once your reports are deployed to the service, you can use row-level security to see data at a granular level, allowing a sales manager to only see their own territory, for example. The data can also be refreshed as often as every 30 minutes. If you're using on-premises data sources, then you can use the on-premises gateway to bring data from on-premises to the cloud.

In the next chapter, we will learn about Power BI dataflows, one of the newest and most powerful self-service options for Power BI users.

Join our community on Discord

Join our community's Discord space for discussions with the authors and other readers:

https://packt.link/ips2H

9

Data Cleansing in the Cloud with Dataflows

Power BI **dataflows** are a new, robust, self-service **extract, transform, load** (ETL) option in the Power BI service. Dataflows allow you to use the Power Query Editor online and leverage your transformational work in a reusable format, both individually and with other people. Currently, you can save dataflows in your Power BI workspaces and your organization's Azure Data Lake Storage account. When created in Power BI, dataflows are always categorized as analytical dataflows, in contrast to the dataflows created in "Power Apps", which may be analytical or standard. These are saved in Microsoft's Dataverse. In this chapter, we cover analytical dataflows created in the Power BI service.

Dataflows help organizations unify data from disparate sources and prepare it for modeling. They provide the familiarity of the Power Query Editor experience using a GUI with M code in the background so that you can create reusable, scalable, and extensible data source solutions for your organization.

Analysts can easily create dataflows using familiar self-service tools. Dataflows are used to ingest, transform, integrate, and enrich big data by defining data source connections, ETL logic, refresh schedules, and more. Power BI dataflows operate with a new model-driven calculation engine based on Microsoft's **Common Data Model** in the backend. Power BI dataflows make the process of data preparation more manageable, more deterministic, and less cumbersome for data analysts and report creators alike. In simplistic terms, Power BI dataflows allow analysts and report creators to create a self-service data mart solution with a few clicks.

In this chapter, we will get you started on your Power BI dataflow journey, covering the following topics on the way:

- Getting started with dataflows
- Creating a dataflow
- Using dataflows as a data source in the desktop

Let's start by covering the basics to build a strong foundation of knowledge that you can build on in your projects!

Getting started with dataflows

Power BI **dataflows** can be simple or complex depending on your needs—and licensing. Licensing and workspace capacity are key factors in how you can leverage Power BI dataflows. It is important to research your organization's governance and overall architecture to conform to best practices. Below is a table from the Microsoft documentation that outlines the features and type of Power BI license needed.

Feature	Power BI
Store data in Dataverse tables (standard dataflow)	N/A
Store data in Azure Data Lake Storage (analytical dataflow)	Power BI Pro / Power BI Premium
Store data in customer-provided Azure Data Lake Storage (analytical dataflow; bring your own Azure Data Lake Storage)	Power BI Pro / Power BI Premium
The enhanced compute engine (running on Power BI Premium capacity / parallel execution of transforms)	Power BI Premium
DirectQuery connection to dataflow	Power BI Premium
AI capabilities in Power BI	Power BI Premium
Linked entities	Power BI Premium
Computed entities (in-storage transformations using M)	Power BI Premium
Schedule refresh	Power BI Pro / Power BI Premium
Dataflow authoring with Power Query Online	Power BI Pro / Power BI Premium
Dataflow management	Power BI

Feature	Power BI
New connectors	Power BI Pro / Power BI Premium
Standardized schema, built-in support for Common Data Model	Power BI Pro / Power BI Premium
Dataflow data connector in Power BI Desktop	Power BI Pro / Power BI Premium
Dataflow incremental refresh	Power BI Premium

For the sake of simplicity, we are giving the basic features with the Power BI Pro license; however, it may be worth a deeper dive into Microsoft's documentation to truly uncover all the dataflow features and administrative requirements needed to use all the Power BI Premium features (find out more at `https://learn.microsoft.com/en-us/power-bi/transform-model/dataflows/dataflows-introduction-self-service`).

In the next section, we will create a practical, reusable dataflow. But before moving to that step, let's review the key differences between a dataflow and a datamart, a new preview feature that will soon be generally available.

Exploring datamarts

Datamarts are available as a preview feature with Power BI Premium (capacity or per user), and it is a self-service, no-code solution that allows citizen developers and business report writers to create a relational database through a GUI in the Power BI service. It allows business groups to bypass the barriers of standard development, while still giving developers the ability to query the data and access it through standard developer tools.

Rather than view **dataflows** and **datamarts** as totally disparate options that compete, it's important to recognize that they may work together right now. Microsoft provides the following guidelines for when to use each feature:

- Use dataflows when you need to build reusable and shareable data prep for items in Power BI. This may feed your datamart, or it may stand alone. Great use cases are calendars, HR employee lists, location tables, and so on.

- Use datamarts when you need to:

  - Sort, filter, and do simple aggregation visually or through expressions defined in SQL

  - Provide outputs that are results, sets, tables, and filtered tables of data

  - Provide accessible data through a SQL endpoint

  - Enable users who don't have access to Power BI Desktop

This next step in Power BI's digital revolution is meant to bridge the gap between IT and business report creators who may not have all the skills, but certainly have the need, for the benefits of a relational database. These benefits include creating row-level security, synching refresh schedules, incremental refreshes, and decoupling the data storage from the report package. Datamarts leverage Azure SQL Database for backend storage of the data, and this is in contrast with dataflows, which are stored as flat files in Azure Data Lake Storage Gen2.

Datamarts use a special dataflow that sends data to a fully managed and automatically provisioned Azure SQL database, which then creates a DirectQuery dataset from Azure SQL Database as its source data. This is all done through a single web UI in the Power BI service and exists as one package. It's suggested that this integrated experience of data modeling and DAX authoring may allow MAC users to more easily leverage Power BI, because it's all online.

Now that we have covered the newest evolution in the Power BI service, let's continue to build our dataflow.

Creating a dataflow

A very common reason to use **dataflows** is the reusability of data among team members. Consistency and having a single source of truth is the main goal for many analysts, and a great application of this is a **Date** table. For this exercise, a Pro license with no additional premium capacity is necessary. In this section, we will explore the Power BI service to see where dataflows are created and then use simple code to produce a dataflow that will work in many different data models.

Dataflows are reusable **extract, transform, and load** (**ETL**) packages created and managed in the Power BI service, while the data you bring into a Power BI dataflow is stored as entities—basically flat tables—in the Common Data Model folders in Azure Data Lake Storage Gen2. These files are stored as CSVs with JSON files containing all the metadata and rules, which unify and standardize your self-service data warehouse. Once created, these dataflows then serve as a data source for Power BI reports, and can also be used with other Azure data services if you bring your own data lake.

In order to create a Power BI dataflow, you need a new **workspace** experience. This has been the default for some time now—you cannot use Power BI dataflows in much older workspaces. When creating the workspace, there are advanced options to set up dedicated dataflow storage capacity—in other words, to connect your own data lake for additional storage capacity and options within the Azure ecosystem. Be sure to read the extensive admin documentation if your goal is to use your own data lake as the backend storage, rather than leveraging the default experience.

One key point is that you will want to ensure your capacity is set to the same region as your other Azure resources. Using My Workspace will never work, regardless of the region and capacity, because My Workspace is a personal folder that's not designed for sharing data organizationally.

First, create a new workspace in your version of Power BI. A key detail is that the creator of the dataflow becomes the owner by default. Previously, ownership could not be transferred, but now there is an option to pass dataflow ownership to another Power BI user. The dataflow owner is the primary admin for dataflow functionality and permissions.

Note in *Figure 9.1* that you are given the option to bring your own storage, versus the default option of using Microsoft's general Azure Data Lake that you cannot customize or monitor:

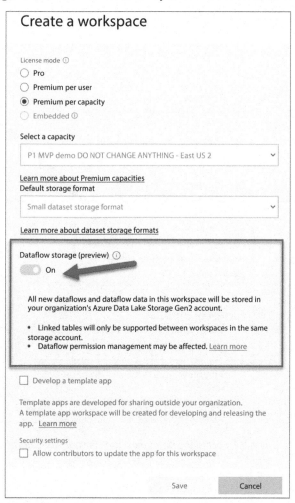

Figure 9.1: Exploring the dataflow settings when creating a PBI workspace

Once the workspace is created (we've created one here called **Dataflow Test 2022**), there is an option for **Dataflow** under **+ New** toward the upper-left corner of your workspace, as shown in *Figure 9.2*:

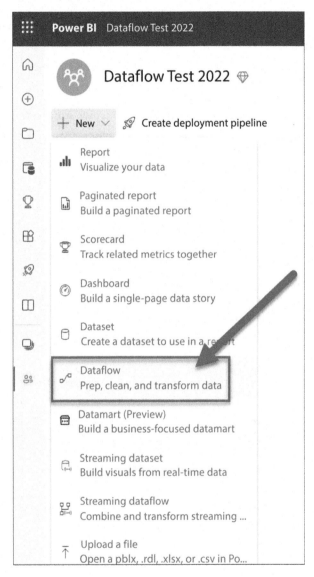

Figure 9.2: Locate the Dataflow option in your workspace

When this option is selected, you will see a popup related to the new datamarts feature:

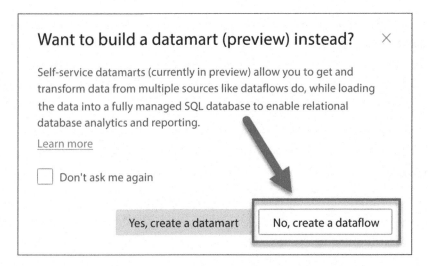

Figure 9.3: Confirm your selection to create a dataflow

Confirm that you want to create a dataflow and not a datamart, to get started. After selecting **No, create a dataflow**, more options appear:

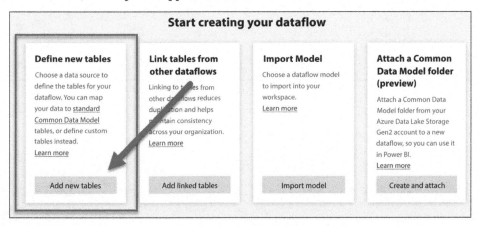

Figure 9.4: Dataflow options

It's worth describing the various options:

- **Define new tables**: Once a dataflow contains data, you can create **computed tables**. Computed tables perform in-storage computations and they may be custom, or they can map to the **Common Data Model** standards.

- **Link tables from other dataflows**: Link to tables that have branched off from existing tables in the same or different workspaces. They are branches that allow transformation, but one key point is that they do not store data. If linked tables exist in the same workspace as the original tables, refreshes may be coordinated between them. However, different workspaces lead to different refresh schedules.

- **Import Model**: Import an existing dataflow from its locally stored JSON file.

- **Attach a Common Data Model folder (preview)**: This is the "bring your own data lake" option.

For the Date table dataflow, there is no need for an enterprise Power BI gateway, because it is a **Blank query** option and the M code will create the table in the Power Query Editor's native language. In almost all other cases, an Enterprise data gateway is needed, which means a Pro license is also needed—although Premium licenses and capacities offer significantly more analytical resources for your dataflows. Power BI dataflows do not work in My Workspace or with a free license.

When defining the new entity, choosing the data source is the first step. For the M code-scripted date table, selecting **Blank query**, one of the options toward the bottom, is key.

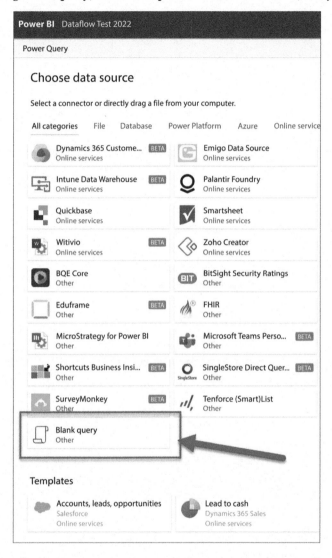

Figure 9.5: Choose the Blank query option to create this dataflow

At that point, copy the following script, which lets you create a date table, into the Power Query Editor, replacing the default query formula:

```
//Create Date Dimension
(StartDate as date, EndDate as date)=>

let
    //Capture the date range from the parameters
    StartDate = #date(Date.Year(StartDate), Date.Month(StartDate),
    Date.Day(StartDate)),
    EndDate = #date(Date.Year(EndDate), Date.Month(EndDate),
    Date.Day(EndDate)),

    //Get the number of dates that will be required for the table
    GetDateCount = Duration.Days(EndDate - StartDate),

    //Take the count of dates and turn it into a list of dates
    GetDateList = List.Dates(StartDate, GetDateCount,
    #duration(1,0,0,0)),

    //Convert the list into a table
    DateListToTable = Table.FromList(GetDateList,
    Splitter.SplitByNothing(), {"Date"}, null, ExtraValues.Error),

    //Create various date attributes from the date column
    //Add Year Column
    YearNumber = Table.AddColumn(DateListToTable, "Year",
    each Date.Year([Date])),

    //Add Quarter Column
    QuarterNumber = Table.AddColumn(YearNumber , "Quarter",
    each "Q" & Number.ToText(Date.QuarterOfYear([Date]))),

    //Add Week Number Column
    WeekNumber= Table.AddColumn(QuarterNumber , "Week Number",
    each Date.WeekOfYear([Date])),

    //Add Month Number Column
```

```
        MonthNumber = Table.AddColumn(WeekNumber, "Month Number",
        each Date.Month([Date])),

        //Add Month Name Column
        MonthName = Table.AddColumn(MonthNumber , "Month",
        each Date.ToText([Date],"MMMM")),

        //Add Day of Week Column
        DayOfWeek = Table.AddColumn(MonthName , "Day of Week",
        each Date.ToText([Date],"dddd"))

    in

        DayOfWeek
```

 You can also go to `https://devinknightsql.com/2015/06/16/creating-a-date-dimension-with-power-query/` to access this code.

After pasting, click **Next**:

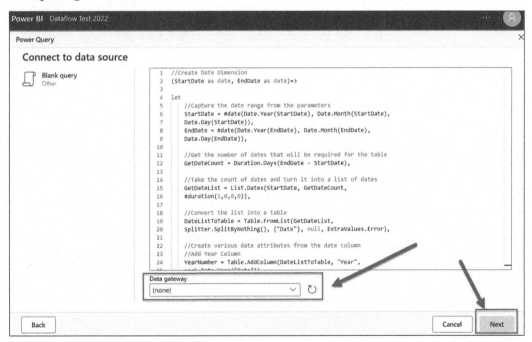

Figure 9.6: Paste the M code and select Next

Clicking **Next** will take us to a screen where date parameters may be specified to determine the length of the table. Take the following steps:

1. Input a date range.

2. Name the query.

3. Select **Invoke** to create the date table.

4. Click **Save & close**:

Figure 9.7: Set the data range and name the table

Once the date table is created, the data type can be set using the little icon in the top-left corner of the columns, as shown in *Figure 9.8*. The layout and options of the online Power Query Editor should generally mirror the Power Query Editor in Power BI Desktop:

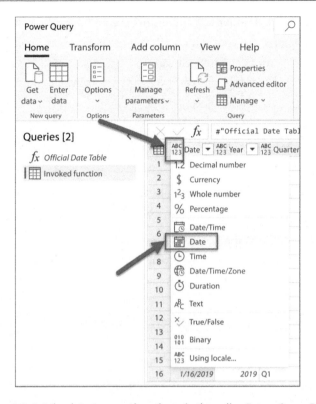

Figure 9.8: Set the data type on the column in the online Power Query Editor

The **graphical user interface (GUI)** is being updated regularly to make the dataflow experience more and more like the Power BI Desktop experience. It is worth taking time to look at the top ribbon with its **Home, Transform, Add column,** and **View** options to explore the GUI because many options are similar, and some are new, such as **Map to entity** and **AI insights**, as shown in *Figure 9.9*.

AI insights is fully leveraged under a Premium license and provides out-of-the-box artificial intelligence options to analyze your data, with things such as sentiment analysis, keyphrase extraction, language detection, and image tagging:

Figure 9.9: New options available for dataflows in Power BI Desktop that are not in the Power Query Editor

Here is the dialog box for the **Map to entity** option, which allows users to take the existing fields in the entities and map them to common data model attributes. Users can choose from a list of common tables (entities) and leverage that metadata if they want:

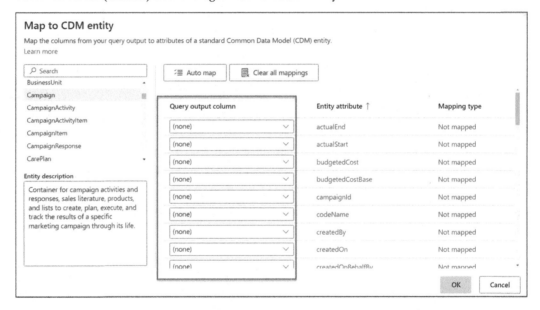

Figure 9.10: New option to map dataflows to the Common Data Model structure

Map to entity does not apply to this date table, but it can be a useful option for other tables, such as sales or accounting tables, where the data types and tables are often very similar across companies, departments, and so forth.

After exploring the options, save the dataflow by selecting the **OK** button in the bottom-right corner. You will see if your query meets all the criteria in a confirmation box, as shown below:

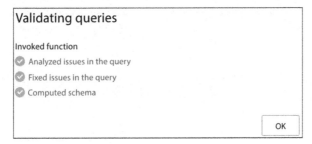

Figure 9.11: Query validation confirmation

Saving will prompt you to enter a name, but does not actually finish the saving process because data is not fully loaded into the dataflow until after it is saved and refreshed:

- **Name** the dataflow.

- Provide a **Description**.

- **Save** the dataflow:

Figure 9.12: Save the dataflow

A pop-up box like the one shown in *Figure 9.13* will appear to load the data and finalize the dataflow for use. **Refresh now** is a one-time option that manually loads the latest data. Dataflows can leverage multiple data sources and allow the unification of disparate sources.

Under a Premium license, incremental data refreshes can be set with **Set a refresh schedule** to manage the performance impact of data sources that update at different times and rates:

Figure 9.13: Popup with refresh options

If you miss the pop-up option, simply find the dataflow in your workspace and click on one of the refresh icons to set up a schedule or perform a single refresh.

Now that we've created a Power BI dataflow that will provide a consistent and standard date table for ourselves and others, we can easily connect to this data source from Power BI Desktop.

Using dataflows as a data source in Power BI Desktop

Power BI dataflows act like any other imported data source. In Power BI Desktop, simply select **Get data** and then connect to the **Dataflows** option. From there, all the available dataflows will be available and organized. Once we click **Get data** and select the dataflow option, a familiar dialog box will appear that shows all the available dataflows we can use.

Figure 9.14: Get data to choose dataflows

As shown in *Figure 9.15* below, your table options appear in a list on the left-hand side. Expand the folders and choose the **Date** table, then select **Load** to immediately use the table, or select **Transform Data** if you have more work to do in the Power Query Editor:

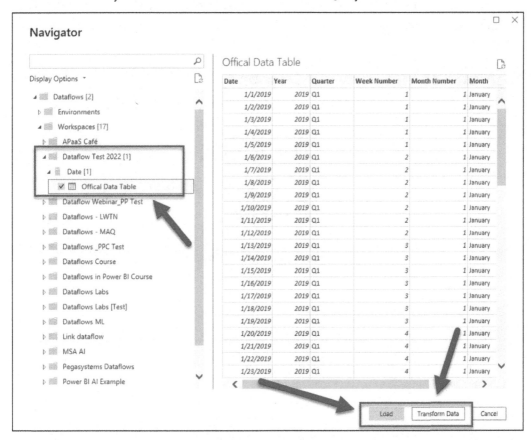

Figure 9.15: Expand the folder options and choose the Date dataflow, then Load to use it immediately

It is important to remember that dataflows are not datasets. Datasets are semantic models on top of data, whereas dataflows are built on top of the dataset in a reusable schema. Additionally, dataflows do not truly replace a data warehouse, but they do allow for lighter self-service "data warehousing" tasks for various integration scenarios.

Summary

Congratulations on exploring an exciting option for reusable, standardized data that can bring great benefits to teams who need single sources of truth. In this chapter, we created a date table dataflow using M code and learned about the mechanics of using the Power Query Editor online.

Join our community on Discord

Join our community's Discord space for discussions with the authors and other readers:

https://packt.link/ips2H

10

On-Premises Solutions with Power BI Report Server

Throughout this book, we've focused on building reports that will ultimately be deployed to the web through the Power BI service or shown in the mobile application. In this chapter, we'll show you how to deploy reports to Power BI Report Server, which is likely being hosted on-premises at your company. For many companies, this is a must-have, since cloud deployments are often not allowed with their type of data or industry.

Power BI Report Server is an on-premises version of the Power BI service that gives you a subset of the features of the full service. Unlike the full service, which is sometimes updated daily with new features, Power BI Report Server is updated every few months. There is also an additional Power BI Desktop specially made for the server.

 Make sure you fully explore the features of the server to ensure it has the critical features that you love. For example, you might find that a connector you can use in the Power BI service is not available on the server. The biggest notable missing feature is the lack of dashboards.

In this chapter, we will cover the following topics:

- Accessing Power BI Report Server
- Deploying to Power BI Report Server
- Securing reports
- Refreshing data

Accessing Power BI Report Server

To get started, you will need to know how your organization's IT governs its servers, hardware, applications, and data. You may need to submit a help desk ticket, or you may be authorized to go directly to Microsoft's Download Center and install it yourself. Regardless of the path forward, it's very important to know and abide by any data governance that's established.

If you are installing it yourself, simply go to https://powerbi.microsoft.com/en-us/report-server/ and select **Download Free Trial** as shown in *Figure 10.1* below, or use **Advanced download options** to specify what you need:

Figure 10.1: Download the free trial or go to Advanced download options to start

If you intend to use the paid version, then you will need Power BI Premium or SQL Server Enterprise **Software Assurance (SA)**—this is why you will want to coordinate with your central IT.

It is very important that you select the right language on the dropdown of the download page. This will impact the specifications assigned to that Report Server based on the language chosen. Additionally, the Microsoft documentation recommends reading through the requirements before installing, and it specifically calls out the following details:

> *While you can install Power BI Report Server in an environment that has a Read-Only Domain Controller (RODC), Power BI Report Server needs access to a Read-Write Domain Controller to function properly. If Power BI Report Server only has access to a RODC, you may encounter errors when trying to administer the service.*

If you've gone down the **Advanced download options** route and have the IT privileges to install, then you will choose the right configuration:

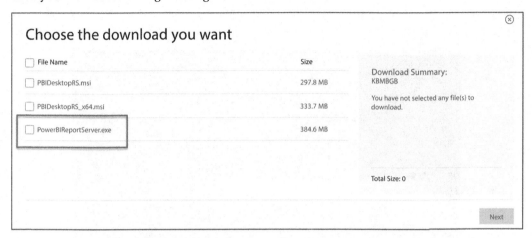

Figure 10.2: Power BI Report Server download options

Once you've made your selection, you can manually launch the setup process by opening it in your **Downloads** folder, or it may appear automatically. The following steps walk through the installation process.

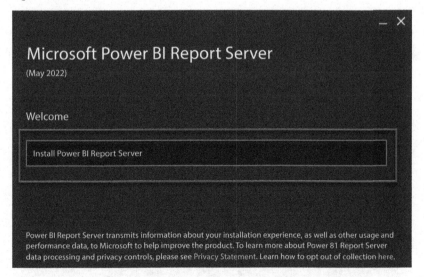

Figure 10.3: Select Install Power BI Report Server

You will need to click on the **Install Power BI Report Server** option to proceed. After you select that, it will provide the options available, and you select the free trial or you can submit your product key, as shown in *Figure 10.4*. It's important that you follow all the standards for installations that your company sets.

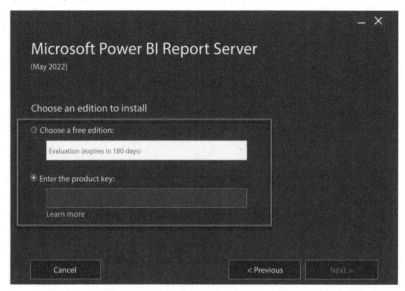

Figure 10.4: Choose your install edition

From there, it's important to choose the best location on your machine. *Figure 10.5* shows that you can use a default location provided, or select **Browse** to specify another path:

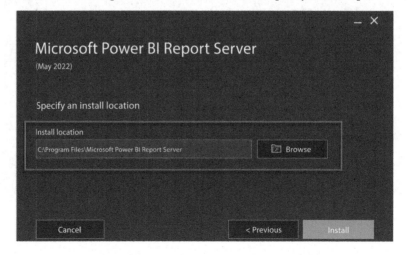

Figure 10.5: Choose the install location

After this, the package will download as specified:

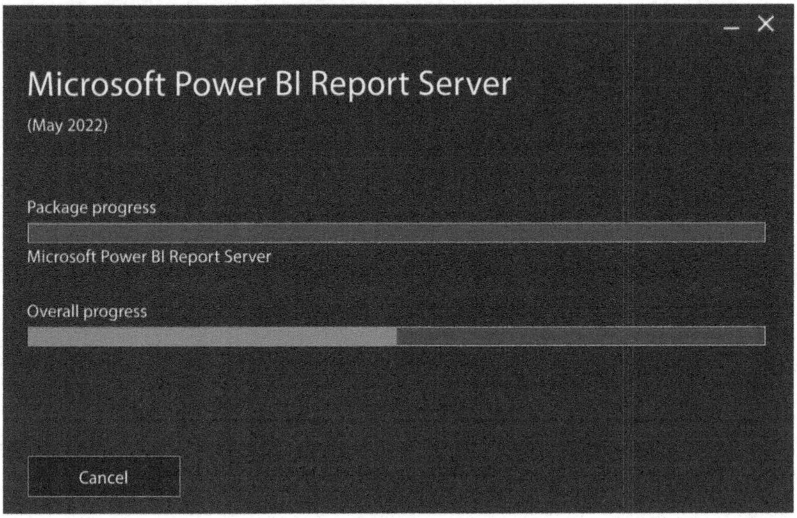

Figure 10.6: Power BI Report Server download options

Deploying to Power BI Report Server

If you're a traditional BI developer who has built Reporting Services reports, you might feel right at home with Power BI Report Server, as the configuration and portals were largely borrowed from Reporting Services. You're going to use a special Power BI desktop that is optimized for the server. The main reason for the separate desktop is to ensure that the desktop doesn't promote a feature that the server does not support. This is an important point to note. One key advantage of using this approach is that Report Server can also host your traditional Reporting Services reports, KPIs, and mobile reports.

Deploying a Power BI report

Before deploying your report, you may want to create some folders to simplify finding your reports later. For example, creating a folder for finance, HR, inventory, IT, operations, and sales is a common starting point. Don't worry, you can always move the reports later if you've already deployed them. Once you've created a folder, if you feel it's needed, you can deploy your Power BI reports in one of two ways, from the Power BI desktop or by uploading:

1. Make sure you have a Power BI Desktop instance installed that supports Power BI Report Server and open the report that you wish to deploy.

This flavor of Power BI Desktop also supports deploying to the cloud, but note that you will be at least 3–4 months behind the main Power BI application. With the quarterly Report Server edition updates, you will not have access to preview features.

2.   Next, click **File | Save As Power BI Server**. If this is your first time deploying your report to the server, everything will be blank. Simply type the Report Server HTTP address in the box to connect to Power BI Report Server. It should look something like `http://servername/reports`. If you have a port number, you'll need to use something like `http://servername:portnumber/reports`. You can find the exact location to enter by going to your Report Server Configuration Manager tool from the server and copying the URL from the **Web Portal URL** section. The port in this screenshot is port **80**, which you don't have to enter as it is the default port:

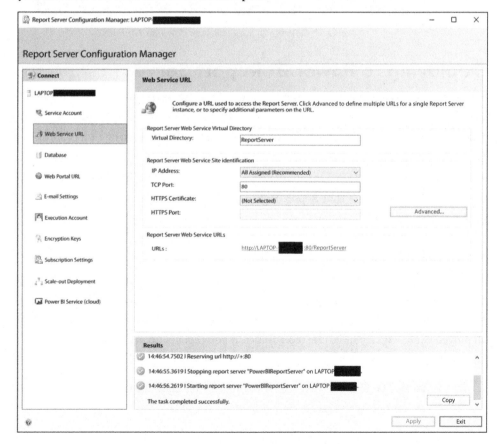

Figure 10.7: Find the location using the Report Server Configuration Manager

3. If the desktop can successfully connect to the server, you will be prompted for the folder name that you want to deploy to and the name of the report you want to use. Typically, you don't want to use this opportunity to change the name of the report since it will become difficult to find your source report later.

4. After clicking **OK**, the report will deploy and provide you with a link that will take you directly to the report that now resides on your server. From this point forward, you can click **Save** without going through this process and it will save directly to the server.

You can also upload the report directly in the browser. To do this, take the following steps:

1. Go to the folder you wish to upload the report to and click **Upload** in the top-right corner.

2. You will then be prompted for the location of the folder, and then you're done. Power BI Report Server will scan to make sure that the report is compatible. For example, if you built the report on a very new version of Power BI Desktop that is using features that aren't supported in Power BI Report Server yet, then you will receive an error before the upload occurs.

3. Once the report is deployed, any user with the appropriate access can also click the **Edit** button in Power BI Desktop to open the report up in Desktop so that they can make changes.

If you wish to move the report to a new folder, you can go to the report listing and click **Move** under the ellipsis button. You will be prompted for the folder you wish to move the report to, and then you're done. You can also do this under **Manage** under the same ellipsis.

In the **Manage** area of a report, you can also hide the report by clicking **Hide this object**. This can be used to hide reports that are built on other reports, for example. It's important to note, though, that this is not a security mechanism. There's nothing to stop a user from seeing the report if they unhide the object.

The next step we will cover is deploying a paginated report from Power BI Report Builder.

Deploying a paginated report

In this section, we will use a sample paginated report provided by Microsoft, as shown in *Figure 10.8* below. To do so, take the following steps:

1. Find the report at `https://github.com/microsoft/Reporting-Services`.

2. Click on the **Code** button in the top-right corner.

3. Choose **Download ZIP**.

4.   Extract the files in a location you will remember:

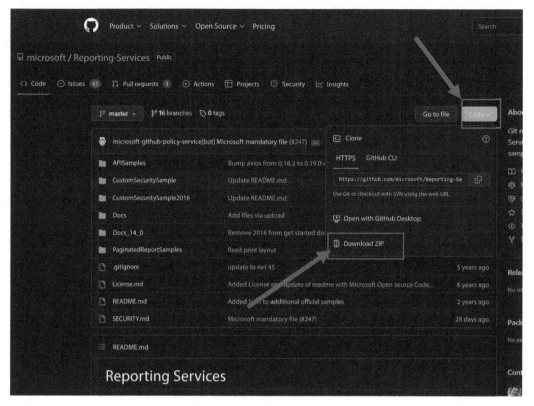

Figure 10.8: Accessing Microsoft's paginated report examples

Once you've downloaded the .rdl file, you could explore it in Power BI Report Builder. For our purposes, we are going to focus on publishing to Power BI Report Server, which is actually done from within Power BI Report Server.

In *Figure 10.9* below, you simply do the following:

1.   Locate the **Upload** button along the top ribbon on the right side of the screen.

2.   Choose the path where you extracted the paginated report's ZIP folder. Do not use the ZIP folder. Choose the **CountrySalesPerformance** .rdl file to upload.

3.   Choose **Open**:

Figure 10.9: Upload the sample paginated report

When this is complete, you will see your report under **Paginated Reports** on the home screen under **Browse**, as seen in *Figure 10.10*:

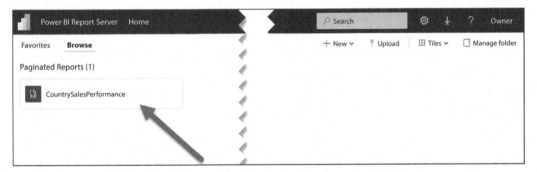

Figure 10.10: The paginated report is found under Paginated Reports

Simply click on the report to open it, and you will see your paginated report in its published form. Now that we know how to publish .pbix and .rdl files to Power BI Report Server, let's cover securing reports.

Securing reports

You can secure a report in the **Manage** screen of a report or folder. To access this area, select a report folder or report, select the ellipsis button, and click **Manage**. Then, go to the **Security** tab. By default, reports and folders inherit security from their parent folder, but this can be undone quickly by clicking **Customize Security**.

Keep in mind that there's quite a bit of overlap in the roles that can be assigned, mainly due to the context of what you're securing (My Reports or the public folder of reports). The security roles that you can select are listed as follows:

- **Browser**: Can view the reports and folders, and subscribe to the reports.
- **Content Manager**: Can manage folders, reports, and resources.
- **My Reports**: Can publish reports and manage folders, reports, and resources in a user's My Reports folder.
- **Publisher**: Can publish reports on your Power BI Report Server.
- **Report Builder**: Can review any definitions or metadata about the report, as well as permissions.

You can also select the gear in the top-right corner of the screen and select **Site Settings** to secure the entire server. Even if you have rights to the folder or report, you may not have rights to the server, which creates a lot of confusion with system administrators and users trying to view their data. When you go to **Site Settings**, you can add a user to one of two roles: **System Administrator** or **System User**. The system administrator can manage the security on the server and the schedules, to name just a couple of options. The system user grants the user rights to log in to the server, and then requires security to view the folders and reports, as shown earlier in this section.

Scheduling data refreshes

Refreshing data in Power BI Report Server comes with a lot more caveats than using the Power BI cloud service. For example, refreshing is contingent on the data source that the report is using. Since you've installed this server inside your firewall, there's no need for a data management gateway to refresh the data either. As you create refreshing schedules, the server will simply create SQL Server Agent jobs to control the refreshes, such as Reporting Services.

If you plan on refreshing data sources that are derived from files, make sure you use a network path for that file (`\\computername\sharename\file.csv`), not a local path (such as `C:\Downloads\File.csv`). You can do this in Power BI Desktop by going to the **Home** ribbon and selecting **Edit Queries** | **Data Source Settings**. Click **Change Source** and change any file references to a network path, such as `\\MyComputer\c$\Downloads\File.csv`.

Once you do that, publish the report to the server again. Then, select the report and select **Manage**. For most data sources, you will need to confirm the source of the data in the **Data Sources** tab. For flat files, confirm that you see the network path and type in the credentials for the machine that's holding those files. This will need to be a Windows Authentication username and password. Click **Test Connection** to confirm that a connection can be successfully achieved. If it tests successfully, click **Save**.

> If you find that there are popular times at which people want to refresh data, you can create shared schedules. Shared schedules can be found in the **Site Settings** administration panel (under the gear in the top-right corner) of the portal. By creating these, you will simplify the scheduling of future jobs for popular scheduled times.

To schedule the refresh, click **Scheduled Refresh** in the report management area. Then, click **New Scheduled Refresh Plan** to create a new schedule. You can also use a shared schedule resource or a one-off schedule. Simply type the time you wish the refresh to occur and the refresh interval. While there are workarounds, the lowest grain of a scheduled refresh is typically hourly.

Test the job by selecting the job and clicking **Refresh Now**. If any errors occur, you will see the error inline in the **Status** column. For example, the following error would show as a data source error: **Login failed for data source 'Unknown'**. This is not nearly enough information to debug with, so click the information icon next to the error to see a more actionable error, such as the following:

```
[0] -1055784932: Could not find file '\\desktop-12qu18g\c$\OneDrive\
Documents\CountyClerksFL.csv'. The exception was raised by the IDbCommand
interface.
```

In many cases, doing a simple search online with the error message will lead you to documentation, blogs, and community forums with solutions that others have found already. In this instance, dozens of articles appear to help the user resolve the connection issue quickly.

Summary

In this short chapter, you learned how to take Power BI service practices on-site with Power BI Report Server. This server has many restrictions on what's available, so be careful that you have the right version of Power BI Desktop so that it matches your version of the server. As you've learned, the server resembles the Reporting Services server and uses SQL Server Agent to handle data refreshes.

Join our community on Discord

Join our community's Discord space for discussions with the authors and other readers:

https://packt.link/ips2H

packt.com

Subscribe to our online digital library for full access to over 7,000 books and videos, as well as industry leading tools to help you plan your personal development and advance your career. For more information, please visit our website.

Why subscribe?

- Spend less time learning and more time coding with practical eBooks and Videos from over 4,000 industry professionals
- Improve your learning with Skill Plans built especially for you
- Get a free eBook or video every month
- Fully searchable for easy access to vital information
- Copy and paste, print, and bookmark content

At www.packt.com, you can also read a collection of free technical articles, sign up for a range of free newsletters, and receive exclusive discounts and offers on Packt books and eBooks.

Other Books
You May Enjoy

If you enjoyed this book, you may be interested in these other books by Packt:

Mastering Microsoft Power BI, Second Edition

Greg Deckler

Brett Powell

ISBN: 9781801811484

- Build efficient data retrieval and transformation processes with the Power Query M language and dataflows
- Design scalable, user-friendly DirectQuery, import, and composite data models
- Create basic and advanced DAX measures
- Add ArcGIS Maps to create interesting data stories

- Build pixel-perfect paginated reports
- Discover the capabilities of Power BI mobile applications
- Manage and monitor a Power BI environment as a Power BI administrator
- Scale up a Power BI solution for an enterprise via Power BI Premium capacity

Microsoft Power BI Cookbook, Second Edition

Greg Deckler

Brett Powell

ISBN: 9781801813044

- Cleanse, stage, and integrate your data sources with Power Query (M)
- Remove data complexities and provide users with intuitive, self-service BI capabilities
- Build business logic and analysis into your solutions via the DAX programming language and dashboard-ready calculations
- Implement aggregation tables to accelerate query performance over large data sources
- Create and integrate paginated reports
- Understand the differences and implications of DirectQuery, live connections, Import, and Composite model datasets
- Integrate other Microsoft data tools into your Power BI solution

Extreme DAX

Michiel Rozema

Henk Vlootman

ISBN: 9781801078511

- Understand data modeling concepts and structures before you start working with DAX
- Grasp how relationships in Power BI models are different from those in RDBMSes
- Secure aggregation levels, attributes, and hierarchies using PATH functions and row-level security
- Get to grips with the crucial concept of context
- Apply advanced context and filtering functions including TREATAS, GENERATE, and SUMMARIZE
- Explore dynamically changing visualizations with helper tables and dynamic labels and axes
- Work with week-based calendars and understand standard time-intelligence
- Evaluate investments intelligently with the XNPV and XIRR financial DAX functions

Packt is searching for authors like you

If you're interested in becoming an author for Packt, please visit authors.packtpub.com and apply today. We have worked with thousands of developers and tech professionals, just like you, to help them share their insight with the global tech community. You can make a general application, apply for a specific hot topic that we are recruiting an author for, or submit your own idea.

Share your thoughts

Now you've finished *Microsoft Power BI Quick Start Guide, Third Edition,* we'd love to hear your thoughts! Scan the QR code below to go straight to the Amazon review page for this book and share your feedback or leave a review on the site that you purchased it from.

https://packt.link/r/1804613495

Your review is important to us and the tech community and will help us make sure we're delivering excellent quality content.

Index

Download a free PDF copy of this book

Thanks for purchasing this book!

Do you like to read on the go but are unable to carry your print books everywhere? Is your eBook purchase not compatible with the device of your choice?

Don't worry, now with every Packt book you get a DRM-free PDF version of that book at no cost.

Read anywhere, any place, on any device. Search, copy, and paste code from your favorite technical books directly into your application.

The perks don't stop there, you can get exclusive access to discounts, newsletters, and great free content in your inbox daily

Follow these simple steps to get the benefits:

1. Scan the QR code or visit the link below

https://packt.link/free-ebook/9781804613498

2. Submit your proof of purchase

3. That's it! We'll send your free PDF and other benefits to your email directly

Made in the USA
Coppell, TX
28 January 2023